Toy Cannon

Toy Cannon

The Autobiography of Baseball's Jimmy Wynn

JIMMY WYNN
with BILL McCURDY

McFarland & Company, Inc., Publishers
Jefferson, North Carolina, and London

Library of Congress Cataloguing-in-Publication Data

Wynn, Jimmy, 1942–
    Toy Cannon : the autobiography of baseball's Jimmy Wynn /
Jimmy Wynn with Bill McCurdy.
        p.   cm.
    Includes bibliographical references and index.

    ISBN 978-0-7864-5856-1

    1. Baseball players—United States—Biography.   2. African
American baseball players—Biography.   I. McCurdy, Bill.
II. Title.
GV865.W97A3   2010
796.357092—dc22
[B]   2010034842

British Library cataloguing data are available

Front cover: Jimmy Wynn; cannon art ©2010 clipart.com
Manufactured in the United States of America

McFarland & Company, Inc., Publishers
Box 611, Jefferson, North Carolina 28640
www.mcfarlandpub.com

To the memory of my loving parents,
Joe and Maude Wynn.
They gave me all I needed.
They made me the man
I turned out to be.

A life is not important except
in the impact it has on other lives.
—*Epitaph of Jackie Robinson*

Acknowledgments

After all these years, finally getting around to putting my story down on paper in black and white is like the lifting of a great weight from my shoulders, heart, and mind. Whether the world needed to hear my story or not is of no great matter to me. I simply needed to tell it. I needed my fans and the general public to know me better, and for my grown children, Kimberly and Jimmy Jr., to have the words on record about how much I care about them and the future of my grandchildren.

It is my humble hope that I may have accomplished most of my aims in writing my story for the benefit of all the Wynn generations who shall come after me. One hundred years from now, when someone asks one of the future Wynn family members, "Didn't you once have an ancestor back there who used to play big league baseball?" they will be able to answer with more certainty than, "You know what? I'm pretty sure I did."

I also want that same lucky and blessed great-great-great-grandchild to be able to explain the meaning of the small toy cannon that rests upon the fireplace mantle of their family home's den. That thought brings me comfort. Even though it really has no bearing on what is important in the long-range plan of God for the soul of Jimmy S. Wynn, I take frail, human consolation in the hope that a more lasting memory of the toy cannon's significance could reduce the prospects that the little artifact could end up out in the yard someday in a weekend garage sale.

I especially want to thank my friend Bill McCurdy, president emeritus of the Texas Baseball Hall of Fame, for patiently helping me put this book into readable good form, from start to finish. Bill and I together want to thank our dear wives, Marie Wynn and Norma McCurdy, for their patience and support over the several months and numerous long days of work we have devoted to this project. Without their backing, this idea for a book about my life in baseball could not have flown high at all. Lucky for us, our ladies have been our spiritual wings from the very beginning of this effort.

Bill and I together also want to thank Sumner Hunnewell of St. Louis,

Missouri, for serving as both our copy editor and specialist in indexing. We have Sumner to thank for the fine job of name indexing that concludes the Appendices section of this work. In addition to some highly developed editorial skills, Sumner is a body and soul baseball man who also cuts a mean path on the vintage baseball fields of Missouri, a place where he plays for the Lafayette Square Cyclones.

Finally, thank you, dear fans and readers, for taking the time to learn more about the baseball life and times of a man that writer John Wilson once nicknamed the Toy Cannon. Thank you for all time, John Wilson.

Other people that Bill and I together and individually want to thank include Bob Aspromonte, Bob Boyd, USA Col. Fred Burley, Richard Coselli, Larry Dierker, Larry Dluhy, Al Doyle, Bob Dorrill, Joel Draut, Gene Elston, Kevin Eschenfelder, Pam Gardner, Nancy Geyer, Bill Gilbert, Howard Green, Milo Hamilton, Marian Harper, Mickey Herskowitz, Bob Hulsey, Jim Hunt, Melvin Hunt, Randy Hunt, Mark Langill, Greg Lucas, Neal McCurdy, Drayton McLane Jr., Larry Miggins, Darrell Pittman, Dr. Sam Quintero, Dave Raymond, Robert Reed, Paul Rogers, Jo Russell, Billy Sanders, Vin Scully, Jeff Share, Tal Smith, Robert C. Turnauckas, USA Major Carroll Teas, Frank Veselka, Curt Walker, Carl Warwick, Charles Willis, and Jerry Witte. Everyone listed here contributed in ways we have neither the time nor the space to completely explain.

May God's love, peace, and blessings be with you all, now and forever.

—Jimmy S. Wynn

Contents

Preface
by Bill McCurdy

Like most other original Houston major league baseball fans, I first heard of Jimmy Wynn when he joined the local club for our city's second season of major league play, way back in spring training of 1963. I didn't know much about him at the time beyond the fact that Houston had drafted him out of the Cincinnati Reds system after his rookie season at Tampa and that he was being touted by some local writers as an excellent hitting prospect.

It didn't take long for the Colt .45 brass to figure out that Jimmy's great arm strength, foot speed, and surprisingly powerful hitting ability might better qualify him as a candidate for the club's effectively open spot in center field.

After spending part of 1963 getting a little more seasoning in minor league ball at San Antonio, and still more at Oklahoma City in 1964, Jimmy rejoined the big league club for good at the end of his second year in Houston.

It was the stuff that fulfilled dreams are made of. Jimmy Wynn had arrived just in time to be the last center fielder for the 1964 Houston Colt .45s and then the first center fielder for the 1965 rechristened Houston Astros.

Jimmy banged out 22 home runs for the 1965 Astros. He followed that first full season in the big leagues by popping 18 more long balls in 1966. Jimmy then virtually blew out the top by taking hope straight through the Astrodome's three-year-old roof, crushing 37 round-trippers and recording 107 RBI in 1967. That same year that he registered the first All-Star Game hit ever registered by any member of the Houston Astros over the course of their then six-year history.

"Houston, we have a baseball icon, and his name is Jimmy Wynn!"

Houston fans swelled with pride over the thought of Jimmy Wynn as one of their own. Jimmy's growing stature in the community also grew in the same orbit as the one traveled by the new astronaut citizens of Houston. Jimmy Wynn had arrived in time to get caught up in the city's glowing new dual love affair with the original NASA astronauts and the major leagues' brand-new Houston Astros.

The hustling, bustling new space race challenged NASA to make sure that the United States of America beat the Soviet Union to the goal of putting a man on the moon. All the Houston Astros had to do, by comparison, was to beat their cousin expansion club buddies, the New York Mets, to the World Series.

Our Houston baseball astronaut-equivalents were men like Jimmy Wynn, Larry Dierker, Joe Morgan, Bob Aspromonte, Carl Warwick, and Turk Farrell. Alas, we were not as successful in baseball as people like John Glenn, Alan Shepard, Buzz Aldrin, and Neil Armstrong were in space.

Ironically, both the space and local baseball races were decided in 1969. In that same year, the USA beat the Soviets to the moon, but the Mets beat the Astros to their first World Series appearance and victory.

The Astros' 1969 strong run at the National League pennant was very much boosted by the man the media now called *the* "Toy Cannon." The small-in-stature Jimmy Wynn stood taller than ever by his performance as a power hitter that special year, cracking out another 33 home runs in a season that saw the Astros come close before sliding away in September.

When Jimmy Wynn was dealt to the Los Angeles Dodgers after the 1973 season, it was a dark day for those of us in Houston who still loved him as a player through thick and thin. Those of us who really cared as fans about Jimmy were consoled by the fact that this trade, at least, opened the door for Jimmy Wynn to appear the following year with the Dodgers in the 1974 World Series. He would've missed that golden opportunity completely had he remained to play another heartbreaking year in Houston.

Years passed from there. Jimmy Wynn's playing career ended quietly in Milwaukee in 1977. After that closing chapter, we ordinary baseball fans didn't hear much about Jimmy Wynn for several years. Then, in the mid–1980s, Jimmy Wynn moved quietly back to Houston from Los Angeles.

By the early 1990s, Jimmy Wynn started reappearing in Houston as a public figure. As a rediscovered asset of the Houston Astros, Jimmy was again working for the club and making community service talks at local schools in the Houston area. Word gets around. Jimmy Wynn was doing some good work with the kids.

In 1993, Jimmy Wynn was inducted into the Texas Baseball Hall of Fame for his work over eleven seasons (1963–1973) as a Houston Colt .45/Astro player. At the time of Jimmy's induction, his 223 home runs as a Houston player were then the franchise record.

In February 2004, I met Jimmy Wynn personally for the first time at the annual Fanfest gathering at Minute Maid Park. By this time, I was beginning my tour of volunteer service as board president (2004–08) for the Texas Baseball Hall of Fame.

Meeting Jimmy Wynn at age sixty-two, when I was already sixty-six, was more like running into one of the kids I once played sandlot baseball with in the East End of Houston back in the post–World War II years. Had our old Pecan Park Eagles sandlot club been blessed with Jimmy Wynn in our lineup back in 1950, we really could have done some serious damage to the opposition. As it was a later-in-life meeting, our friendship grew simply as a naturally forming river, one that flowed from our shared common values in life and our mutual love for the game of baseball.

During the summer of 2004, I called Jimmy to ask him if he would consider allowing the Texas Baseball Hall of Fame to establish an annual banquet award for exceptional community service in his name. With his consent, the Jimmy Wynn Toy Cannon Award for Exceptional Community Service was established in 2004 as an annual feature of our Texas Baseball Hall of Fame (TBHOF) Induction Banquet.

Fittingly, and upon the insistence of our selection committee, Jimmy Wynn was chosen over his own modest protests as the first Toy Cannon Award winner in 2004. Since that time, Jimmy Wynn has become the annual presenter of this award: to broadcaster Milo Hamilton in 2005; writer Mickey Herskowitz in 2006; and Astros Community Relations Vice President Marian Harper in 2007. Because of the recent economic slump, no Toy Cannon Awards were made in 2008 or 2009 due to the temporary suspension of TBHOF banquet activities, but the selection of a new honoree is expected to take place again once the new board for the state baseball hall of fame resumes its normal scheduling of celebration activities.

On June 25, 2005, the Houston Astros recognized the franchise value and serious playing contributions of Jimmy Wynn by retiring his Number 24 prior to a Saturday afternoon game played at Minute Maid Park. It was a beautifully correct tribute to Jimmy Wynn, one only made possible by Mr. Drayton McLane Jr., the dynamically-wound, hands-on owner and president of the Houston Astros.

In January 2007, Jimmy Wynn joined the Board of the Texas Baseball Hall of Fame. He previously had served as a member of the organization's Advisory Board since 2004.

The 2007 season also saw Jimmy Wynn moving into television broadcasting as one of the pre–and post–game commentators for FOX Sports Network Houston. He has continued in that role through the 2010 season, while also continuing to work for the Houston Astros through a wide range of community service roles.

Jimmy Wynn also has remained active nationally, doing charity appearance performances on behalf of the Major League Baseball Players Alumni Association since the 1990s. He also has conducted his own annual golf tourney in Houston since 2002 for the benefit of the Urban League.

Over the past four years, my wife Norma McCurdy and I have become close friends with both Jimmy and Marie Wynn. When Jimmy asked me to work with him in the telling of his story, I was both honored and humbled by the invitation.

I didn't have to think about it long. I already knew that Jimmy and I shared a matching set of values on the importance of truth and personal responsibility for the accurate recording of history. I've only helped on one book of this kind previously, but the match existed there as well when I worked with the late Houston Buff slugger Jerry Witte in *A Kid from St. Louis* (2003).

What are those shared values? They were, still are, and always will be: (1) Tell the truth every time; (2) Don't make anything up; (3) Don't leave anything important out of the story; and (4) If it's something tough that the public already knows about, be prepared to deal with it, or otherwise, don't bother to write.

None of us is perfect, but people are forgiving if we can be honest with them on the facts and take personal responsibility for our own behavior. I told Jimmy from the start: I'll help you organize the time frame for looking at your life from childhood forward, and I'll try to help too by asking questions that will allow you to tell your story into a tape recording. Your job is to tell it like it was and is. That was the simple bottom line we started and finished with.

What I've tried to do here is to help Jimmy Wynn tell his own story and then get myself out of the way. This story had to come from Jimmy. It could not have been written objectively about him by a disinterested third party and still have moved forward with the same gravitas of credibility that he reveals every day in his ordinary dealings with people.

In the pages that follow, most of you will get to know the Jimmy Wynn that you never before had a chance to meet. You will meet a man of hope, heart, and unyielding faith and loyalty to the goal of giving and self-sacrifice. You will also meet the Jimmy Wynn who owns up to his own mistakes and walks away with a wheelbarrow load of wisdom. It is a lifetime of wisdom that Jimmy openly shares with all those who have eyes to see and ears to listen beyond the walls of any personal bias that leads them to only think of baseball stars as perfect human beings.

Jimmy Wynn makes no remote claim for personal perfection, but he comes through here in this book, in my estimation, as one of the most honest personal storytellers who ever decided to share his baseball experience and life history. When it comes down to taking personal responsibility for the outcomes and lessons of his important life decision-making, Jimmy Wynn owns everything he sees to own.

In the writing of this book, Jimmy Wynn approaches the subject of his whole life as he did the game of baseball. He leaves everything on the field.

James Sherman "Jimmy" Wynn is the walking embodiment of all that we sometimes like to say about old houses: "They don't build 'em like they used to." Jimmy Wynn bears just such a character as that strong and reliable old house. He was put together with the finest materials from a plan that flowed from divine hands. He was assembled with love and care by two loving parents to be strong enough to weather both the expected and the unexpected storms of life. After a lifetime of sunrises and sunsets, time and the elements of life didn't push him to the ground. They just gave him character.

Friends, fans, and fellow readers, over the pages that follow, it is my honor to present to you the one and only James Sherman "Jimmy" Wynn.

Introduction

I grew up close to old Crosley Field in Cincinnati. Baseball was in my blood from the age of five years on. Beyond my dad, the Cincinnati Reds were my heroes.

My dad was a good ballplayer in his time. He didn't have much chance due to the color line, but that didn't stop him from teaching me all he could about hitting, especially. He didn't teach me how to run or catch the ball. Those skills just came naturally to me, but he taught me about hitting, and I mean hitting with an attitude.

God gave me the kind of body that would allow me to hit for power, even though I had a *toy cannon* physique in the making, even back then. On the sandlot, the teams that chose up sides always wanted me because I hit those big long rainbow drives that won ballgames. I never got bigheaded about my ability, even as a kid, but I wasn't deaf either. I heard what people were saying about me, especially if they were grown men I respected as fellows who knew something about baseball.

"That kid is really going to be something someday!"

When someone you respect says that about you as a kid ballplayer, you don't ever forget it.

Humility about your own gifts and respect for what you could learn from older people were two important lessons I got strongly from both my parents. We were very close and I miss each of them dearly to this day. You don't ever get over the loss of people you really love. You just make your peace with loss being the part of God's plan for all of us who survive longer than those we love on this earth. In my heart and Christian faith, I know this much: We'll be together again.

When you're a kid, you don't always, or usually, see the whole picture of how far the arms of love and respect extend out from and back into your little world. One of my strongest early memories was of the time we spent hanging out in the front of our house, especially when my dad was home. People would come and go past our house, waving and honking their horns.

And taking our lead from dad, we'd always wave back with a smile. I used to wonder why we got all that attention. As I grew older, the answer came easy. People were just giving back the caring and respect to my dad that they also got from him. Knowing that fact today just makes the sweet memory all the sweeter. There is no price tag you can put on the love and loyalty we get from family, and a few other good people. I grew up rich on love and all the faithfulness that comes with it. Thank the Lord. Without those gifts, I wouldn't be who I am today.

What I'm going to try my best to do in the pages that follow in this book is to tell you the story of my life in baseball and beyond. Thank you for deciding to read what I have to say. Along the way, it is my hope that I will be able to help you get to know me a little better too as a human being.

I won't mince words, and I won't leave out the mistakes and parts of my life that would be easier to skip because of their offensiveness to right thinking and plain common sense, but I will neither excuse nor glorify these things either. I will just try my best to deal with them honestly here for what they were: painful life lessons.

Thank you for your patience and understanding. And God Bless!

CHAPTER 1

The Cincinnati Kid

How many people get the opportunity to start their story trying to correct for the umpteen-hundredth time the most basic fact of their lives, their place of birth? Well, however many there are out there, count me among them.

That's right. My *won't-stay-dead* mistaken fact is over my place of birth. And I will do all I am able to do right here to not only set the record straight, but to tell you in plain English, if you read anything else otherwise, any place else, no matter how official the source appears to be, that whatever you're reading elsewhere that is contrary to my next official word on the subject is flat-out wrong. What goes down here in the next "breath" of ink is the truth, and the only truth, about where I was born.

I was born in the Cincinnati General Hospital in Cincinnati, Ohio, and not in Hamilton, Ohio, or anyplace else. I am a *Cincinnati Kid* all the way, in spite of the fact that articles keep coming out placing me and Mama in Hamilton, Ohio, on a certain first day of light for me back on March 12, 1942. Even at this writing, a couple of big Internet baseball statistics sites still carry forth the misstated and very much in error "born in Hamilton, Ohio" false information. There are even some baseball cards of me floating around out there with the "Hamilton, Ohio" birthplace tag on them.

Years ago, I thought I could clear this mistake up, but now I'm not so sure if that's even possible. The original reason for this birthplace error is easy enough to explain, but something happens to false information once it finds its infernal way into print: It starts to take on a life of its own as people read it and then sit down and write other things based on the same faulty facts. It didn't take all that long for "born in Hamilton, Ohio" to become the unwanted wave that kept landing on the beach of my life.

Here's how it got started:

The late broadcaster for the Cincinnati Reds, Joe Nuxhall, is a name you probably recall. Nuxie was a pretty fair left-handed pitcher for the Reds around the time the club was trying to sign me out of high school back in

Joe and Maude Wynn, Jimmy's parents.

1960. He is best remembered, however, as the fifteen-year-old kid the Reds trotted out to the mound to make his major league pitching debut on June 10, 1944. It was pretty much a publicity stunt, but it was one of those things that people would associate with Joe Nuxhall for the rest of his life, no matter what else he did or didn't do.

At any rate, Joe Nuxhall was born in Hamilton, Ohio. For some reason, he either got the idea, or made up the idea, that I also had been born in Hamilton. When I came around the Reds at Crosley Field during that time, Joe Nuxhall liked to tell everybody in earshot that they needed to "meet Jimmy Wynn, a future Red and the second major leaguer to be born in Hamilton, Ohio!"

First of all, I don't know if Joe Nuxhall was the first and only major leaguer ever born in Hamilton, Ohio, but I do know for sure that I wasn't the second or any other number in that line. I just went along with it back then as a sort of shy high school kid suddenly thrown into the company of big leaguers, and some of the same big leaguers I had followed for years as a kid fan of the Cincinnati Reds.

All the while, I kept thinking to myself: "Why is Joe Nuxhall saying that stuff about me being born in Hamilton, Ohio? Oh well, if it makes him happy to think that way, so what!"

Today, at the age of 68, I understand the "so what" part a whole lot better. I've spent this much time all these years later trying to straighten out the truth about one of the most basic facts in anyone's life—the name of the place where they were born.

Wish I had asked Joe Nuxhall why he did that in the first place, but it's too late now. Joe passed away on November 15, 2007. With his passing, Cincinnati lost a longtime, loyal Reds man and a really fine broadcaster. And baseball lost a good friend.

I was born in Cincinnati all right. I got to be a Cincinnati kid because of the two most wonderful people in the world, my parents, Joe and Maude Wynn. My parents moved to Cincinnati after my dad got out of the service. I'm not sure how they met, but Dad was originally from Georgia and Mom was from Kentucky. I was the firstborn child, but Mama and Dad didn't stop there.

After me came my brother, Charles, whom we called Chuck. He was born in 1944, but sadly, he passed away in 2002 at the age of fifty-eight.

After Chuck came Ronald and Joe Jr.; then came my sister Marie and our youngest sister, Lynette. A seventh Wynn child came along by way of adoption. (Brother William had been a neighborhood kid who was at our house every day; he spent the night with us every night; and he ate at our kitchen table with us every meal time.) Finally, one day, Mama said, "We may as well go ahead and adopt this kid. He's here every day, as it is. We may as well make him an official member of the Wynn family."

What was behind Mama's words was a whole lot of heart and caring for William. We all knew that he lived alone with a single mom who was up to a lot of no-good things, and that William wasn't going to have much chance in life without the love and support of a real family. So, somehow, Mama got William's biological mother to release him for adoption. He's been a Wynn ever since and he now is doing OK for himself at his present home in Indianapolis, Indiana. William fits in age between Chuck and Ronald, and he's as much a Wynn today as any of us who were born blood kin.

The adoption of William is just a taste of the family love and caring that surrounded all of us when I was growing up. William became one of us because he fell in love with us and we fell in love with him. Explanations sometimes don't get any simpler or truer than that. That's how there got to be a William Wynn in our household.

We weren't alone in Cincinnati. We had aunts, uncles, and cousins that we saw pretty regularly, and Christmas was a really special gathering time in the two-story brick residence of the Wynn family at 1917 Colerain Avenue in Cincinnati near old Crosley Field. We did the whole Christmas celebration the old-fashioned way. The tree went up about two weeks before Christmas and it stayed up until about the first week in January.

Santa Claus came on Christmas morning, usually landing on a roof covered with snow and probably accompanied by Bing Crosby singing "White Christmas." Snow at Christmastime was normal for Cincinnati and I still miss it on that special holiday, even after all of my snow-free years of life in Houston and, for awhile, in southern California. I mean, how were Santa Claus and Rudolph the Red-Nosed Reindeer even going to land at our house without that blanket of snow that covered the roof? Have you ever thought of that? As a kid, I sure did. I also thought of it again as an adult going through his first ninety-degree Christmas Day in Houston. I had to wonder: How do Houston kids even buy into the idea that there's a way for Santa's sleigh to land at their houses? Houston kids even get cheated out of building snowmen in their yards. They miss out on snowball fights too.

I guess another thing I'm saying down deep is this—I still miss Mom and Dad and our early life together. I still have their love, even if I no longer have their physical presence in my life today. The love and wisdom they gave me flows on through me every day as I carry on with my own branch of the Wynn family in this very different climate from Cincinnati. It's just that Christmas reminds me most of the time when I thought of everything with a child's mind.

Back then I thought that Mom and Dad would just be there for me forever. Like everyone else who lives long enough, however, I had to get through finding out that some things we take for granted as kids turn out to be not true, but that you never lose the love that was given to you as my Mom and Dad gave it to my brothers and sisters and me.

That's how I look at it, anyway.

We lived pretty typically of many families from our era. For most of the time I was growing up, Mom was a stay-at-home mom, but she later took on some outside work to help meet family expenses. For a while, she worked for the telephone company and then she took a job with the Internal Revenue

Service. The IRS position lasted long enough to help us get by. God bless Mom! Dad worked as a garbage collector. He was very proud of what he did, too, and I, in turn, was very proud of him. When they came up with the newer, cleaner term "sanitation worker," I still called him a garbage man because that's really what he was doing and there was no shame in that work at all.

If it were not for people like my dad, people who do the really essential work that has to be done, our cities would stink to high heaven and slow down to a dead stop. The world can survive a baseball strike that cancels the season, but try having a garbage man strike that lasts just as long. In the latter case, you would have to cancel the city where it was taking place too. So, was I proud of my dad for what he did? Ask me forever and the answer will always come back the same: "Yes and always!"

There's no way I can really put into words all that my dad meant to me. He was my father, my teacher, my coach, my guide to life, my hero, and my best friend—all rolled into one. And he taught me everything I needed to know about getting started in baseball. As my Little League coach, Dad drew upon his own experience as a former baseball player to teach me the fundamental things you need to know to play the game right.

Dad also had a colorful way of making his point when it came to teaching me what I needed to take into account as I set up my goals as a hitter. This, of course, is something he only said once I was a little older, when it was obvious to him that I had the talent to become a really good baseball player.

"Jimmy," Dad used to say, "if you want to drive a Chevy some day, you will need to become really good at hitting singles. If, on the other hand, you hope to drive a Cadillac in the future, you will need to become very good at hitting home runs."

Dad really knew how to tilt me in the direction I was leaning anyway. In spite of my small size and compact stature, I had been blasting home runs on the sandlots of Cincinnati from my earliest summers of opportunity. I had heard the comments of older men observers at my games, men who knew baseball, and their words had only served to fire my spirit for trying harder and getting better.

"Look at this kid hit! He's really going to be something someday!"

Those words heated my soul when I was little kid. They didn't give me the big head. They gave me the motivation to work hard and let nothing else stand in the way. I think that was because I heard both parts of that whispered bleacher message: (1) be something, and (2) someday.

I was going to have to work hard to get there, and I was going to have to stay away from anything that would derail my dream of becoming a big league baseball player. A lot of my schoolmates were getting into devious things in those days, but I was blessed to see that where they were going was not for me.

Mom and Dad were spiritual people, but that didn't turn either of them into superhuman parents. They just did their best. Mom was a Catholic and Dad was a Baptist. I was raised a Baptist, but I also sometimes went to a Catholic church as a young kid. I had a lot of aunts and uncles that were also Catholic. By the time the dust cleared on my childhood years, I was still a Baptist, but one who also had been strongly influenced by my attendance over the years at Catholic masses.

As hard as they tried, Mom and Dad couldn't protect us all the time from all the false beliefs and temptations that have always been out there in the world, just waiting for everyone's kids. They just tried to show us by both their words and actions what we were all going to have to learn to deal with out there on our own in the world.

Mom and Dad understood a truth that I've always tried to keep in mind as a parent myself: No child ever got preached or "speeched" into living and thinking right. Unless a kid sees a parent living by the words they use, they pay no mind to whatever is being said. And sometimes, kids just go their own way, anyway. With no fire burning within them for some goal that matters, most kids, most people, are just driven by the winds of whatever feels good right now. There's a whole lot of no-good-for-nothing stuff that is going to happen to you in life, whenever those feels-good-now winds are blowing.

I can only speak for myself here. From early on, I was saved by my burning fire for baseball. Dad didn't make me play or force me to learn the game. I wanted to learn all the things he had the power to teach me. For whatever reason, I just knew from a very early age that I wanted to be a major league baseball player when I grew up.

The only way I could hope to reach the big leagues was to follow what I was taught to believe in by my parents. And what I believed in was myself and my God-given abilities. I also knew that my father and mother believed in me. Mom and Dad taught me to believe that I could achieve my goal, if I became willing to follow a set of rules they set forth for me. These basic rules would become the cornerstone of anything good I've ever done. Simple as they are, they remain in my life to this day as the key to my focus on anything I'm trying to accomplish.

When I was first presented with these ideas, Mom and Dad put my rules to me this way—If you want to be a ballplayer, these are the rules that you have to abide by:

Rule Number One was: "Your education comes first!"
Rule Number Two was: "If you don't understand something, you have to go
    back to the teacher right away and ask for help!"
Rule Number Three was: "As much as you can, as the oldest, behave as a
    third parent to your younger brothers and sisters." And so I did as they
    asked. When Mom and Dad gave me an order for something that we had

to get done, it was my job to take this order to the younger kids and see that it was carried out in the best way. The others knew too that Mom and Dad had given me the authority to see that their work orders were carried out as fairly as possible.

As the years have gone by, I have grown to appreciate even more how much this simple little plan, this gift from my parents, has carried forward into every corner of my life. It's helped me understand why things have gone well in certain areas, and it's also helped me get the lesson after the fact from certain things I had to learn the hard way.

Today I boil the old rules down into these terms. For me, these rules apply to all situations in life:

Rule Number One: "Your education comes first!" Before you start a new business, a new career, or a new marriage—learn everything you can over time first before making a big jump. If you fail to follow Rule One, you've just enrolled in the School of Hard Knocks by default.

Rule Number Two: If you don't understand something about a new situation, or if you begin to see that things are changing from how they first looked, speak up to the other people involved. Ask questions. Have an opinion. Look for answers you can live with.

Rule Number Three: Take responsibility for yourself in any life situation. Do what has to be done to reach the goal you have defined. Early on, be prepared to deal with things that don't turn out as you first thought they would. Have the patience to persevere through the work of succeeding at love or labor but also maintain and act upon the courage to get away from anything or anyone that proves to be a poison to your God-intended purpose in this world.

Back in my old neighborhood, I had no such visions of how far Mom and Dad's rules would travel with me through my life, even during the times I later may have forgotten them for a while. I just knew that I wanted to be a ballplayer and that I was surrounded by loving family who believed in me too.

Mom loved to cook. It was pretty much an all-the-time thing that aunts and uncles would drop by and take meals with us. She'd have prepared everything in her own way, and I'm talking about all the food that was the soul to my body while I was growing up: fried chicken, sweet corn, greens, cabbage, iced tea, homemade lemonade, and my all-time favorite—pork chops. Good conversation and family togetherness just went down easy at our house because it was all based on food prepared in the name of love. It didn't hurt either that my mom also was one terrific cook.

By the time I reached Robert A. Taft High School, my closest friends were the seven other student athletes who went on to professional sports careers from our senior year class of 1960. Jinx Martin went on from Taft as a boxer. He ended up as manager for the great Sugar Ray Leonard. Another Taft guy was a fellow with the already famous baseball name of Walter Johnson. This Walter Johnson, however, was a football player who went on to an NFL career as a tackle for the Cleveland Browns. Carl Ward was another football guy. Carl departed Taft to eventually play defensive back for the Cincinnati Bengals. O.C. Mack was one of my baseball teammates. He later pitched for the Cincinnati Reds. We also had Tom Dinkens, who later played center for the Detroit Pistons of the NBA, one other guy whose name escapes me for the moment, and, of course, me.

A lot of kids today are specialized on one sport by the time they reach high school. It wasn't that way during my era. Back then, student athletes played as many sports as their grades could stand. I was captain of the baseball team for four years, but I was also co-captain of the basketball team for three years. I ran cross-country in track, which was a requirement at Taft for those of us who played baseball, and I also played football. I lettered in all four sports.

By the time I got to Taft, I had been a shortstop since elementary school. I played shortstop in Little League, Pony League, and right on through high school. I did play catcher once as a younger kid, but I didn't like it very much. I turned my head at the wrong time while I was catching in that game and the ball hit me in the neck. I called time and told Dad, who was also my coach, that catching was not for me, that I had to go back to shortstop.

Dad never pushed me anyway, but he sure never tried to get me to play catcher again either. As far as I'm concerned, they don't call the catcher's gear "the tools of ignorance" for no reason.

On the other hand, I loved playing shortstop. I patterned myself after Roy McMillan, the smooth-fielding shortstop of the Cincinnati Reds and, for a long while, I patterned my defensive game completely upon the way I saw him playing the game. After a time, I made some adjustments that worked better for me. And that's when I started coming into my own with a style that I considered to be pure Jimmy Wynn. That felt good.

Another thing that felt good back in high school was the fact that we just lived a few blocks from Crosley Field. In fact, on game days, several of my Reds heroes had to pass down my street on their way to the ballpark. The timing of these passages was such that a quick scamper home from school at 3:00 p.m. would put me there with just enough time to see them and say hello as they passed our house. We're talking about Frank Robinson, Vada Pinson, and Ted Kluszewski here, folks. For a kid from Cincinnati in the late 1950s, the names didn't get any bigger.

While some kids my age were walking a mile for a Camel cigarette back in those days, I was running smoke-free a full mile and a half home from school in time to catch up with the guys as they made their way to work at the only job I ever aspired to hold down.

At the same time this was going on, I was too young, naïve, and modest to be aware that the Reds players' friendly behavior toward me was being influenced by my growing reputation as a prospect. That attention even heated up after I performed really well at a private Reds tryout at Crosley Field. I saw the possibility then that I might even be running home to greet my future teammates by these mad dashes home from school.

At any rate, one day something happened to sort of bring the Reds players' friendliness and the Reds club's interest in me home under the same roof. Frank Robinson and Vada Pinson stopped at my house and got out of Frank's white Thunderbird convertible. They wanted to speak to my parents. They asked my folks if it would be OK for them to take me down to the ballpark and show me their clubhouse—and how they prepare for a game. Mom and Dad said it would be very much OK. Dad understood.

My head still swims from the thrill of that day. I got to meet everybody on the Reds club that afternoon, even getting a chance to shake hands with their manager, the legendary Fred Hutchinson.

The highlight of my visit with the Reds at Crosley Field came when Frank Robinson handed me this glove and said, "Here, Jimmy! This glove is yours. It's just my gift to you."

Whoa! I wasn't on Cloud 9. I was on Cloud 999!

Needless to add, the events of that day only accelerated my attempts to be there every time I could when the Reds were likely to go marching by. Any shade of doubt about my baseball career goals also was erased. Although I think that goal was already pretty much sitting in solid sunlight anyway, it just pumped me up all the more.

Once my high school baseball season got into high gear, I couldn't make it home everyday to greet the Reds. I was too busy taking on some of the local future greats of baseball and other sports.

The Cincinnati area was loaded with athletic talent during the time I played high school ball there in the late 1950s. Pete Rose of Western Hills High School was undoubtedly the most famous of us all back then, at least among those who went on to play professional baseball. Pete was a little skinny guy back then, but he built himself up over the winter months working at the Post Office, lifting heavy boxes and bags. He was a fierce competitor, even then, and I got to take him on as a rival in high school in both baseball and football. That fieriness that blazed in Pete Rose, as I'm sure you've already read or heard, came straight from his dad. The apple didn't fall far from that tree when Pete Rose came along.

Pete Rose wasn't the only super-famous athlete I played against back in high school. I played baseball and football against the great Roger Staubach of Roger Bacon Catholic High School in Cincinnati. I also played against the much lesser known shortstop Eddie Brinkman. Brinkman was some kind of smooth-fielding shortstop back then. He was good enough to later sign and play for the Washington Senators for a short while.

I didn't spend any time thinking about Pete Rose's future back then. I had a fire of my own to fan, and, by my graduation year, other people were beginning to pay attention to my future possibilities too.

The assistant principal/athletic director at Taft High was also a "bird dog" scout for the Reds. For those who may not be familiar with that term, a bird dog scout is a guy who checks out potential talent on his own, or by special request, and then reports his findings back to the professional scouts employed by clubs. If a bird dog scouting report leads to a signing, he gets paid a little fee for his contribution to the final result.

At any rate, the bird dog scout at Taft, of course, had been watching me play right there under his nose at Taft and he was able to easily line up a tryout for me with the Cincinnati Reds, right there at Crosley Field. How lucky for me! How many baseball-struck kids even get a tryout, let alone a tryout with their favorite club at a ballpark located only blocks away from home?

The tryout went great. As a batter, I was hitting balls out of the park in every direction—left field, left center, center field, over the scoreboard, and even to right field! After I'd nearly finished batting, I got a nod from Jerry Lynch, a hard-hitting Reds outfielder who was there and paying close attention as I batted.

Jerry Lynch nodded at me; then he nodded at Reds General Manager Gabe Paul, as he quickly added: "Mr. Paul, sign this kid now! Don't let him get away!"

Well, there was still some fielding to demonstrate, but that went well too. I went out to shortstop and took on everything they hit to me. I showed range and athleticism. And my fundamentals were rock-solid on footwork, positioning, and catching all the different kinds of balls they hit to me, I worked the double play flawlessly and, as the final demonstration and final word on any shortstop's future, I showed the Reds the big thing, other than range, that can't be taught: I fired every throw to first strong, hard, straight, and true. There could be no doubt that I had both the arm and the range needed by any worthwhile major league shortstop.

Once I had taken my last grounder in the field, Mr. Paul and the Reds people called me in as they then proceeded to bubble with enthusiasm while talking among themselves on the importance of contacting my parents about signing me to a contract. Since I had yet to reach my eighteenth birthday, the Reds would need parental consent to sign me to a professional baseball contract. And they really wanted to sign me before some other club swooped down and stole me away from my hometown Reds.

The Reds scout quickly made a date to come speak with my parents. And here's where the rain starts to fall on my too-quickly-celebrating parade.

After hearing all the good things the Reds had to say about me, and how much they want to sign me now, Mom took over the meeting. She had a different idea about what was going to happen next, even as Dad lent an interested and more openly laid-back ear to the Reds' contract proposal. I think he was pretty much waiting on Mom's reaction too, and I believe he pretty much knew what it was going to be.

"Hold on, everybody," Mom said, "there's just one thing wrong with this offer. There's no way Jimmy's father and I are giving our permission to this contract proposal!"

"Why not, Mom?" I pleaded. "This is my big chance! You know how I want to play professional baseball, and all of a sudden, here we are, talking with the Cincinnati Reds! They want me, Mom! And this is what I want! This is what I've *always* wanted!"

A moment of silence hung in the air as Mom gave me a long stare, before turning the same firm gaze into the eyes of the Cincinnati scout.

"Our son is going to college, sir," Mom said evenly. "If you still want him as a baseball player when he's done, and that's still what he wants to do, you can get together with him then. By that time, he will be of age and totally responsible for making a decision this big all on his own."

I remember that moment so well. You could almost feel the air leave the room on its own, at least the air that had been floating the balloons of my big dream.

"Jimmy," Mom said, as she turned to me, "the program you've been aiming for at Central State College is only two years long. You will also be playing baseball there. If the Reds still want you in two years, their offer tonight will still be good."

"Your mother's right, Jimmy," the scout added, as he shook hands with Mom and Dad, and soon departed.

The matter was settled, and it wasn't just Dad going along with Mom. Dad always valued education too. He often told me that education was the key to me having another line of work beyond baseball. And he was also the one who stayed on me about my homework until I both did it—and did it right. So, when the door closed on my first opportunity to sign with the Reds, Dad was right there with Mom on that decision.

I left for Central State College in the fall that followed my June 1960 graduation from Taft High. My enrollment had been arranged by my parents and by my namesake, Uncle Jimmy. I gave it my best shot academically, and I played baseball and basketball during my short time there. In fact, my baseball coach at Central State was a fellow named Ben Waterman. Ben had been my baseball coach at Taft before going on ahead of me to Central State. He pretty much is the one who recruited me to go there too.

I think Mom and Dad both knew that I had gone as far as my motivation was going to carry me with formal education during the time I was at Central

State. They also could see that I had accepted Mom's veto of my first Reds offer and gone on to college as we had planned prior to the tryout. Making the effort in the proper spirit counted heavily in the Wynn household.

Two years later, in 1962, Mom called me up one day. "Now's the time for you to sign onto your dream, Jimmy," she said. The Reds were still interested in me, and again, Mom was right. The extra time I spent away at college was good for me, and now I was ready at age 19 to decide the next step for myself. I right away returned to Cincinnati and signed a professional baseball contract with the Cincinnati Reds.

I signed with Reds scout Chris Polking for a bonus payment of $500.00 and a monthly salary of $375.00. The money wasn't all that important to me, but signing that contract sure as heck was. It meant that my lifelong dream had finally come true. I was now a professional baseball player. Now I would be in a position to do some things to help my mother and father.

Signing on with Cincinnati just prior to my twentieth birthday wasn't like going to Central State College, a mere fifty miles from home. In the middle of my joy was the realization also that this was one of those life-changing moments. I didn't know at first where the Reds would be sending me for minor league seasoning, but I did know that it was going to be far, far away from home.

If I succeeded as a professional baseball player, which I fully intended to do, I would never be living at home again with Mom and Dad and my little brothers and sisters, in quite the same way, ever again.

That's as it should be, but I still felt the impending separation right down to the bones of my soul. I also knew deep down inside: For as long as we are all living on this earth, breathing God's good air on the same day, no matter where we each may be at any given time of day, I will never really be far away from these people who raised me, these people I grew up with, these people I love.

Mom and Dad tried to prepare me for my journey into the world. That preparation started from the time I was old enough to understand anything. Their message came down to these elements:

1. Be yourself.
2. Treat other people with dignity and respect, regardless of race, creed, or color.
3. Try understanding what other people are about and what they are going through.
4. Live love, not hate, for others.

Dad always told me: "Look! You are going to run into some people and things out there that will be hurtful and very hard to understand. Remember too, when these things happen, give me a call. We will do our best to sort them out so that you can learn from them and strengthen yourself into an even better, more grown-up person."

As I headed from home on the train that would take me through the Deep South and into my first assignment with the Tampa Tarpons of the Class D Florida State League, I would soon enough need to make that call to Dad. The Deep South of 1962 was still a place that sadly brimmed with violent racism and hateful words from many whites toward black people.

And here I came into this bubbling arena of social change, a 20-year-old kid from Cincinnati who had been raised to love life and the game of baseball. I had no desire to bring pain or misery to anyone, but I was black—and my legal middle name was Sherman.

My simple young life was about to get a whole lot more complicated.

Chapter 2

A Tempest in Tampa

Nobody, not even my loving mom and dad, could have spared me the pain I was going to feel from people who hate blindly. All I was trying to do was start my professional baseball life, but I was doing it in the Deep South, and the year was 1962.

Remember: This was two years prior to the passage of the Civil Rights Act of 1964. That new federal law would make segregation illegal, but it didn't come about early enough to cover my start in baseball. In 1962, everything down South was segregated by race—right down to the business of where you could drink water or go to the bathroom. In the fall of 1962, a black student named James Meredith would need the protection of federal troops as he enrolled and began classes at Ole Miss over in Oxford, Mississippi.

It was crazy, but it's how it was. Some whites didn't want blacks to follow their dreams, if it meant rubbing elbows with whites. It didn't matter if a black person had the talent for engineering or baseball. He or she was just supposed to do it somewhere away from white people. Same as eating, eliminating, or going to the movies. "Do it someplace else" was the name of the segregation game. We blacks were supposed to be as invisible as possible, and just show up when the white man had some work he needed done cheap.

The Negro Leagues had been the black man's answer to segregation in baseball until Jackie Robinson broke the color line in professional baseball back in 1946, when he took the field with the Montreal Royals, a AAA farm club of the Brooklyn Dodgers. In 1947, Jackie would then break the major league color line for all the rest of us who came after him wearing black skin. And that was only fifteen years prior to the start of my career.

A lot of things hadn't yet changed in support of fair play for all people in 1962. And I'm not just talking baseball here. Remember, there wasn't anything out there like a Negro League for black engineers. You had to either qualify yourself for jobs in the world at large, or else bury your dream for want of an opportunity, and that just wasn't right. James Meredith would go on to take his degree in political science from Ole Miss. There wasn't any Negro League for political scientists either, and that idea no longer even worked in baseball.

I learned the ins and outs—and mostly *outs*—of segregation as I made my way south to Florida for spring training in late February of my 1962 rookie season. Fortunately for me, the Reds had assigned a fairly big group of other black players to the roster of their Class D Tampa Tarpons ball club. From the start, I felt right at home in the company of guys like the big bopper first baseman Lee May.

The Reds had arranged for us black members of the Tampa club to stay in an un-air-conditioned black motel during spring training while the white players all stayed on the beach in posh all-white air-conditioned hotels. See how it was? Or maybe you remember.

I didn't mind. We stayed there at the motel on a several-players-to-each-room basis and drew three good-tasting square meals a day. The motel was owned by a sweet lady whose name I've unfortunately forgotten, but she could really cook. She relied upon the motel to support her and her two little girls. I'm sure the money that the Reds gave her for taking care of us was a big help. She cooked breakfast, lunch, and dinner for us, and she made every effort she could to fix the foods we liked, too. Man! Could she ever cook some great meals!

It was sort of like living in a college dormitory and we all got along pretty good. As I look back now across the years, that condition of closeness among us black players was no doubt helped by the fact of our "you and me against the world" living conditions.

We only had two rules. We had to be in our rooms by midnight and we had to be on time for meals. If you showed up late for meals, you missed out. Believe me, I was never late.

We had about twelve black guys on the Tampa roster in 1962. The most famous of these would be Lee May, the fellow they later called the "Big Bopper" when he became a great-slugging first baseman for the Reds. As you probably know, Lee May later also joined us on the Astros, coming over to Houston in the Joe Morgan trade.

Not all of us were on the road up back in 1962. Our center fielder, Willie Kern, was in his third and last year of pro ball at the lower minor league level. He could run as fast as Vada Pinson. He just couldn't hit like him.

Another guy I liked was Nate Thurmond. Nate was not to be confused with the famous basketball player of the same name. Our Nate didn't make the club, but he was a big part of our spring training group at the motel in Tampa.

Crazy as this may seem today, we all sat around the motel at night, for the most part, and talked baseball. We talked about the game we played that same day, and we talked about baseball fundamentals. By and large we were a group who wanted to learn and make progress. A fire burned in our bellies for baseball.

After the Florida State League season started, those of us who made the team were placed as boarders in the homes of various families in Tampa. The Reds worked all this out, as they had the motel/hotel lodgings for spring training. As was the case when we got there, the Reds went with the flow of the locals, placing black players with black families, and white players with white families. At the Class D ball level, we were all pretty much in the same boat as young kids starting out. We all had different levels of talent and, as the years progressed, it turns out that we each came with different levels of commitment to the idea of becoming a professional baseball player.

Some of us just had to start our playing careers with the extra weight of doing our jobs under the watchful eyes of subtle and not-so-subtle racial hatred for us because of our skin color. Fortunately for me, I came armed with talent, desire, and the powerful support of my family back home, whom I talked to by long distance at least a couple of times each week. The voice and wisdom of my dad was my shield against the ignorance and blind hatred of racist whites. He told me to keep in mind my own worth and value as a child of God, and he encouraged me to pray for those people who said terrible things to me simply because I was black. Most of the time, those were the only thoughts I needed to keep in mind, but I'm human, and there came a time later in the year that could've been a breaking point for me, had I not had the support of my second manager at Tampa, a fellow named Hershell Freeman, and a champion of goodness that I shall never forget.

But let's not get ahead of ourselves. We'll cover the Freeman story later. I don't want to jump past the first manager I had at Tampa because I liked him too. He also happened to be one of the great stories in baseball history.

Johnny Vander Meer started the 1962 season as manager for the Tampa Tarpons. As you probably remember, or know, Johnny Vander Meer is the only pitcher in major league history to have pitched two straight no-hit games. He did that amazing thing in 1938 as a pitcher for the Cincinnati Reds in consecutive appearances against the Boston Braves and the Brooklyn Dodgers. It was the sort of feat that puts all other memories of a player in the shade for all time. Baseball has a few people like that, and Vander Meer is one of them. Pitcher Don Larsen is another. Do I need to tell you why people remember Larsen? I didn't think so.

No matter what else Johnny Vander Meer did as a pitcher, and he had a pretty fair career, people remember him for those two straight "no-no" games. All I can add is that Vander Meer was a pretty fair manager of us young guys too. He was patient and he had some things to teach us about moving on from losses and mistakes and getting ready for the next game. My dad had always stressed the importance of learning the fundamentals because he believed strongly that a lot of errors occur because players don't have their heads straight in advance about what to do with the baseball in various game situations. Vander Meer was the kind of manager who thought that way too, making it real easy for me to listen to what he had to say.

As human beings who happen to be baseball players, we are going to make mistakes in life and baseball. The important thing is to learn from our mistakes and make fundamental corrections in the way we approach similar situations in the future. I knew that much in my head back in 1962. It just didn't spare me the ride into certain errors of personal judgment in the years that lay ahead. Now, at age 68, I see the light on this subject a little brighter.

Making a good life decision is both logical and emotional, and these two elements are tied to each other like lightning and thunder. Like viewing lightning, it's always easier to see the logic of what we need to do, but we won't really get the lesson of why that choice is so important until we hear the loud thunder of our personal experience. I can look at the hot stove and understand that it's hot, but when I touch the thing, I know it's hot in ways that go beyond all words. The hope is that we don't have to touch all the different hot stoves to get all of the different lessons we need to survive and thrive.

Back in 1962, I'm just trying to get my feet on the ground when Manager Vander Meer decided to move me to third base, a position I had not really played in high school, where I was strictly a shortstop. It didn't take me long to discover the thunder of this learning experience. I always knew that third base was different from shortstop. When I moved over to play the very aptly named "hot corner," I got the thunder boom fast on this learning experience. Yes, indeed, third base was a different deal altogether.

My move to third base was helped along by the fact that the regular Tampa guy at third, a legendary older Latin player whose name now escapes me, was having visa trouble getting out of his country in time for spring training. In his absence, I was asked to take his place. The move also was helped by the fact that Len Boehmer was their holdover shortstop at Tampa from 1961. Len Boehmer had excellent defensive skills, but he had batted only .202 in his rookie year. The Reds wanted to rule him in or out as a prospect, I now suppose. I guess they figured they could always move me back to short if Boehmer didn't show any improvement. In the meanwhile, it set me up for moving fast down a whole new learning path.

Whereas shortstop required you to have good speed, range, a strong arm, and a whole lot of athleticism, third base demanded that you have agile, quick feet, strong and suddenly working reflexes, a strong arm too, and some kind of special sense about how many batters use the position of the third baseman to determine where and how they will attack the pitch. A good bunter and slugger, one who was capable of suckering you deep or shallow, could take a great big advantage of you, if you were not aware of what he was doing.

As a third baseman, I participated in executing what I think was the only triple play of the year in the 1962 Florida State League season. It was equal parts of easy and fun. Here's how it worked: The other club had runners on first and second while I was playing only about two or three steps off the bag. When a sharp one-bouncer came straight into my glove, I just stepped on third and fired to second, where the second baseman made the base tag there and quickly fired to first for the third out. A 5–4–3 triple play was in the books, just like that. We were out of the inning with a feather in our cap.

It was a simple play, but its execution really started with the lesson that both my managers at Tampa drilled into us at Tampa from Day One: "Know the game situation at all times," manager Vander Meer used to say, over and over again. "Before the ball comes to you, you've got to know what you're going to do with it, if it's hit to you in that particular game situation."

Playing third base really brought home the lesson too of how much we have to rely upon our reflexes, once a play goes in motion. There's no time to think and make new decisions, once a hard ball is hit to you. You had to get your thinking done before the play started. That's the hard lesson that Vander Meer preached. And that's the same lesson today that we need to teach, even young kids, from the very start.

Making the adjustment was helped by the fact that I stayed in close touch with my dad by phone about what was going on. By this time, just the sound of his voice was enough to help me keep focused on the only career life goal I ever had, that of becoming a successful professional baseball player. Dad's presence, even from afar by long distance, was the flame of wisdom and support that kept my dream alive.

I never loosened my grip on the dream. Even then, I knew. I knew because, more and more, as I moved into the world on my own, I saw it happening to other people. Those who loosened their grip, or their level of dedication to the dream of being a ballplayer, fell by the wayside. The picture came together for me, even if I couldn't put it into words at that time: If you let it go for a single day, you will never get it back. A dream is like a helium balloon in that respect.

My dedication extended to trying to learn a little something new every day, and to obeying the rules that the Reds set forth for us as members of the Tampa ball club, and that included how I responded to the people that the club had paid to help us. The older lady who boarded a few of us that season was awfully sweet and another great cook. She had the same strict rules about being on time for meals and being in the house by midnight, but neither was ever a problem for me. After all, I had grown up as the son of a lady named Maude Wynn. I arrived in Tampa already knowledgeable of how to show respect for women in authority.

If showing the baseball world I had a talking bat, playing third base well, and doing the right thing on and off the field was going to get me to the big leagues, I was on my way to somewhere better. I was convinced of that fact. I was also long on believing that I was holding my own, with and against some other pretty good prospects. Of course, our side of this formula was easy to see. Our first baseman was Lee May. The Big Bopper was on his way to great things with the Reds and Astros.

On the other side, the league had players like All-Star outfielder Alex Johnson of the Miami Marlins. Alex was headed for a long big league career with the Phillies and several other clubs. The Lakeland Giants also featured an All-Star second baseman named Tito Fuentes. As you probably remember, Tito Fuentes went on from his rookie minor league year to a successful big league career with the San Francisco Giants and others.

When he retired from the game in the late '70s, Tito Fuentes was the Latin player who will be remembered for this famous one-sentence retirement speech: "Baseball has been very good to me!"

I must have been doing a few things right. By year's end, I was named as the Florida State League All-Star third baseman with a .290 batting average. I also led the league in home runs with fourteen and in runs batted in with eighty-one.

Len Boehmer did OK at shortstop too. Boehmer was named as the 1962 Florida State League All-Star shortstop with a .293 batting average, one home run, and forty-four runs batted in. Boehmer would have a minor league career that carried him through a cup of coffee with the Reds in 1967 and he would also see some action for the Yankees in 1969 and 1971. By 1972, Boehmer would be out of baseball as a player, but for the 1962 season, he helped make an All-Star third baseman out of a fellow named Jimmy Wynn.

My rookie season of 1962 also taught me another of baseball's universal lessons. That is, that nothing is ever guaranteed or forever. People come and people go. And sometimes, change takes place overnight.

For whatever reason, Johnny Vander Meer did not finish the season as manager of the Tampa Tarpons. He moved on up to take over as manager of the Class AAA International League's Syracuse Chiefs. As his replacement, the Reds brought in a fellow named Hershell Freeman from their Class B Carolina League Rocky Mount Chiefs to take over our Tampa club.

The appointment of Hershell Freeman as the new manager for the Tampa Tarpons turned out to be one of those critical moments in my early baseball life. Freeman was a former big league pitcher and still pretty young when I met him. At age thirty-four, and at 6' 3", Manager Freeman towered over me. He was still in pretty good shape too. We hit it off well together right away, but I still had no idea of how important he was going to be for me just a short time after he took over the reins of the club.

It happened on a road trip game we played against the Palatka Cubs. These Cubs hailed from a Florida town that already had a very bad reputation among black players as a really tough place to be, let alone play a baseball game against the local club. I guess it was just my time to catch the hell that comes from the cowardly voice of racial hatred yelling at you from the shadows of the crowd.

I was playing third base, of course, and that made me an easy target for one of those bigots on the third base side.

"Hey, monkey," this guy starts yelling, "Where's your tail?"

The man moved quickly to calling me the "n" word and just about every other offensive name ever laid down upon black people by ignoramuses, but I couldn't stand it. In spite of everything my dad had taught me about people of this type, this was my first time to come under such a close and personally mean attack, simply for being black. The man was creating a thunder in my experience that threatened to take me to a place where I said, "This isn't worth it." Still, my dream and my dad's words fought back from the inside: "You don't allow ignorant people to step on your dream because of their hatefulness. Forgive them. Pray for them. And get on with what you need to do to succeed. With God's help, nothing can stop you from using the abilities He gave you to play baseball."

For innings in the field, it was a like a fight in which I wasn't allowed to punch back. I thought of Jackie Robinson and I wondered, almost aloud: "How did you put up with this stuff, Jackie?"

Tears came to my eyes, but I fought hard to push them back. I didn't want to give the man the satisfaction of seeing that he was getting to me, but I guess that wasn't going to work out as an escape plan. The next thing I knew, someone had called timeout. And here came my manager, Hershell Freeman, walking out to talk with me.

"What's going on here, Jimmy?" Hershell Freeman asked. From the dugout, he either had not seen the man or heard all that was being said.

When I told my manager what the man in the stands had been saying to me, I thought he was going to explode, but he didn't. He very calmly assured me that he would take care of this situation right away.

"Point this guy out to me, Jimmy!" Hershell Freeman stated flatly.

When I pointed to a man sitting several rows back of the third base dugout, Hershell Freeman asked the umpire for an extension of his timeout. After a few words with the umpire, the tall and imposing figure that was Freeman started walking directly toward the stands, with the umpire trailing behind him.

The next thing I knew, Hershell Freeman had climbed over the bar and into the stands, walking straight toward the racist heckler. Standing straight above the now-silent "fan," Freeman made his point. As best I recall, this is what he said: "You see that man out there, mister? Well, that's my third baseman and he has a job to do. He didn't come here to put up with your insults, but to play his best for our ball club. I'm here to tell you to shut up and watch the game. If I hear one more insulting word out of your mouth directed toward any of my players, I'm coming back up here to punch you out personally! Do I make myself clear?"

The man said nothing as several policemen now joined the scene, making no effort to contradict anything Hershell Freeman said. The man also said nothing else to me the rest of the night. We even rallied to win the game, but that night, the win we celebrated was even more important than the outcome of a baseball game. It was a win for decency over disgrace.

Looking back, which I do a lot of these days, it just makes me happy to have a chance to tell you this story of another quiet baseball hero, Hershell Freeman. It also reminds me of how many chances we all have to give up on our dream when we're young because of some obstacle that gets in our way. We just can't let it happen if we want to avoid a lifetime of wonder and regret. We have to hang in there and persevere, if we want to sleep well in our old age.

There will be some sadness if we fail to achieve some goal that is part of our dream, but sadness is not the poison. Sadness just comes from doing all we can and still not getting there. The real poison is regret. And regret comes from knowing that we either didn't try, or we let the dream go, or we simply backed away in the face of some adversity that plopped itself down on our path. My dad knew that I couldn't live with regret and so too did Hershell Freeman. They each taught me well that I had to live with the same truth. It's fight back or die inside.

Hershell Freeman had an interesting last name. It really fit well to the role he played in the rookie year of my professional baseball life. I will never forget what he did for me. He was the difference-maker for me on a hot night long ago in Palatka, Florida. He was the difference that allowed decency to win over disgrace.

The 1962 season ended with the Tampa Tarpons finishing in third place with a 66–54 record. On the heels of my rookie year going into the books, I took nothing for granted. Leading the Florida State League in home runs and runs batted in and also being named to the All-Star team would mean nothing next year.

I had no idea what the Reds had planned for me in 1963, but I decided to do everything within my power to help them see the most positive side of my potential as a ballplayer. I decided to return to Tampa over the off-season and play in the winter league they conducted down there.

My dad's words burned brightly in my brain. His wisdom was there like the sunshine, both before and after the Palatka incident. And that wisdom resided within me when my 1962 rookie season ended. The more it spoke to me in my mind, the more it seemed to ooze out and fill every cell of my body. I would just hear his words, without ever intending to hit any kind of internal play button, and the same message from Dad would speak and repeat: "You know what to do. You know how to do it. Just always remember these things:

Love the game. And try to love the people who are out there on the field with you as teammates."

Dad's wisdom went from here to forever, but I was now walking down a path in organized baseball that wasn't totally like any that he had traveled as a young man. Organized baseball had a way back then of pouring hot and cold water upon you at the same time, but in different spots. I would soon get my first taste of another fact about baseball life back in the reserve clause era: No matter how well you do, it's not up to you where you play baseball next year.

CHAPTER 3

"Houston, We Have a New Ballplayer!"

The date was November 26, 1962. I arrived in camp in Tampa for winter league play, but all the other Reds prospects were already assembled on the field and really talking up a storm. Then I saw the usually smiling face of Lee May. He motioned at me to come on over as though he had something to say. With my curiosity peaked to a high level, I made a beeline to him.

"I hate to break the news to you, Roomie," Lee May said, "but we've just learned the bad news about you a few moments ago."

"What bad news?" I asked. May's words hit me as disturbing.

"The Reds have released you," he said.

Lee May's message may as well have been a gunshot. I was speechless, but soon on the brink of tears. I never cried. I guess the sight of my horrified face was just too much, even for a skilled practical joker like Lee May.

"I'm sorry, Jimmy," Lee May countered, as he reached out to me. "I should never have kidded you about a thing like that. Please forgive me. The Reds have not released you, but you have been drafted out of the Reds organization today by the Houston Colt .45s, that new expansion team over in Texas."

Whoa! What a roller coaster ride that was for my whole nervous system!

I was only at "you have been released" long enough to hurt real bad. Now I had to come back and figure out what the other news in truth really meant. For a while I just got mad enough to fight anybody and everybody. Somebody or some kind of baseball thing had just turned my dream all around and upside down. I didn't even know where Houston was located, and I sure as heck didn't have any idea what a Colt .45 was!

At any rate, the owner of the Tampa club soon pulled me aside and started explaining what the drafting of my contract by Houston meant to my future. That discussion made me feel a whole lot better, even if I still held onto the normal fear about going into a situation I didn't know. By going into an expansion club organization, I was moving into a faster lane for reaching my big league dream. Had I stayed with the Reds, chances are that it might have taken four to five years to break into their roster. At Houston, the club had just finished the 1962 National League season in 8th place, playing with drafted rookies and a bunch of over-the-hill veterans. If I continued to improve, which I planned to do, I might get to the big leagues as early as the 1963 season. That prospect sounded pretty good to me.

Later that same day, my first contact with Houston came ringing at me by way of the telephone. I got a call from Mr. Paul Richards, the general manager of the Colt .45s. It was pretty much of a formality call, with Mr. Richards welcoming me to the organization and saying that he would be looking forward to meeting me in person when I came to Houston. "Welcome aboard!" was good enough for me on that day of news that I soon enough saw for what it was—good news!

I wanted to shout for joy, but I did the next best thing. I called my parents in Cincinnati. They were, of course, very, very happy for me. I just couldn't wait to get back home and see the faces that I knew came with all those smiles I heard over the phone.

I wouldn't be staying to play for the Tampa Reds winter league club now. No need. My contract was now the property of the Houston Colt .45s, whatever that was.

Jimmy Wynn joined the Colt .45s in 1963 (National Baseball Hall of Fame Library, Cooperstown, NY).

My pursuit of the major league dream was to continue in Houston. Nothing would ever be guaranteed, nor would I let up on my approach to hard work, but I would allow myself a little floating-on-a-cloud-with-joy time during the winter of 1962–63.

When I got home to Cincinnati, all my family and friends came around to greet and congratulate me on my season in Tampa—and on my draft selection by the Houston Colt .45s. It was more wonderful in real time than I had imagined in my mind.

I didn't take a job that off-season. I had made enough money playing ball to both help out and get by at home, and I didn't want to do anything to cause injury to my chances at Houston in 1963 on a manual labor job over the winter months. If I was going to get hurt, which I didn't, thank God, it was going to be doing work around the house for my family. I went back to some familiar chores at home. I mowed the grass for as long as it kept growing. Then I shoveled snow off the porch once the white stuff started falling.

I didn't have much of a social life during this period of time, but I did meet a Cincinnati girl who would soon become important to me. Her name was Ruth.

Christmas and New Year's passed like holiday postcards at the Wynn home in Cincinnati and all seemed well and right with the world. It *seemed* that way because it *was* that way. I just didn't realize that it would be the last Christmas at home under the old conditions of my childhood, of me being around my family. As time goes by, life changes all things for all of us and, sometimes, it especially first changes the little routines we grew up feeling good about at holiday time.

Once spring training time rolled around in 1963, I traveled to Houston to meet all of the new people who were about to become big parts of my new life. By then I already knew that I would be starting the season with the Houston Class AA Texas League farm club, the San Antonio Bullets, but there was no shortage of people in Houston who wanted to meet me in person on my way to work.

My head still swims at all the greeters who came over to the Colt .45s office to shake my hand in Houston upon my arrival. The city was a big sprawling place and full of big-talking men that wore cowboy hats. Prominently, the one who did the most talking was the man who best represented the face of ownership, Judge Roy Hofheinz himself. I also met Paul Richards, the GM, of course, and Tal Smith, who was then the farm club director, and Harry Craft, the Colt .45 manager. I also shook hands with the other Houston icons as well. It was only later that I learned how important R.E. "Bob" Smith, Craig Cullinan, and George Kirksey were to the establishment of big league baseball in Houston. At that moment in time, I was just a twenty-one-year-old kid from Ohio, following his dream, and hoping I'd taken a new big step to the big time.

I also met the local media while I was in Houston for the first time. Two of these people stand out in memory today, one because of how he later put a name to my public image as a ballplayer, and the other because he was the only writer in the group that was shorter than me. I'm talking here about the late John Wilson of the *Houston Chronicle* and the wonderfully sharp and witty Mickey Herskowitz, then of the old *Houston Post*. I am seriously grateful to both of these writers for how fairly they each treated me over the years but, again, back in the early part of 1963, they were just two more hands to shake.

The 1963 San Antonio Bullets were managed by a career minor league guy named Lou Fitzgerald. Lou had just the right touch with our bunch. And we were quite a good ball club too, if I do say so myself.

For black ballplayers, the living conditions in San Antonio back in 1963 were just awful. Because of segregation, there were only a few places open to us for eating out, going to movies, or even getting haircuts. Our choices of places to live were just as restricted. Jim Pendleton and I roomed and took our meals at the Air Force base there in San Antonio. I think the ball club worked that deal out for us. Living on the base wasn't a bad deal. Just knowing that we were living in a town where we weren't welcome in most places felt really bad. Having grown up in Cincinnati, I wasn't accustomed to being told that the color of my skin was reason enough to keep me from even drinking water from the same fountains as whites.

Thank God again that social change was on the way in 1963. And thank God forever too that my dad had prepared me mentally for this kind of challenge. That foundation allowed me the growing freedom to focus on my baseball dream and the changes I needed to make in my game. In other words, I was free to go to school on everything I still needed to learn about playing the game of baseball.

One coach and a part-time catcher was Clint Courtney, the old St. Louis Browns receiver, plus a young fellow who would develop strong and go on to catch for the 1969 World Series champion New York Mets, a fellow named Jerry Grote. Houston lost the services of Jerry Grote when the club dealt him off to the Mets on October 19, 1965, for a pitcher named Tom Parsons. Our third catcher was Dave Adlesh, who did make it up to the Houston club for a while.

We had some boppers on that San Antonio club too. In fact, seven of us were in double figures for home runs at San Antonio in 1963: Ed Olivares (23), Chuck Harrison and Aaron Pointer (18 each), Ron Davis and Jimmy Wynn (16 each), Jerry Grote (14), and Mike White (10).

It's funny how that works out in baseball. Of San Antonio's "Magnificent Power Seven," Jerry Grote and I were the only ones who ended up with long-term careers in the big leagues. Harrison, Pointer, and Davis made it to the bigs in the short term, but Olivares (.292) and White (.324) never even got another call. Even being named as the Texas League All-Star second baseman didn't help Mike White. As for Ed Olivares, he had caught an earlier cup of coffee with the St. Louis Cardinals, but his nice year for the '63 Bullets still failed to restore him to prospect status.

There's an old saying in baseball: If you stay in the minors too long, it's easy to move almost overnight in the eyes of scouts from *prospect* to *suspect*. It isn't always fair, but it is the way it is. Maybe a player's only crime is being a slow developer. One scout sees that factor and still values the player as a *prospect*. Another scout may simply see how long the same guy has been in the minors and write him off as a *suspect*.

All I knew as a twenty-one-year-old kid in 1963 was that I wanted to reach the major leagues as fast as possible. The Colt .45s weren't in a great position to write many players off as suspects, and I sure wasn't planning on being one of those who caught that label. I should add that no club avoids the occasional mistake on the prospect/suspect assessment. Make a note that on April 4, 1963, the Astros dealt away a young outfielder they had earlier acquired from the Giants to Pittsburgh in exchange for a center fielder named Howie Goss.

Goss played one season for the '63 Colt .45s, batting .209 with 9 homers and 128 strikeouts at the plate. He was out of baseball for good by season's end. The other kid, the one that Houston traded away, was a little fellow named Manny Mota, an excellent batter who went on to become one of the greatest pinch hitters of all time.

As future Astros pitcher Joaquin Andujar would someday say: "I can sum up the mystery of baseball in two words: You never know!" If you have a crystal ball, or halfway decent scouting, you don't trade away a Manny Mota for a Howie Goss at any time of the year.

Could the same club that was so wrong about Howie Goss be all that right about Jimmy Wynn? In the spring of 1963, we were all on our way to finding out. I was ready to give the opportunity my best shot, and ready to learn from anyone who could teach me what I needed to do to improve my game. Fortunately for me, and for anyone else who cared to listen or just watch him perform, we had such a veteran teammate with us on that '63 Bullets club. His name was Bob Boyd, a fellow who turned out to be my first real veteran teammate teacher.

On the '63 San Antonio Bullets club, they called lefty first baseman Bob Boyd "The Rope," and for the best of all baseball reasons: His nickname almost totally summarized his skill between the lines. My dad always loved baseball nicknames. He used to say, "You will know when you've arrived in baseball on the day that someone gives you a nickname that sticks."

Bob Boyd earned his nickname, the Rope, for all of those line drives he swatted off countless baseball walls across America in right and right center field. Boyd had one of the sweetest, most even swings I ever saw, and practically every ball he hit was a line drive rope to right, although he was capable of lining one to left on defenses that played him to pull right.

A lot of times, Boyd would hit a line drive that barely escaped the leaping grasp of the second baseman. Once clear, the ball would just keep on slowly rising until it either cleared the park or landed forty feet high against an outfield wall.

Now, that's a baseball rope, my friends.

Bob Boyd taught me by the character of his game. He played baseball with ability, care, and respect. He was an old-school gentleman who literally spoke gently and carried a big stick. At age 43 in 1963, Boyd still managed to hit .336 for San Antonio. He also batted .293 over a nine-season big league career that only began at age 32 because of the old color line that kept him out of organized baseball earlier.

I only recently learned that Bob Boyd was the first black athlete to break the color line in all of Houston's sports history. It happened when he came to town to play baseball for the 1954 Houston Buffs of the Texas League. If he even knew of this distinction, Bob Boyd never mentioned it. Quiet men are like that. Bob Boyd knew that people would judge him by what he did, and by how he conducted himself on the field, and not by what he said. Quiet men are often heroes. The late Bob Boyd will always be one of mine.

There is one thing about Bullets outfielder Aaron Pointer that I'd love to mention here. That's to point out the musical pedigree that his Pointer sisters earned for his family. Even though Aaron Pointer never became a household name in baseball, his singing sisters, the Pointer Sisters ("You Bet Your Sweet Bippy") did all right for themselves on the record charts, didn't they? The Houston clubhouse joke for years was that the Pointer Sisters had more hits as a singing group than all of the Colt .45 players as a baseball club did in the three years the team played by that name.

Behind the pitching of guys like Joe Hoerner and Cliff Davis, the San Antonio Bullets would take the straight away title in the '63 Texas League race with a 79–61 record, but they would then fall in the league championship playoff finals to third-place Tulsa.

Hoerner did some serious big league time as a pitcher. He later gained an early reputation, once the Astrodome opened, as one of the few fungo experts who could hit the top of the inside roof with a batted ball. Future big league outfielder Jim Beauchamp of Tulsa would be named as the Texas League MVP in 1963. That All-Star outfield would also include Jose Cardenal of El Paso and Rico Carty of Austin. Sandy Alomar of Austin would also be named as the shortstop and Randy Hundley of El Paso would get the nod as our All-Star catcher.

All-Star outfielder Arlo Engel of El Paso is another of our "history mystery" guys from the 1963 season. Playing in his fourth year of a nine-season, all minor league action career, all Engel did in 1963 was hit .320 and lead the Texas League with 41 HR and 126 RBI. None of that production earned the guy even a single future time at bat with a big league club.

Go figure that one!

By early July 1963, I got the call that probably would not have come so soon had I still been toiling in the minors for the talent-loaded Cincinnati Reds. Wearing my own skin as a player in the Houston organization, my .288 batting average with 16 homers and 49 runs batted in at San Antonio, plus the big club's crying needs, had won me a plane ticket to join the Houston Colt .45s in Pittsburgh, where they were getting ready to play the Pirates in a four-game series at old Forbes Field.

I was excited, but tempered by the thought that I really had only won a plane ticket to join the roster of the Houston Colt .45s. To stay, I was going to have to play well, both at bat and in the field.

When I got there, they gave me uniform number 18, and manager Harry Craft plugged me into the number six hole at shortstop. The series opener on July 10, 1963, marked my debut game as a big leaguer. I was so excited that day that I hardly remember a thing that Harry, and others, tried to tell me.

I got my first big league hit in that July 10 first big league game. I singled off Pirates starter Bob Friend for one of the only six safeties we collected off the Pittsburgh ace. Friend went all the way that day in a losing cause. Ken Johnson started for us, going seven and two-thirds innings and giving up only goose eggs and five hits to the Bucs. Hal Woodeshick finished the game and picked up the save in Johnson's 2–0 win over Pittsburgh.

That win in my first big league game pulled the Colt .45s to within twenty games of .500 at a record of 34 wins and 54 losses. It may as well have been the seventh game of the World Series to me. I was nothing less than quietly excited about landing in the big leagues, getting my first hit, and, at least, finding a sweet temporary parking spot for my major league baseball dream. I sure didn't want to make too much of a big deal about it. The rest of the guys, as you would expect, were pretty much taking the win in stride. I didn't want to come off like a kid in the candy shop. So I tried hard to play it cool.

One fact about big league life came home hard in my first game. The ball just seems to come at you faster on the infield, and especially on a steel-hard surface like they had at old Forbes Field. Roberto Clemente lashed a wicked hop-and-skip grounder to me that I stopped and played all right, but I stopped it with my shin. Man! Did that thing ever sting! It's a wonder I even made the play.

Four days later, on July 14, 1963, I got my first major league home run off a fellow named Don Rowe of the Mets. We had moved on to New York and the Polo Grounds after dropping the last three games of the Pittsburgh series. I guess I may have been getting a better idea of why the Colt .45s didn't get too excited after a win, even a pretty one. Still, I kept telling myself that I would never become OK with the idea of losing on a regular basis. And I didn't, in spite of the fact that I had a few losing clubs looming in my future that I really couldn't foresee back in the summer of 1963.

Galen Cisco started that June 14 game for the Mets against our veteran righty, Skinny Brown. Cisco didn't survive the first. He was taken out by Casey Stengel after giving up five runs, four earned, and replaced by Don Rowe, who pitched the rest of the game. I homered to left with a one-out solo shot in the top of the fifth. Although I didn't think about it at the time, I later realized that I had hit my first major league home run into the same stands that Bobby Thomson had blasted his "Shot Heard 'Round the World" homer into for the old New York Giants in that famous playoff game against the Brooklyn Dodgers back in 1951. Put my first home run at the Polo Grounds on a timeline basis: It came less than eleven years past the time that Bobby Thomson hit his famous home run to the same spot.

Because of Thomson's homer, "The Giants win the pennant! The Giants win the pennant!" My first big league home run helped the Colt .45s to an 8–3 everyday regular season win over the worst team in baseball, the New York Mets.

How's that for rookie perspective? Even if I were trying real hard on June 14 not to show anybody up, I pretty much floated around the bases after my first big league homer. Who wouldn't have? Only somebody without a soul, or a man from Mars, could've managed that level of coolness and felt nothing!

Through my first thirteen games at shortstop, I felt I was getting the hang of it and that my reflexes and range were improving. I had made three errors in the field, but two of those had occurred in my first three games. I'd had only one boot play over my next ten starts at shortstop.

Everything changed on July 23, 1963. Manager Craft put me in center field for the first time in my life. He and Spec Richardson, the general manager, had been talking, Harry Craft said. They both wanted to see how I used my speed and arm in the outfield before they spent any further developmental time working with me as a shortstop.

How could the club have moved me from shortstop so fast? Easy. We had a capable fielding veteran shortstop in Bob Lillis already on the roster and we had a hot shortstop prospect in the minor leagues named Sonny Jackson moving fast to the top. Trying me in the outfield made sense, even to me.

Jimmy's power was obvious from his 1963 start. (National Baseball Hall of Fame Library, Cooperstown, NY.)

I recall the July 23 game as being pretty easy for me. I could run, catch, and throw—and I did all these things routinely that day. Of course, I plugged in the oldest lesson my dad ever taught me in general to the specific job of playing center field. After each pitch, I would mentally review the game situation and think out my best options on every kind of play that might come my way. I was OK at the plate that day too, banging out three singles in six appearances, scoring one run, and knocking in another. On the bottom line of the actual ball game, we edged the Phillies at Colt Stadium by a score of 6–5.

My second major league home run came against one of the all-time greats, Don Drysdale, on Friday, August 2, 1963, at Colt Stadium in Houston. As a matter of fact, I went three for four against Drysdale and the Dodgers that night, with my homer and a double off Drysdale helping Houston to a 4–1 win.

Everybody told me to watch out, that Drysdale was going to make me pay for having that kind of rookie-good luck game against him, but that's not what happened at all. As a matter of fact, Drysdale came up during our pre–game workout the next day and even congratulated me. "Jimmy," Don said, "you did great last night. Now hang in there. You're going to be a good player."

From that moment on, Don Drysdale never threw at me in any game. There would also be many times ahead in which he showed me the goose egg collar in critical contests. We both just did our jobs, playing out our careers in clear mutual respect for each other, but back in 1963, I was just an up-and-coming rookie and one who was also trying to get a handle on the business of playing center field.

Carl Warwick was a great deal of support to me as I made my move to the outfield. He had a kidding way of making it easier for me. One day we were all out shagging fly balls prior to a game when Carl ran up to outfielder Al Spangler and shouted that he had better keep an eye on me. "If this kid keeps hitting and fielding as I think he's capable," Carl yelled out to Al, "one of us is going to be looking for a job somewhere else!"

You have to be careful of baseball prophecies, even when you're kidding.

When the winter of 1963–64 came around, Houston traded Carl Warwick back to the St. Louis Cardinals, the same club with whom they traded Bobby Shantz to acquire Carl back in 1962. As a result, Carl Warwick became an important member of that great St. Louis Cardinals comeback ball club that defeated the New York Yankees in a seven-game 1964 World Series. Carl Warwick got to be a St. Louis hero in the Series by coming through with three pinch hits in clutch game situations, becoming one of the big reasons the Cardinals won that year.

Ever since then, I've remembered Carl's joking words to Al Spangler and tried to remind my old friend of his reason he should be grateful to me. "Just remember, Carl," I like to kid back with him, "if it hadn't been for me, you never would've gone back to the Cardinals in time to be a World Series hero!"

Carl Warwick smiles at that mention. We both know the truth about that one, and we both understand the importance of good old baseball story humor between old friends and former teammates over the years. For whatever their own reasons were, the Colt .45s club traded Carl Warwick back to the Cardinals on February 17, 1964, in exchange for outfielder Jim Beauchamp and pitcher Chuck Taylor. Carl arrived just in time to play a big part in one of the most exciting years in St. Louis Cardinals baseball history.

Bob Aspromonte was another of my old teammates from the Colt .45 days. "Aspro" was the tall, suave, and good-looking ladies' man member of our Colt .45 club and a neatness freak like no other player I ever knew. Aside from being so handsome, that's why he looked so darn good all the time. Even his playing spikes had to be completely dirt-free before he went out on the field for each game. Of course, when we traveled, or when we went out to dinner, or to some new public function, we could always count on our Bobby Aspromonte being the leader of the club pack on style and neatness. I always admired him for that quality.

Here are few other tidbits about Bob Aspromonte:

1. Bob Aspromonte was the first official game batter in Houston big league baseball history. He also got the first franchise hit and scored the first franchise run in history in that same April 10, 1962, Opening Day game at Colt Stadium.
2. Over two seasons, Bob Aspromonte hit three promised home runs for a little kid named Bradley who was in Houston to have surgeries that restored his eyesight from a vision loss caused by a lightning strike. The last two HRs were grand slams. Years later, the same kid came back to Houston as a grown man to offer support to Bob Aspromonte when the latter was having his own vision worked on by the same doctor due to harm he had suffered from an exploding car battery.
3. Bob Aspromonte appeared in one game for the Brooklyn Dodgers back in 1956. Because he did, he is on record today for all time as the "last Brooklyn Dodger standing" as an active player. Bob's last major league game was played on September 28, 1971. No other original Brooklyn Dodger played that long past the team's move to Los Angeles.

If I had the time and space to talk about all my special old teammates, I would. Back in the early 1960s, however, I was just busy trying to learn a new position that would give me a better chance of sticking with the club. By late September 1963, my move to the outfield was working out OK, but I was knee-deep into the reality check on my readiness as a consistent hitter of big league pitching. I was hovering in the .240s batting average range and I also only had four home runs to my credit. All I knew to do was stay after it, grind out the days, and let the chips fall where they may. No matter what else, I knew I had the ability to make it, and I knew for sure that I would never give up on my dream.

Then something happened near the end of the '63 season that would change my life forever. I met the man who was to become my best friend in baseball when second baseman Joe Morgan joined the club as a late-season call-up from the Durham Bulls of the Class A Carolina League. Joe had compiled an impressive .332 batting average with 13 homers for Durham after coming over there from Modesto earlier in the '63 season. He was quiet and reserved, as were most of us rookies, but he was very smart, and very aware of the chance he had with the Colt .45s.

Joe had broken in as a pinch hitter against the Phillies in a game played at Colt Stadium on September 21, 1963, but he had failed to hit in a contest we lost by 4–3. I didn't play that day, but I was back in the lineup as the left fielder against the Phils the next day, September 22. When Joe Morgan entered the game late as a pinch runner for Johnny Temple, and then remained in the game to play second base, it marked the first time our names appeared in the same big league box score. Joe later came up and singled in the tying or winning run, I forget which, but it was a nice start, and the first of many good days in the big leagues for the man who would soon enough become the club's little field general. "Little Joe" Morgan and I both had high goals. We just lacked vertical lift while standing.

Thinking of that "Little Joe" moniker always brings tears of gratitude to my now weathered and ancient eyes. Had Joe Morgan not come along when he did, I might have ended up as "Little Jimmy" and then missed out on another nickname that I came to treasure. The Lord moves in mysterious ways, and He sometimes acts with a sense of humor. Hope you're laughing as you read this part, Joe!

As the days wound down to a precious few in the 1963 season, the ball club faced a potential gate disaster at Colt Stadium. Our ninth-place Colt .45s were way back in the pack, floating some thirty-plus games out of first place. We were set to close out the season against the tenth-place New York Mets, who were fifteen or so games back of us. Throw in the fact that we now had to compete in late September against live and televised professional and college football here in Houston and the problem spoke for itself.

At any rate, manager Harry Craft decided, and probably with some help from Paul Richards, the GM, and Judge Hofheinz, the face of ownership, that we would square off in Game One of the Mets series with an all-rookie lineup. That sounded pretty good to us rookies. It gave us an extra opportunity to show what we each could do and, this time, under the spotlight of the novelty promotion.

Our lineup looked good to those of us who started the game as rookies. We had Sonny Jackson at shortstop; Ernie Fazio at third base; Joe Morgan at second base; me, Jimmy Wynn in center field; Rusty Staub at first base; Aaron Pointer in right field; Brock Davis in left field; Jerry Grote at catcher; and Jay Dahl as pitcher.

The first failure of September 27 was the promotion itself. All the hype in the world couldn't have made this game sound attractive. Need proof? Only 5,802 fans showed up to be overwhelmed by "great rookie baseball."

Those who did show up were underwhelmed. Starting pitcher Jay Dahl got clobbered for seven runs in only two and two-thirds innings. Another rookie, lefty Danny Coombs, relieved Jay Dahl, surrendering another run in his one-third inning of work. At the end of three innings, the score was lopsiding all over us as the New York Met Regulars led the Houston Colt .45 Rookies 8–0.

Joe Morgan and I picked up two hits each in the rookie game, as did Rusty Staub and rookie sub Glenn Vaughan, but the whole plan for using only rookies for the entire game, if there were such a plan, was flat-out dead in the water as the game moved to the fourth inning. The Mets finally won, 10–3, with no big gain or loss in the standings going to either of our two lost expansion teams as a result of the gate promotion.

We then knocked off the Mets by 9–1 and 13–4 in the last two games to finish the 1963 season in ninth place. Our record was 66 wins and 96 losses.

Bigger fish were frying in America as the Colt .45s ended their second losing season in 1963. Back in Cincinnati, I could almost feel the change from how things had been there while I was growing up.

The black community was up in arms, demanding a guarantee of civil rights and equal treatment under the law. The Rev. Martin Luther King Jr. was fast becoming a familiar face on nightly television as the leader of a movement for Southern black voter registration and peaceful change. Black militant leaders, people like Malcolm X and the Black Panthers, were demanding an angry response from all blacks toward the institutions of support for racist oppression. Larger groups of all races were also beginning to speak up in protest against the war in Vietnam.

As for me, I'm just trying to keep my twenty-one-year-old head about me during these difficult times and to focus on the things I can do something about. I had been out there in the world at large for a couple of years now. I had seen and experienced the humiliation of segregation, and I had personally endured and survived the words of unfounded racist hate from strangers in the crowd. My fulfillment of the baseball dream seemed like the best place for me to put my energies in this world of harum-scarum insanity.

My goal was to become the best Jimmy S. Wynn I knew how to be. That goal included going down to South America to play winter ball in Venezuela over the 1963–64 off-season. The Houston club decided that the winter ball time could help me sharpen my skills and give me a little more seasoning, and I was willing to go through anything that could help me stay in the big leagues. The problems in American politics would continue to heat, but my contribution to anything like a solution was just going to have to fall on the side of personal self-improvement.

On November 22, 1963, something happened in Dallas, Texas, that made all of us who cared about building a better America wonder how bad things had to get before good change could take place in our country.

The answer, my friend, was blowing in the wind.

CHAPTER 4

Destiny Meets the Dalton Gang

There are a lot of ways in life to slip off the track. You can just get there faster if you have someone around to give you a little push. We had a couple of guys who fit that bill on those early Colt .45 teams, but I was fortunate to miss out on them until sometime midway through the 1964 season.

Nineteen sixty-four was the ball club's first year to train in Cocoa Beach, Florida, after spending our first two years baking in the desert at the legendary digs of Apache Junction, Arizona. While at Apache Junction in 1963, I had heard tales about rattlesnakes slithering across the infield, and I had been told about all the various ways that different players sought out the possibility of night life on the western wasteland.

Somehow, I had managed to escape being taken on a snipe hunt in Arizona. Maybe that was because none of the veterans took me seriously as a candidate for making the big club during my first season in the organization. If that were the case, it was fine with me. Even I knew that I was headed for San Antonio that year.

Spring Training 1964 loomed as a different proposition. I'd been called up from San Antonio to the Colt .45s in July 1963. I had performed OK and had just spent the winter playing ball in Venezuela at the club's expense. I was now being viewed as a serious candidate for making the club as an outfielder.

All of this possibility as a serious prospect added up to only one certain thing: I was now living in the crosshairs of the club's notorious "Dalton Gang." I just had no idea what was in store for me later in the year on the road.

The Dalton Gang was a transplant bunch from the Philadelphia Phillies that drew its name from the famous outlaw family that terrorized banks and trains with robberies in the Midwest back during the late nineteenth century. Most, if not all, of the original Daltons were wiped out in a botched bank robbery in Coffeyville, Kansas, way back in the Wild West days.

The Dalton Gang on the Houston Colt .45s was a lot smaller and not quite so violent or illegal about things, but they did aim to terrorize rookies, and they tried hard to intimidate anybody who got in their way.

The whole Dalton Gang consisted of only two pitchers who once had been teammates and previous "partners in crime" as members of the Philadelphia Phillies. Dick "Turk" Farrell had joined the Colt .45s from the Phillies through the expansion roster draft of 1961. Jim "The Bear" Owens had signed with the Colt .45s as a free agent after receiving his release from the Cincinnati Reds following the 1963 season. Both Farrell and Owens were old-school tough. Either one of them would have sent his mother into the dust had she batted against her son and tried to crowd the plate. Both were old-school guys who thought of muscle training as a waste of time, unless it involved the repetitious bending of elbows at whatever local bar was handy.

They were loud laughing galoots who had no clear idea or caring for where a good practical joke blurred over into an act of outright meanness. Some people made excuses for their actions toward others, but these were the people who also enjoyed watching others suffer, with a sprinkling of others who just did not want to cross either the Turk or the Bear thrown in for good measure.

At nearly age 22, I arrived at camp in 1964 with all of the same dull and routine habits that had served me well in life up to this point in time. I didn't drink. I didn't smoke. And I didn't fool around with women all that much. There was a girl back in Cincinnati that I was starting to like, a girl named Ruth that I mentioned earlier, but I wasn't out chasing women. The only thing I chased to this point in time, and I hope you're not tired of me saying it by now, was my dream of playing big league baseball.

My eating habits were balanced and my simple pleasures were incredibly tame. I enjoyed relaxing with a glass of cold milk in the evening. Everybody who lived around me quickly learned that much about me. By the way I lived, I may as well have been sending everybody a telegraph that read: "Jimmy's day is almost done. He's having his glass of milk now. Pretty soon he will be in the sack and getting a good night's sleep in preparation for tomorrow."

I was a pretty exciting guy, all right, but I also must have looked like a lost lamb to the two wolves that made up the Dalton Gang. They didn't waste much salivation time on me in spring training. I think they were either too busy with the job of tormenting other people or else, they were just saving me for dessert later in the season.

The 1964 season started on notes of sadness and hope. Pitcher Jim Umbricht died of cancer on April 8. The club later retired his number 32 from the 1963 season. On the hope side, the Colt .45s had added two big names in American League history (Pete Runnels of the Red Sox and Senators, and Nellie Fox of the White Sox), to their '64 roster. Fox would soon enough become an important mentor to my friend Joe Morgan on the art of playing second base. Pete Runnels would stand tall with Fox as another veteran

His power quickly moved Jimmy from shortstop to centerfield (National Baseball Hall of Fame Library, Cooperstown, NY).

inspiration to all of us young guys on how the great game of baseball is supposed to be played.

The 1964 season opened in Cincinnati as it always used to start, with the Reds hosting the first game of the new season in traditional respect for their club as the oldest professional franchise in the major leagues. The date was April 13, 1964, and I was starting in center field, batting sixth, for the Houston Colt .45s. The right-handed knuckleballer Ken Johnson, the roommate of the late Jim Umbricht from 1963, took the mound as our starting pitcher. The Reds' ace, Jim Maloney, was our opposing pitcher. Mom, Dad, and just about everyone else in my whole family was there to watch me play. For me, it was like I was starring in a movie in which my baseball dream had come true.

The biggest surprise for me at the start of the 1964 season awaited me at my locker on Opening Day in Crosley Field. Instead of a jersey with the uniform number 18 that I had worn since joining the Colt .45s, there was a Houston road uniform with the number 24 on it hanging in my locker. Before I could even get out my first full gasp of "What's this all about?" forced to the surface, there was Spec Richardson, standing behind me and ready to explain.

"Jimmy," Spec spoke out as he steadied me and his words with a right hand placed firmly on my left shoulder, "we have high expectations and great plans for you. Now I think you know that another great player for another National League club already wears number 24, and he wears this special number with pride and distinction. Our assignment of the number 24 to you is simply our way of saying that we want you to go out there and do for the Houston Colt .45s what Willie Mays has done for the San Francisco Giants."

Man! Talk about frontloading a guy's career with great, hard-to-live-up-to expectations. This took the cake. I thanked Spec for the confidence the club had in me, but down deep it felt as though I had been tied to a sandbag and told to go steal second base. I wasn't really comfortable with #24 until San Francisco finally came up on our schedule and the media got me together with Willie Mays for some pictures of the two number 24 center fielders. The media-guided photo op gave me a chance to talk with Willie about the pressure I felt about the number.

"Number 24 is a very good number," Willie offered. "Just don't get caught up in trying to be what the owners, managers, or anyone else wants you to be. You don't have to be the next Willie Mays anyway because that's not who you are. I watched you a little, kid, and I can tell you this much right now: You've got what it takes on your own. Just wear number 24 with pride. Now go out there and simply be the best Jimmy Wynn that you know how to be!"

The date and location of my pre–game meeting with Willie Mays was May 5, 1964, and on the road in San Francisco. Thanks to Willie, it was also the date I started wearing number 24 in the right spirit and understanding,

That being said, I did put an exclamation point on wearing number 24 back on the Opening Day date of April 13, 1964, that I actually wore it for the first time back at Crosley Field. For me it came about in the sixth inning when I blasted a two-run homer to left field with one out against starter Jim

Maloney. My first number 24 long ball gave the Colt .45s a 6–0 lead through the top of the sixth inning. We were well on our way to a 6–3 Opening Day win. Johnson tired and gave up all three of the Reds' runs in the ninth, but lefty Hal Woodeshick came in to get the last out and save the game for Kenny.

Sure, it was only one game, but the win put us in first place all by ourselves until the other clubs started playing, and it also made Bob Skinner of the Reds and me the home run leaders in the majors, each with one, if only for a day. Bob had belted a two-run shot of his own in that big Reds rally in the ninth. Our Nellie Fox also had a couple of runs batted in during the game. That meant that three of us were tied for the lead in that category. I had my flights of fancy, but I really didn't think that way too much or very often. OK, remember that I was only 22 years old at the time. Didn't you ever think that larger-than-life kind of way as a kid in the backyard when you were growing up? Pete Rose sure did. He never stopped thinking that way, and here he was, sitting in the Reds dugout on Opening Day. As best I recall, he didn't do much in that game. (Rose was 0 for 4.)

Not long after that Opening Day game against the Reds, I was involved in one of the most unusual games in big league history, and it was played right here in Houston at old Colt Stadium against that same club of my childhood heroes, the one that also included my fiery old high school baseball rival Pete Rose.

On the night of April 23, 1964, Ken Johnson of our Colt .45s pitched another very nice game against the Reds, this time giving up no hits while walking only two and striking out nine. The problem was—*we lost the game.* Our pitcher threw a nine-inning complete game no-hitter, but we still lost to the Reds on a run in the ninth inning by the score of 1–0.

Here's how it happened. And this time, Pete Rose was center stage as the spoiler of all good things for Ken Johnson and the Houston Colt .45s.

Going into the top of the ninth, Ken Johnson of Houston and Joe Nuxhall of Cincinnati were locked in a classic pitchers' duel, with the exceptional effort nod going to Johnson for having given up no hits through eight. Then fate stepped in.

And fate's other name was Pete Rose.

When Pete Rose tried to bunt his way on, pitcher Johnson mishandled the ball. His errant throw to first base allowed Rose to reach second base on a two-base error. Rose then advanced to third base on a groundout by Chico Ruiz to the right side. Rose then came home to score when second baseman Nellie Fox couldn't find the handle on another trickling grounder to the right side. Nuxhall then shut us down in the ninth and the final line score read like something out of *Ripley's Believe It or Not*:

Reds: 1 Run, 0 Hits, 2 Errors
Colt .45s: 0 Runs, 5 Hits, 2 Errors.

Poor old unlucky Ken Johnson! He's the only pitcher in baseball history to lose a complete nine-inning game no-hitter! Good old lucky Ken Johnson! He's the only pitcher in baseball history to lose a complete nine-inning game no-hitter!

I had a double in that game, but it didn't spare our guy his fated but noted place in the history of pitching. Think about that "lost no-hitter" outcome for a moment. Sometimes we are more easily remembered for the things we don't quite get done. Although I know of no pitcher who would aspire to it, what if a guy comes along someday who pitches and loses seven no-hitters? Who would we likely remember best then? Mr. "I Lost Seven" No Hitters? Or the fellow who won seven no-no's, Mr. Nolan Ryan?

I couldn't complain about playing time at the start of the '64 season. We were 7–9 in wins and losses for April and I had played in all but one of our sixteen games and almost as evenly as possible on defense. I played eight games in center field and seven games in left field. My hitting needed to improve: I was batting .250 (12 for 48) with only three home runs. I'd had only one multiple hit game.

Green as I was, I didn't need manager Harry Craft to tell me that my production needed to improve. If it didn't get better in May, I figured, I'd soon be checking my mail in either AA-level San Antonio again, or at the AAA-level farm club in Oklahoma City.

The month of May produced no improvement in my hitting. I struggled with a .230 hitting percentage for May (20 for 87) that dropped my '63 season batting average to .237. Just as bad as the average, or worse, I hit only one HR in May.

Three homers for the season, going into June, weren't exactly boosting my status as a prospect. All I could figure is that I was pressing too hard, going for too many balls out of the zone that I normally would have passed on. I tried to explain to Dad over the phone what I was doing at the plate. It would have been easier had he been able to see for himself. About all he could do was offer his support and remind me not to get down on myself.

Then one night, after a game in Philadelphia and in the middle of this painful struggle with my hitting production, something happened that changed the course of my life. It involved the Dalton Gang, but it had nothing to do with making me a better ballplayer, or even a better human being, for that matter.

I already knew this much from watching the Daltons do their work on others. They were most effective when you didn't see them coming after you in the moment. It happened to me as we were all gearing down and cleaning up in the visitors' clubhouse at Connie Mack Stadium after a series-opening night game. Before I knew what hit me, the Daltons were on me in full-gnash mode.

I was having a glass of milk late when Turk Farrell and Jim Owens came over to me. It was a planned move on their part, but I was naive enough to think at the time that their sudden appearance was simply coincidence.

"What are you up to, Jimmy?" Turk Farrell asked.

"Nothing much, Turk," I said. "Just relaxing a little before I go back to my room and settle in for the night."

"Settle in for the night?" Bear Owens asked. "What do you mean, 'settle in?' The night hasn't even started!"

"It has for me, Jim," I answered. "I'm ready to go back to my room."

"Oh no, you don't," they both said, almost in unison. "Not tonight, Jimmy! We're going to teach you how to enjoy your nights a little better! We're tired of watching you chugalug milk after games! It's time you were introduced to what real men drink!"

They weren't kidding, but I really wasn't prepared for what happened next. The next thing I knew, the Daltons had picked me up and they were physically forcing me to go with them by cab to some favorite Philly bar. I don't know if our being back in Philadelphia, the place where all their shared hell-raising together started years earlier, had anything to do with the timing of their attack on me, but I've always supposed it did. The other very discouraging thing to me about this kidnapping was the fact that it unfolded and flat-out happened in plain view of all my teammates, and nobody on the club, nobody, so much as even made a move to answer my pleas for help, not even my good friend Joe Morgan.

What was written off as "good bull" back then would probably be treated as criminal assault today. There's no way that this kind of behavior could go on in today's major league clubhouses without somebody getting killed or sued, and everybody getting written up by the media, but this was then, not now.

When we got to the bar, the Dalton Gang ordered me to drink a glass of Chivas Regal scotch on the rocks. I had no choice, but to take the first drink of alcohol I'd ever consumed.

Unfortunately, I liked it. Or I liked the way it made me feel, at first.

Unlike cold milk, a drink of alcohol seemed to instantly calm me down and smooth away the tensions of the day. All of a sudden, even if it had been forced upon me, I was having a Christopher Columbus experience with alcohol. From my involuntary "discovery" of Chivas Regal, I was suddenly aware of a new mindset to want to use alcohol on a regular basis as a way of relaxing and having fun.

As others have learned before me, I was on the way to some lessons about the not-so-pleasant effects of alcohol over time. Give me some credit, please. I learned, also in time, that alcohol had the power to affect my judgment and influence my decisions. It also had the power to create anger, slow reflexes, and rob me of a good night's sleep.

Let's be reasonable here. None of these direct side effects of alcohol are there to help a person become better at what he or she does. They just lead you down the wide highway of greater diversion from your true purpose in life.

I got away from alcohol, in time, with God's help. And I've often wondered how my life might have gone differently, had it not been for the actions of the Dalton Gang and my own vulnerability to alcohol back in 1964.

On the other hand, I really don't waste time blaming Farrell or Owens, or even regretting the fact I once drank. I have some pleasant memories associated with my drinking days too. I just don't recommend alcohol as the road to lasting happiness or good decision-making for anybody.

Bottom line: Anybody can come up with a Dalton Gang excuse in their past to blame their bad choices on. In the end, things just are what they are. And we are all each responsible for the choices we make in our own behalf, for better and for worse. The Daltons weren't responsible for any drinks I took on my own.

Sadly, we lost Turk Farrell to a road accident in England back in 1977. I have no idea if alcohol was involved in his death, but that's always a serious possibility when a guy has a drinking history.

In spite of it all, Turk Farrell was one heck of an intimidating pitcher. Farrell lost twenty games for the original 1962 version of the Colt .45s, but his version of that season was typical Turk. "Do you realize how good a pitcher I had to be to have enough chances to lose 20 games in one season?" Farrell used to ask. That question became his stock answer to anyone who asked about his loss record in 1962.

Jim Owens, who must be doing something right because he's still living, was cut from the same cloth as Dick Farrell. He controlled the inside part of the plate and he brushed back any hitter who tried to take over the whole strike zone.

Getting past the Dalton Gang initiation, but adding alcohol to the mix of my 1964 recreational pursuits, I still faced the problem of my disappointing year at the plate. By the middle of June, I was hitting .236 (37 for 157). I had been stuck on four homers since May 3. I got the news from manager Harry Craft that I had been expecting. I was going out for a little more seasoning against minor league pitching, but this time I was headed for the Oklahoma City 89ers of the AAA–level Pacific Coast League to spend some time playing under manager Grady Hatton.

The decision came as a relief, even though I had successfully hit twice in a row as a pinch hitter during my last two plate appearances for Houston prior to my demotion. It was June 15 and I looked forward to some work away from the big league spotlight. I felt that I just needed to relax and find my groove again.

Oklahoma City proved to be a good tonic for me. I didn't set the world on fire in the Pacific Coast League, but I did manage to hit .275 with ten homers and forty runs batted in while I was there.

We had some good ballplayers at Oklahoma City back in '64. Outfielder Jim Beauchamp, whom the Colt .45s had acquired from the Cardinals for Carl Warwick, was tearing up the league with 34 homers and 83 RBI. Outfielder Rusty Staub hit .314 with 20 homers while he was there and a third outfielder, Carroll Hardy, hit .321 with 14 homers during his time with the club.

The message to me was clear. The other competition was outdoing me statistically, all over the place. None of these guys had my speed or athleticism, but they were putting up the numbers. I would have to devote myself to doing everything I could to improve my performance and bring it up closer to the level of an ability I knew deep inside I had to show to get back to the big leagues and stick. I knew I could do it. My belief in that positive outcome was unshakeable.

I returned to Houston at season's end from Oklahoma City. The games didn't mean much to the club's final standing by this time, but they were big ones for me in the performance department. I wasn't all that impressive, finishing with a National League batting average of .224 (49 for 219) and only one extra homer after my return. That one gave me a grand total of five HR on the year.

One unexpected other opportunity came about upon my return from OKC. A guy who would become a good friend, Dick Oppenheimer, approached me about doing some interviews with other ballplayers for his mainly black audience radio station KYOK in Houston. Here I am, this young player, just back from AAA ball, and the owner of a radio station is asking me to do something this public.

Well, partly because I liked the idea, and partly because I wanted to learn something new, I agreed to the challenge. I started carrying around this portable tape recorder and sticking it in the faces of other players after games to get their comments on whatever may have happened that particular day.

I took to talking to people on tape like white on rice. Today I understand even better why Dick Oppenheimer was ahead of his time in recruiting me for this job. As a uniformed player, even if I was still pretty much a green rookie, I could get to players for comments that the regular media couldn't hope to reach. I even got to the players from other clubs for taped commentary whenever that seemed like the interview people might most want to hear.

The radio extra job went on for the rest of 1964 and throughout 1965. It only ended because Oppenheimer sold his radio station and the new owners went to a new format with their own program ideas. I liked it while it lasted. I've always felt that it helped me build the confidence and experience I needed in the future for other kinds of broadcasting and reporting opportunities.

Unfortunately, I have no idea where those old tapes are today. They may have been destroyed a thousand years ago, for all I know. When Oppenheimer sold KYOK, the tapes disappeared with him.

Meanwhile, I rejoined the Colt .45s in time for a special moment in club history. On September 22, 1964, a Houston pitching icon, Larry Dierker, made his debut with the Colt .45s at Colt Stadium, on his eighteenth birthday, facing off against a lefty named Dick Estelle of the San Francisco Giants. Dierker was gone prior to the third inning, and he would take the loss in our 7–2 fall, but he would also be on his way to a big career for the franchise.

After the game, we celebrated Larry Dierker's birthday in the clubhouse with a cake, candles, and the birthday song. Maybe we were getting a little too happy beyond the lines with our habit of losing. Who knows? And who cares? We just wanted to help "the kid" recall his birthday pitching start.

Another game ended in a special way for me too, and that was the last game ever played at Colt Stadium on September 27, 1964, as we prepared to move over to the new domed stadium in 1965. On that day of last hurrahs, we squared off against the Los Angeles Dodgers, with our Bob Bruce going up against their Don Drysdale. What a game that turned out to be! For ten innings, Bruce and Drysdale hooked up in a total run goose egg (0–0) pitchers' duel.

Drysdale left for a pinch hitter in the top of the twelfth inning, but Bruce stayed in there, hanging two more goose egg innings on LA before we came to bat against lefty ace reliever Ron Perranoski in the bottom of the twelfth. I came to bat with two outs, with Rusty Staub on second base and Bob Aspromonte on first base. As fate would have it, I cracked a single down the left field line that drove Staub home for the winning run in the last major league game ever played in the place some fans loved calling "The Skillet." My walk-off hit and run batted in brought Bob Bruce up to a record of 15 wins and 9 losses on the year.

Bob Bruce was the first to run out and hug me for that winning hit. The win not only gave him a club high (for the time) fifteen wins, but, as I later learned, it put Bruce down for pitching twenty-two straight innings without giving up a run. That's some pretty fair country pitching for a guy who ended up on a two-year-old expansion club.

What a game that was for Bob Bruce! No way you will see today's pitchers go twelve innings, let alone pitch twelve innings of shutout ball while giving up only five hits in the same game. Nobody was keeping pitch counts in those days.

Today's pitch count fascination makes you wonder, especially when you look at what guys like Bruce and Drysdale used to produce. Are one hundred pitches really all we can expect pitchers to throw in one game? Or does telling young starters that one hundred pitches is the most a club expects just teach them to think of themselves in a limited way?

After the last Colt Stadium game, we finished the season on the west coast, flaming out with a 1–5 record against the Giants and Dodgers. Our season record of 66–96 in 1964 was only good enough for ninth place in the ten-club National League. Thank God for those early New York Met clubs. They were only amazing in their "awfulness," but they took much of the heat off the Colt .45s.

At least, nobody in Houston was trying to sell us to the fans as lovable losers. People just tolerated our losing ways as a two-year-old expansion club. As individual players, we all knew that we either had to find ways to produce in the near future or face the pretty sure consequence of being gone. In that harsh light, Venezuela and the winter league probably would have been my next best choice after our last game, but that's not what I did as we headed into the 1964–65 off-season.

When the 1964 season ended, I asked Ruth, the girl in Cincinnati, to marry me, and she accepted my proposal. Neither of us really understood the penalty on our decision to get married, but we would soon enough learn.

How little we knew. How little we understood. By our quick decision to get married, we had just checked ourselves into the Heartbreak Hotel. Now, forty-six years later, it's high time for me to take full responsibility for what happened back then.

It boils down to this: I had proposed marriage to a girl I hardly knew for all the wrong reasons back in 1964. It's something I've felt bad about for a very long time, and I only own up to it now because I've come to understand deep in my soul over the years that there is nothing to fear from the truth. None of us is perfect. Only Jesus Christ fills that bill.

For years, I've worried that my two grown children by Ruth, my lovely daughter Kimberly and my fine handsome son Jimmy S. Wynn Jr., would turn away from me if they knew, flat-out, what originally motivated my proposal to their mother.

Now I'm placing my faith in the greater reality that they love me as their dad and that they already know too how much I love them as my children.

Beyond regret, my apologies to both my children are what matters here.

For their understanding, here's how my decision to get married the first time unfolded. I'm not proud of it, but it is what it is. I was 22 years old; I had a whole lot of growing up yet to do; and I was still struggling, above all other things, to make it in the major leagues of baseball with the Houston Colt .45s.

One day, late in the 1964 season, and this was still during the time that Paul Richards served as general manager of the club, Spec Richardson, who was then with the Colt .45s in a lower-level administrative position, came to me to explain a concern he was having.

Spec was afraid that I was coming up as a military draft candidate at age 22 and still single. The Vietnam War was heating up and the army was grabbing every man they could get their hands on to send over there.

Well, all I knew about Vietnam was that a lot people were stepping up in opposition to the war and that a lot of guys my age were dying over there for reasons that seemed to have more to do with politics than they did with common sense or any real defense of our country. I sure had no problem with serving my country militarily for the right reasons, but Vietnam didn't seem to be on the list of right reasons in my book.

Having read that, you may now be inclined to ask: "If you were opposed to the war in Vietnam, why didn't you do as Muhammad Ali did and simply wait for the draft call and then refuse to serve as a 'conscientious objector'?"

First of all, I am not Muhammad Ali, or Cassius Clay, as he was then known. Next I'd say this: I didn't think about things in that way back in 1964. I don't even think about things in that way now. I wasn't ever out working in Mississippi and Alabama for black voter registration back in 1964–65, nor am I now out there today trying to run for political office so I can change the world.

All I've ever known how to do in behalf of the world is to get up each day and try to be the best Jimmy S. Wynn I know how to be. Today that involves doing a lot of things through programs that reach out to disadvantaged kids, but back in 1964, being the best Jimmy S. Wynn I could be meant making it successfully as a big league ballplayer.

At any rate, Spec Richardson came to me in 1964 and put it to me this way: "Jimmy, as a single man at age 22, they are going to draft you into the army early next year and send you to Vietnam. If you get married before December 22, 1964 [I now forget what was so magical about that date], you will be eligible for a draft deferment that will keep you out of military service and free you to continue your baseball career."

Making a decision of that type hit me hard. I didn't like the idea of being forced to prove my patriotism by serving in a war I didn't support. I didn't like the idea of demonstrating in the streets against the war. I didn't like the idea of going to jail for political reasons. I didn't like the idea of losing my best chance at the big leagues. And I didn't like the prospect of getting married and settling down for all the wrong reasons.

In the end, and after talking it over with my dad, and hearing him leave this very big grown-up decision squarely in my own lap, I went with the prospect of getting married for the sake of avoiding the draft.

Ruth and I married in Cincinnati on December 21, 1964. The next day, I took proof of our marriage to my Cincinnati draft board and filed the necessary papers for my deferment. Ruth and I returned after the holidays to Houston, where we moved back into the house we already had purchased in the southwest area.

Ruth and I didn't know each other that well back in the fall of 1964, but she had accepted my proposal, never knowing all the facts that drove my motives for getting married. I knew that my feelings for her were not as strong as they should have been toward a girl I planned to marry, but I allowed my selfish interests to outweigh the whole truth. Immaturely, I thought that things would work themselves out in time.

Was I ever wrong! The only two things that ever worked out well for Ruth and me were our two beautiful children!

For all the harm our marriage caused to Ruth, and for all the pain that fell over upon our kids because of how Ruth and I lived in marriage and beyond our divorce, I have always felt guilty. After all, it was my original need that set this whole train of tears in motion down the track. Please forgive me, Ruth, wherever you may be in God's eternal embrace.

Ruth died many years ago from cancer, long after our 1971 divorce. All I can hope for now is for the forgiveness of my children, whom I shall continue to love forever and completely, no matter what they decide about me in this now very open public disclosure of my reasons for getting married to their mother.

Based on the clock, these events took place a very long time ago. Based on my heart, this has been a matter I've needed to get off my chest ever since the day it went into motion. I can only hope that my children, and those who really know and care about me, will understand and be forgiving. Those who choose to judge me otherwise can't be helped. I did what I did.

Like anything else about my life, all I can bring to you now is the whole truth. Nobody's perfect. All any of us can do is either live up to our mistakes, or else spend the rest of our lives trying to hide from them. Life unfolds by each thing we do, from moment to moment, under almighty God's watchful eye.

It was what it was. And it is what it is. It will be whatever it will be.

CHAPTER 5

The Eighth Wonder of the World!

Even if I had not gotten married in December, the 1965 season was set to be like no other in my career, and for a reason I shared with every other member of the Houston ball club and the whole National League. For the first time in big league baseball history, an enclosed stadium was opening and right here in our own home town of Houston. At least, I hoped it was my town to call home. I'd married and bought a house here, and I also held out every hope of establishing myself in Houston as an everyday outfielder.

There's more to the stadium story, much more. Those of you who are longtime Houston fans already know the basics, but it deserves telling again anyway. My personal baseball history ran straight through this period, and, for any of us who played there (especially, if we turned out to be power hitters), our careers were about to be seriously affected by the presence of the new domed stadium.

To really appreciate the monumental step that the Dome was back in 1965, we first have to go back to how the idea started. I didn't know a lot of these facts at the time, but I've since learned a little about how it all began.

The first indoor baseball games were played in some northern cities during the latter part of the nineteenth century. These hardly count due to all the special rules that had to be made governing balls bouncing off walls and ceilings in auditorium and gymnasium facilities.

Nothing else along the lines of indoor baseball happened until the early 1950s, when Brooklyn Dodgers owner Peter O'Malley proposed the construction of a domed stadium in Brooklyn as a replacement for Ebbets Field. When the Dodgers couldn't get the approval from New York mass transit and public works construction mogul Robert Moses for acquiring land in Brooklyn on a prime subway line for any kind of closed or open ballpark, that inaction on the part of the city became the turnkey on the dual move of the Dodgers and Giants to California in 1958.

Branch Rickey brought the idea up again for Pittsburgh during the late

1950s' talk of starting a new major loop called the Continental League. When Major League Baseball killed that attempted start of a new big league by awarding expansion franchises to New York and Houston, Judge Roy Hofheinz picked up the charge for building a domed stadium in Houston as part of the package deal for the National League's approving the city as a new club.

I don't know if Judge Roy Hofheinz gave any mention to the Brooklyn and Pittsburgh efforts prior to his own plans for a domed stadium, but he wasn't the kind of man who sprinkled credit very far from home, unless it was to someplace in ancient history. I've heard the two local stories about how the Judge came up with the idea for a domed stadium in Houston. One version is that the Judge's young daughter, Dene, had inspired him into coming up with the idea back in 1952. Following a series of rainouts for Texas League Houston Buffs games at old Buff Stadium, Dene supposedly had voiced this idea-crunching question to her genius father: "Daddy, why can't they play baseball games indoors?" A second version had the Judge going to Italy and finding inspiration among ancient plans for covering the Coliseum of Rome.

However it happened, Judge Roy Hofheinz was the man who made it real. As Houston slipped into early 1965, the Harris County Domed Stadium was about to open its doors to an era of total change in American sports history. For about thirty million dollars, Harris County had built the world's first domed stadium on property south of the Texas Medical Center that the Judge and his friends had acquired from one of Houston baseball's other founding fathers, R.E. "Bob" Smith. The new place was planned as a "multi-purpose" stadium with movable seats that would make it adjustable to baseball and football, the rodeo, and other events. The Dome was to be the first of what came to be known as "cookie cutter" stadiums that dominated new sports venue construction during the 1960s and 1970s.

Jimmy was there when the Colt .45s became the Astros in 1965 (National Baseball Hall of Fame Library, Cooperstown, NY).

From the baseball side,

Tal Smith was placed in charge of making sure that the new domed stadium was going up in a way that would make playing the game of baseball work out OK. Balls hitting the roof and the fielders' being able to see fly balls were the major questions. Tal did as good a job as possible, working on the kind of stadium for baseball that had never before existed.

The main need was to see if we could follow the flight of batted balls during games under all those glass panels in the roof. On February 8, 1965, a few players were asked to take the field for the first practice inside the new domed stadium, just to get a feel for the place more than anything else. Pitchers were relieved to find that their breaking pitches still worked indoors. That had been a concern for pitchers, of course, but no one complained back then that they were having any trouble following the flight of baseballs. On the hitting side, Rusty Staub was the only batter to hit a ball over the wall, but no one expressed concern about how well the ball might carry in general.

The practice was more of a media circus. About 250 members of the press showed up to cover the event. Singer Anita Bryant was even brought in to throw out a ceremonial first practice pitch. That was a little bit much.

The off-season of 1964–65 saw another change in plans for the club. Judge Hofheinz and the Houston Sports Association had come under fire from a lawsuit filed against them by the Colt gun company for trademark infringement. It seems that back in that day, some people weren't quite as careful about seeking legal permission before they publicly used the names of products belonging to others. The Judge had gone with the name "Houston Colt .45s" without seeking approval from the gun company. At some time during the 1964–65 winter, the gun company came after Hofheinz and the ballclub to either stop using the name or start sharing the revenues from "Colt .45s" baseball.

The Judge apparently wasn't real warm to the idea of sharing revenues with the gun company, so he came up with something that went way beyond a mere name change. Here's the best example I can think of that shows the full genius of Judge Roy Hofheinz for coming up with ideas that were not only larger than life, but ideas that would also create instantaneous public fascination and big profits.

The Colt .45s named disappeared overnight. The ball club was rechristened by the NASA-approved name of the "Houston Astros," and the team would now play their games in a new stadium that had now been renamed the "Astrodome."

The old 19th-century circus ballyhoo artist P.T. Barnum apparently wasn't dead. Judge Roy Hofheinz began to promote the opening of the Astrodome as the "Eighth Wonder of the World!" How sweet a sound was that? Even all of us ballplayers couldn't wait to go inside and see what the "Eighth Wonder" was all about. You just had to be young and alive during that time to fully appreciate how excited everybody was over the opening of the new domed stadium. With the name changes to Astros and Astrodome, we also now had an identity that was as slick as the idea of a futuristic domed stadium itself.

Opening night for the very first Astrodome game ever played finally came to pass on April 9, 1965, as an exhibition contest between the hometown Houston Astros and the visiting New York Yankees. Literally, everybody who was anybody was on the list of invited guests, starting with President Lyndon Baines Johnson and the First Lady, Mrs. Lady Bird Johnson. The President and Mrs. Johnson, and other major dignitaries, would watch the game from Judge Hofheinz's suite, located high and mighty as it could be above the wall down the right field line.

Leave it to Houston sportswriter Mickey Herskowitz to bring us all back down to a funny planet called Earth the next morning in the *Houston Post* with his written first impression of the Astrodome's first night: "The Astrodome looks like a giant underarm deodorant bottle that's been buried, standing up, with only its neck and roller head top now visible above the ground!"

No extra touches went uncovered. The usherettes dressed in golden-colored space girl outfits. And the groundskeepers all wore bubble glass helmets, as though they may as well have been scraping the surface of Mars or the moon as they smoothed the infield from the danger of earthly clods.

Governor John Connally and his wife Nellie Connally, the First Lady of Texas, were on hand to throw out the first pitch.

President and Mrs. Johnson arrived a little late, but they made up for it after the seventh inning by leaving early.

The club's public reverence for the Old West past was now relegated to the exploding scoreboard. Designed to blast off with a great big Texas celebration every time an Astros player homered, or the team won, the scoreboard was set off that first time especially for the benefit of the departing President and Mrs. Johnson in the eighth inning of a 1–1 tie game that had featured no Astro homers to make it happen any earlier.

What the Johnsons witnessed in that scoreboard show was pretty darn impressive. Even I watched from my position in center field. The all-lights display started with a baseball bursting through the dome roof and then going through the scoreboard to set off more explosions. When that happened, a cowboy on each side of the scoreboard started firing bullets that ricocheted all over the big board. Then a steer appeared at both ends of the scoreboard, with American and Texas flags unfurling from each of both animals' two horns. Wait! That's not the end of the road. The show concluded with more fireworks bursting across the scoreboard as "The Eyes of Texas" boomed proudly and the sounds of fresh pistol bullets ricocheting everywhere exploded loud as could be. Finally, we heard a horse neighing forth with a really loud whinny and the sound of thundering hooves, like the stamping herd of horses and cattle during a John Wayne western movie.

It was as obvious as could be. The scoreboard was designed for a club that had fully expected to come into the new Dome as the Houston Colt .45s.

Things had changed. We were the Houston Colt .45s no more.

Notwithstanding the scoreboard, praise for the future and the new era of space exploration were now in style. By the club's ability to shift its identity on a dime, based on legal pressures and new marketing strategies, the Houston Astros had proven themselves totally fit as a worthy new major league representative of America's fourth largest city and the brand-newest National League geographical location.

The first Astrodome game did not disappoint.

Houstonian Johnny Keane was now the manager of the New York Yankees and he came prepared to play the game as a serious entry into baseball history. By placing Mickey Mantle in the leadoff spot, the great Yankee future Hall of Famer took advantage by lining the second pitch off Astros starter Turk Farrell into left field for the first hit in Astrodome history, but he didn't score.

With one out in the bottom of the third in a 0–0 tie game, Astros catcher Ron Brand tripled down the right field line for the first Astros hit in Astrodome history. Brand died at third base and the game moved to the top of the sixth as a scoreless tie.

Mel Stottlemyre of the Yankees and Turk Farrell of our very own, still-thriving Dalton Gang were locked hard in one heck of a pitchers' duel when Mickey Mantle came to bat to lead off the top of the sixth. Mantle broke the ice with a mighty blast that sailed far over my head and way beyond the center field wall for the first home run in Astrodome history and a 1–0 Yankees lead. The Mantle homer didn't trigger the big scoreboard, of course, but it brought Mickey a standing "O" and a roaring cheer from Houston fans for being the first to do it, and, I think, for attaching the Mantle name to Houston baseball history.

The Astros tied the game in the bottom half of the sixth. After Turk Farrell walked, Joe Morgan also reached on an error by first baseman Joe Pepitone, sending Farrell to second base. Al Spangler then beat out an infield hit to third base that loaded the bases. Rusty Staub then grounded into a 3–6 force out on Spangler at second base, but Farrell scored to tie the game at 1–1. Walt Bond then ended our threat by bouncing into a 6–3 double play that ended the inning.

I got to play a humble part in keeping the game tied in the top of the seventh. After Yankee catcher Johnny Blanchard doubled to left with two outs, he then tried to score from second base on a single up the middle by pitcher Stottlemyre. I was able to retrieve the ball cleanly, running in for it, and I got off a clothesline throw to catcher Brand that was on the mark. Blanchard was tagged out and we escaped the threat of falling behind again.

Lefty Hal Woodeshick took over in relief of Farrell in the top of the eighth. Going into the bottom of the twelfth of a game still tied at 1–1, Woody had held the fort, giving up only 2 hits and 2 walks, while fanning 5.

Hal Reniff of the Yankees had relieved Stottlemyre after the eighth and held us to only 3 hits in his three innings of work, but one of those was my first Astrodome hit, a two-out single in the ninth. Sadly, it led to nothing as Bob Lillis then hit into a force play on me at second base. That play ended our time at bat and sent the game into extra innings.

Now, as we moved to the bottom of the twelfth, Pete Mikkelsen was taking the mound for New York.

As luck or fate would have it, I led off the bottom of the twelfth with my second hit of the game, an infield hit to deep shortstop. After Bob Lillis struck out, I stole second base. Then Brand also fanned and I started feeling edgy. We really wanted this first Dome game. I'm the winning run on second, I thought. Don't waste me out here. Somebody get a hit, please. Let's not waste the opportunity.

We really wanted to become the first big league team to ever win an indoor baseball game played by regular rules. We also wanted to take our first home game ever played as the Astros, and we sure as heck wanted to be the first team to ever win a game in our new Astrodome.

"Let's do it!" I said in my head as I stood on second base, waiting to see who manager Lum Harris was bringing into the game as a pinch hitter for pitcher Hal Woodeshick.

The pinch hitter was Nellie Fox, one of the biggest tobacco-chewing, clutch-hitting players in baseball annals. Nellie was just the guy we needed up there to write a happy Houston ending on a night marked for history. Nellie Fox slashed a looping single to center and I took off running like the Roadrunner, determined as never before to score from second base on a clean single up the middle. I made it easy. The throw from Yankee center fielder Tom Tresh was way late with "no chance" written all over it. The moment my foot touched home, the deed was done. We had won in twelve innings by a squeaking close score of 2–1.

As midnight soon enough rang away the end of April 9, 1965, the Houston Astros were now free to boast of a perfect 1–0 record in the world's newest wonder place, the Astrodome!

Nobody stays perfect forever, but the Judge did his part in trying to keep it that way as we opened the first regular season Opening Day at the Astrodome on April 12, 1965, against the Philadelphia Phillies. This time the ballclub was ready to give the full bear treatment to the new space theme.

Twenty-two NASA astronauts were on hand, all there to throw out the first pitch simultaneously. We almost ran short of Astro players to serve as ceremonial catchers, but we got the job done, with the stunt coming off OK. Unfortunately, the game was another matter.

Our Bob Bruce got the starting pitcher nod on Opening Day 1965 against Chris Short of the Phillies. In the top of the 3rd, Richie Allen of the Phils blasted the first official game home run in the Astrodome off Bob Bruce. With Ruben Amaro on base at the time, Allen's blast made it 2–0, and that turned out to be all the firing by everybody and also the final score.

To hear the giant scoreboard explode again as planned, Houston fans had to wait another day. After a strange day off on the 13th, the Astros would start writing some official history in our second game against the Phillies on April 14.

The big news of that first official game, however, was not Allen's homer, Short's pitching, or the Phillies' winning. It was the fly balls that we couldn't see. We had seen a little of the problem in the Yankee game, but daylight made it something that couldn't be overlooked.

I remember running in on a short fly ball, then looking up to see it nowhere. The next thing I knew, the ball was falling to the ground beside me for a "lost-in-the-sky-on-the-way-up-or-down" base hit. Everybody else was having the same problem. You just couldn't see the ball a lot of the times once it blended into all those clear glass panels and close-to-ball-color girders in the Astrodome roof.

"What are we going to do about the fly ball problem?" became the question on everybody's mind, whether you were owner Roy Hofheinz or outfielder Jimmy Wynn. In the meanwhile, we had games to try to play.

Fortunately, we left town for an eight-game road trip following the single game opener against the Phillies. During the road trip, the club decided to paint the two larger pie sections of clear panels behind home plate at the Astrodome as a first fix solution to the lost-fly-ball vision problem.

When we came back to the Astrodome to play the Pittsburgh Pirates on April 23, everybody noted that the paint job definitely had helped us with the lost fly ball problem. We also won our first official Astrodome game that night, taking the Pirates 4–3 behind some steady pitching. Dave Giusti worked the last two innings to pick up the first official Astros pitching victory in the Astrodome.

The following night, April 24, we took the Pirates again behind a complete game 5–0 shutout effort by Turk Farrell. Another landmark notched its way into Astros history during that game when third baseman Bob Aspromonte slammed the first Astros home run in the Dome in the sixth inning, a two-run shot to left field off Vernon Law. I followed up in the seventh by also taking Law deep on a solo shot to left for the second Astros homer in the Dome. It felt great to see and hear the scoreboard explode after all this time of anticipating what it might be like. It was awesome.

I felt good in 1965. What caused it, I really can't say, but I was seeing the ball better, and adjusting better to how they were trying to pitch to me. It made me feel more confident in my arrival as a major league ballplayer.

Winning as a ballclub, for spurts, and playing like a really good ballclub in streaks helped all of us, both as individuals and as a team.

From a single game 11–3 win on the road over the Phillies on April 21 through a doubleheader sweep of the Chicago Cubs in the Dome by 6–4 and 6–1 on May 1, the Astros set a ten-game consecutive win record that would be tied but never broken until 1999. During the win streak, I batted .270 (10 for 37) with 11 runs scored, 6 RBI, 3 doubles, 1 homer, and 3 stolen bases. I wasn't setting the woods on fire, but I was establishing myself as a consistent hitter. Over the year, I would go on to lead the Astros in batting average (.275), home runs (22), RBI (73) and steals (43). All these stats were a step up from my struggles of the previous two years with the big club. I was starting to believe that I could do even better, and to think of myself as a guy who could both hit for power and play the running game.

Unfortunately, I would later encounter a manager who would almost ruin me by his efforts to make me over into a player of his own image, but that was not a problem in 1965 with Luman Harris. Jimmy Wynn and several other young Astros were coming of age. We were not yet a winning ballclub over the length of the season, but we could see ourselves getting there.

Joe Morgan (.271 BA, 14 HR, 40 RBI), Walt Bond (.263 BA, 7 HR, 47 RBI), and Bob Aspromonte (.263 BA, 5 HR, 52 RBI) also produced decent years in 1965 and we shared a common hope for better days.

Part of that future hope was dashed for some of us on May 13, 1965, when GM Paul Richards traded away pitcher Ken Johnson and outfielder Jim Beauchamp to the Milwaukee Braves for a hot young outfield hitting prospect named Lee Maye.

Johnson was the loss we grieved. Kenny had been one of our top pitchers and he was 3–2 when the trade went down. He went on to go 13–8 in 1965 as a Brave. Meanwhile, Lee Maye batted only .251 with 3 homers and 36 RBI with the '65 Astros. This would not be the only time I experienced frustration with Astros management and their trade decisions, not by a long shot. As most of you older Astros fans already know, this was only 1965. The worst was yet to come.

I enjoyed some personal accomplishments in 1965. On June 30, 1965, in a 6–4 winning game against the San Francisco Giants at the Astrodome, I was on third base in the eighth inning, with right-hander Frank Linzy pitching and Tom Haller catching as the opposition battery. I picked up something in the timing of Linzy's pitching, and because of his inattention, that all added up to, "Go for it. You can steal home on this guy." Well, I tried and I did, and my steal of home gave us a two-run margin for victory that we held onto during the ninth. I never brag because there's too much luck that also has to go your way on a play of this type, but I do cite it only as a sign that my confidence in my own abilities was simply armed and growing. It felt good to steal home in a game in which it really meant something.

In the end, the first Houston Astros club would finish the year with a record of 65–97, bad enough for ninth place in a ten-team league again, but still fifteen games better than the dead-last amazingly awful New York Mets.

Meanwhile, the story of Houston's unintentional contributions to baseball history continued to unfold during the 1965 season. Just as the fierce heat and heartless mosquitoes at Colt Stadium once led indirectly into

Jimmy Wynn gets Dizzy Dean's autograph at Astrodome in '65.

the everyday notion of Sunday Night Baseball, the painting of the ceiling in Houston's pristine baseball chapel was now creating another need for change.

Because a considerable portion of the ceiling had been painted, the lack of light coming through was now killing the grass. The ballclub even took to spray-painting the dead brown grass green, but that was only a short-term cosmetic solution until the dead grass rotted and started falling away in clumps. It was neither a pretty sight nor an easy ground to play ball on as conditions continued to deteriorate into something on the level of a sandlot ball field. You don't ever get a true bounce on fields that are unevenly hard, soft, and covered with deflecting dirt clods. Heck! Most Class D baseball teams back then played under field conditions that were superior to ours in the Astrodome during the 1965 season.

The reputation and survival of the world's eighth wonder hung in the balance. Something had to be done to solve the turf problem before the start of the 1966 season.

Layered onto the turf problem, the Astros also entered into the off-season of 1965–66 with some even deeper leadership problems at the top. Judge Roy Hofheinz and his main partner, Mr. R.E. "Bob" Smith, who actually owned most of the stock in the club, weren't getting along well, but I wasn't involved in that fight then and I don't plan to join it now. I just couldn't ignore one big change, and neither could the other ballplayers.

On December 14, 1965, Judge Hofheinz fired Luman Harris as manager and Paul Richards as general manager of the Houston Astros. Instead of appointing a replacement GM, the Judge turned over the general administration of the club by vice president sectors to Tal Smith (player personnel), Spec Richardson (business), and Grady Hatton (field manager).

I didn't care about all this stuff back then. All it meant to me was that (1) the guy who talked me into getting married, Spec Richardson, was now a vice president; and (2) my new Astros manager, and old Oklahoma City manager, Grady Hatton, also came on board with a vice president title. My job wasn't to figure out all this maneuvering. My job was to play baseball as best I knew how.

Paul Richards took his own firing pretty hard. In this light, we have another great line from Mickey Herskowitz to lighten up the winter gloom of a figure at the top getting cut down by the baseball axe man. Herskowitz wrote that he told Richards something like, "Don't let it get to you personally, Paul. Sometimes the Judge is his own worst enemy."

"Not while I'm alive, he isn't," Richards answered, on his way out the door.

CHAPTER 6

Violation in Venezuela!

The winter of 1965–66 remains in my memory as my worst experience in baseball or in life, period. There isn't much to tell, but what there is of it, is pretty gruesome and ugly. To those of us young American ballplayers and their families who went through it, the sad part is that we just didn't have the sense to report it to our ball clubs or to the Commissioner of Baseball. Things happened to us during the winter ball season in Venezuela of 1965–66 that should never have happened to anyone, anywhere. The guilty parties should have been identified, apprehended, tried, and punished, but I guess it stands as an example of what happens in a country that has fallen under the control of a ruthless dictatorial government.

In respect for the rights of others who suffered these offenses to remain silent, I will not divulge the names of any other players who went through this ordeal with me, but this is my story, and I do choose to talk about how it played out in my own life.

First of all, be clear on this point. Winter ball for most of us young guys who had just finished a 162-game regular season schedule was not something we saw as a picnic or the easiest way to spend the winter months. For us Americans, it's a big adjustment to go live in another country where everything from the language to the food to the housing to the general way of living is different from and most often substandard to how we live back here in the USA. If you played winter ball, you had to be going there to learn more about the game and get better, to maybe pick up something from the experience that gave you a leg up on the competition the next spring.

That's pretty much how I saw it during my first winter ball season in Venezuela a couple of years earlier, but things had been different then. I was single and the country was stable. That was not true during the winter of 1965–66.

The country was on the brink of something like a revolution. Now that I look back on it, I think they should've either canceled the winter ball season, or else the American ball clubs should have held their players back from going down there. In effect, we were flying into a war zone, and most of us who were married had brought our wives and kids with us. I brought my wife Ruth and my little baby daughter Kimberly with me into this situation. We didn't know that we were flying into a state of guerilla warfare between the Venezuelan federal army and the guerilla revolutionaries.

It didn't take us long to sense the new dangers we faced. Army troops were stationed everywhere on the highways and byways and especially on the main roads into the capital of Caracas, where we played many of our games for the little country town we represented.

It only took us one trip through the Caracas inspection stop to find out that we weren't driving into the middle of a John Wayne movie, where you could count on the men in badges being the good guys—and the bearded devils in the hills being the bad guys.

When they stopped our team bus on the way into Caracas, we expected to move on as soon as our baseball business was explained, but that's not what happened at all. Soldiers armed with rifles came aboard our bus and quickly noted that many of us were traveling with women. Thank God none of the children were with us on the bus trip. The kids were being watched and taken care of back at the places where we stayed in the country.

The next thing we know, we are being told in pidgin English that a physical search and inspection will be required before we can be allowed into the city. No explanation is given, but not much is required when the main speaker is all those loaded guns now cocked and pointed at our noses.

Oh yeah, these guys are really decent and brave soldiers. They don't want to search us. They want to search our wives. While my teammates and I are held at gunpoint, these Venezuelan military bullies take our women outside and begin to hand-search them in the most obscene and violating ways imaginable.

By the time our crying wives are allowed back on the bus, we are all about to burst with anger and a fairly equal desire for either escape or revenge. Even we could figure out that a bunch of guys armed with baseball bats were outmatched by guys bearing semi-automatic rifles and handguns.

We tried as best we could to put it behind us, but there was no way to do it. We had been marked as victims by everyone from the troops to the police to the street criminals. When the original insult was then followed by a mass group robbery of our wives while they were shopping, we just all said, "That's it! Let's get out of here! Let them have their winter season for the sham that it is! We want no part of it!"

Somehow we managed to book flights back to the USA and just pull out of Venezuela without alerting the local club of our intentions. By this time, we didn't trust them either.

We went home, but, as far as I know, we all just shoved it under the rug and tried to treat it as something that never happened. Today I can't even remember how I handled my early return to Houston with the Astros. I may have just played dodgeball with them and stayed away from the places where I might have run into someone like Spec Richardson.

All I know for sure is that it didn't help my relationship with Ruth. Today I understand even better how difficult that must have been for her. I didn't like the fact either that it showed me how vulnerable we all can be to the actions of evil people in authority when they have the physical upper hand on what happens next. That was a scary fact that I've never forgotten.

Coming on the heels of a rather joyful first season in the Astrodome, the memories of Venezuela left a very bad lingering pain in the lives of all who were there to endure it. Even now, it hurts to write about it, but I feel I must for the sake of my own peace of mind and spiritual deliverance from ancient anger.

Not everything that happens in life is either fair or easy. Some stuff lodges in your chest and belly like a hot coal from Satan that's hell-bent on simmering for a lifetime. I don't need that torture, nor do I deserve it.

Believe me, I never push my religious beliefs on anyone else, but give me the space here to say briefly what I believe and embrace about this sort of thing. It's important to me in this telling of my life in baseball.

Here and now, and once again for firm affirmation, I renounce the hot coal of the devil's temptations in the name of Jesus Christ! I will give the devil his due, but I will never give him my life by staying lost in resentment.

Satan has no power over me. I belong only to God Almighty, and He wants me to tell my baseball story, even if there are a few more bumps in the road that was my life from this point forward.

Chapter 7

Astro Turf Toes
and Top Spins

The dying grass at the Astrodome didn't hang around long beyond the 1965 season as an unsolved problem. Judge Hofheinz learned of an artificial surface product at Monsanto called Chemgrass that he bought as the answer to the unexpected surface problems that came with his version of indoor baseball. He even worked it out with Monsanto to call the green plastic grass by the name of Astro Turf upon its installation in the Dome in zipper-interlocking sections prior to the 1966 baseball season.

When Monsanto patented the popular new product for broader sale in 1967, it was, by then, identified by the name that would grow to be a synonym for artificial surfaces of all kinds. When the public thought of an artificial surface, they came to think of it as Astro Turf, whether it came from Monsanto or not. No doubt that's what you call good marketing.

As the bright green Astro Turf was being installed in the Astrodome prior to the 1966 season, writer Mickey Herskowitz watched the process, in boredom and awe, no doubt, as the new field began to unfold, section by section, and zipper by zipper.

Leave it to Mickey to sum things up in a way that brought a smile or a laugh to everyone around him, and to his readers.

"Houston now has the only infield in baseball with its own built-in infield fly!" Mickey Herskowitz observed.

Monsanto couldn't make enough Astro Turf to do the whole field prior to Opening Day, so they just did the infield in time for the April 18 home opener against the Los Angeles Dodgers. By June 10, the outfield was also covered for our game with the Chicago Cubs.

This is important to remember too about that first installation. The old dirt part of the infield was left as it always was, creating a really uneven speed bounce for batted infield balls, depending upon where they landed first, on Astro Turf or dirt. That problem would not be fixed until 1970, when the Cincinnati Reds installed Astro Turf over most of their playing surface at the new Riverfront Stadium, while leaving only dirt sliding areas near the bases. With that correction, the complete new feel of the artificial-surface game was in place for another big change in the way game played out. As the grass substitution course in Houston and other places soon followed the Reds' lead of almost total coverage in Astro Turf, we soon found ourselves playing on infields that turned yesterday's easy ground outs into today's seeing-eye and blue darter singles. These batted balls skipped across the much faster surface like the second coming of Bugs Bunny.

Yes, Astro Turf may have solved the dying-grass ugliness problem, but it was one of those things that changed the beautiful game of baseball in ways we could only have imagined a year earlier. And it all started with the problem of fielders being unable to see fly balls under unmovable glass panels in the stationary roof. Just think about it for a second. If we could have afforded to build retractable roofs on these stadiums from the get-go, there never would have been any need for Astro Turf because we could have kept the natural grass alive. But that's not how life works, is it? Even with domed stadiums planned by some pretty smart people from the very start, a lot was left to trial and error.

Once they installed it everywhere, it didn't take us players long to realize that Astro Turf was going to expose all of us to a brand new ball game. We saw that Astro Turf was going to speed up the charge of ground balls racing through the infield, and that it was going to really accelerate the movement of line drives into the outfield gaps. Any infielder without range and reflex, and any outfielder who was slow afoot (and not a good enough hitter to overcome that fact), was going to be dead in the water and soon looking for some other kind of job.

I may be wrong, but I've often thought the introduction of Astro Turf in 1966 was the cutting edge for providing baseball with its first group of designated hitters when the American League came up with that new position in 1972. Guys who could still hit, but who no longer had the range and speeds to play defense on the new turfs, were natural candidates for the "DH" jobs. Add to the idea the fact that most players worth their salt who can still play the whole game don't want to "DH" anyway, and my whole theory makes sense.

I knew I had the speed and athleticism to make the adjustment in the field on Astro Turf. I also figured that the turf would help me get a few extra safeties as a hitter. Nonetheless, we were all in for a period of adjustment.

A one-bounce, slashing base hit off Astro Turf took a truer directional bounce, but it also came at you with a lot of top spin. The spin and the spongy surface (installed over a layer of sand and on top of a concrete base) caused bounces to arc higher and faster, and to go longer between hops. If an outfielder wasn't careful, or if he had trouble judging balls hit straight at him, he risked the danger of embarrassment from the ones that bounced over his head and went all the way to the wall.

So-called turf toes were another new problem. On Astro Turf, a fielder couldn't always tell when he was running over a soft spot that was going to catch his toe and jam it enough to make running hard or impossible. There was no instant cure for this issue. You just had to get to know the surface of the field where you were playing and be careful, which isn't always possible when you're playing all-out baseball.

Astro Turf also came along at a time when a lot of players still chewed a lot of tobacco on the field. That wasn't such a problem when we were playing ball on natural surfaces. Nature and the elements quickly took care of the juicy tobacco wads that had been deposited on the playing surfaces of America's old regular grass playing fields, but Astro Turf posed a new problem.

Nellie Fox summed up the Astro Turf problem for tobacco chewers: "Where am I supposed to spit?"

Nellie Fox and others provided their own answers to that obvious question soon enough. They spat wherever they mainly played—and their deposits stayed there like a brown territorial marker that was easily visible from the stands.

Ain't baseball wonderful?

Of course, baseball is wonderful, but it can be a bittersweet pill too. I would learn more about that lesson before the 1966 season was done.

After starting the season with six games in Los Angeles and San Francisco, we came home to play our season opener for the first time on Astro Turf against the Dodgers on April 18, 1966. As I said earlier, they only had the Astrodome infield covered with Astro Turf for that first game, but you could already tell the difference in how quickly the ball moved when it took its first good roll or hard bounce off that surface. It occurred to me that big changes were coming.

Players were going to have to be faster and quicker to play this game on the new Astro Turf. Guys who were no longer quick enough to play the infield were going to have to look for a job in the outfield. Guys who were no longer fast enough to play in the outfield were going to have to look for a job selling cars or insurance.

I had more than enough quickness and speed to survive in this game. I just went into the 1966 season knowing that my bat had to come alive for me to stand up and survive. I hit the ball hard, anyway. That extra-speed bounce off those balls that first found the Astro Turf could only help me as a hitter.

We went into that 1966 home opener feeling pretty confident. We had won two of three from the Dodgers at their place before going to San Francisco and getting swept, and we had the old future Hall of Famer Robin Roberts going for us on the mound. Our lineup looked pretty good too: Lee Maye led off, playing left field; Sonny Jackson filled the two-hole at shortstop; Jimmy Wynn (me) batted third as the center fielder; Joe Morgan batted cleanup as our second baseman; Rusty Staub took the number five guardian spot as our right fielder; Chuck Harrison, our first baseman, batted sixth; Bob Aspromonte played third base and batted seventh; John Bateman, our catcher, hit in the eighth place; and pitcher Robin Roberts batted ninth.

The 1966 Houston Astros were the product of youth, talent, and timing—a hopeful case of good young kids coming together at just the right time and place for team success. Manager Grady Hatton also was a good man when it came to handling and getting the most out of young guys. I had learned that about him when the club sent me down to Oklahoma City in 1964 for a little more seasoning.

Seasoning I got!

Grady Hatton helped me to refocus on all the things I do well. Grady also helped me to build confidence in my ability to do these same things at the major league level. Now it was 1966 and here we were, together again. It all added up to the sweet smell of success in my mind. All we had to do as a young team was to go out there and make it happen.

Well, we didn't make it happen on opening day. A 21-year-old kid named Don Sutton stopped us for the Dodgers to notch his first major league win. We got to Sutton for three runs and eight hits in eight innings, but Los Angeles did much better against our Robin Roberts, chasing him for five runs and ten hits over the four innings he lasted. The final score was Los Angeles 6, Houston 3.

The Dodgers had won the first official game ever played on Astro Turf. Since they only had the artificial infield in place on opening day, the Dodgers technically only had won the first game played on half–Astro Turf.

By May 21, 1966, the Astros were going great guns, playing as though we were on our way as a team to bigger and better things than just another second-division, always near-the-bottom finish. Our 1966 season record stretched to a high water mark of 21–14 on May 21 when we took the Phillies at home by 4–3. I had a good day at the plate, coming through with three hits, three RBI, and my eighth homer on the year. I was seeing the ball well. It was starting to look like a cantaloupe.

At one point in late May 1966, we even climbed to second place in the National League. We were heading into the summer almost hotter than the season itself. For the first time, our fans had reason to hope for more than a "nice try, good effort" finish from the Houston Astros.

Big crowds were coming to see our Eighth Wonder stadium and the new turf, but now we had a sense of the fact that the fans also were coming to see us play winning baseball too. That was awesome. And it also carried with it a lot of responsibility.

Fans invest their love in a team, but it is never unconditional forever for very many of them. Most expect winning to be the interest the team pays back to the fans for their invested support. I think most of the 1966 Astros were aware of that fact. Our early season success was teasing the Houston fans with a hope that the time for winning was at hand. We knew that many of the fans were already expecting us to lose our expansion team hat right then and there and start playing as pennant contenders.

To the extent that any of us on the club also thought we were ready to win big all year, we had as much yet to learn as the Houston fans. In the meanwhile, we hung in there, playing the games as best we could from pitch to pitch, inning to inning, game to game, and city to city, all the while waiting for the completion of the Astro Turf job at the Astrodome.

Interestingly too, back then, we never referred to our new home field as the ballpark or the stadium. It was a place we knew only as the Astrodome, and then as the Dome, for short. I guess that was simply because, in those early years, there was no other place like it in the world.

By June 10, 1966, additional supplies of the Astro Turf material had arrived and been installed in the outfield areas of the Astrodome. On this date, in the first game of a series against the Chicago Cubs, the first all-Astro Turf field game was finally played in Houston. This time the Astros won a 1–0 squeaker in spite of four errors in the field by third baseman Bob Aspromonte, shortstop Sonny Jackson, second baseman Joe Morgan, and left fielder Rusty Staub.

Did the new turf play a part in those four Houston errors? It's been too long ago now for me to remember for sure, but I'm guessing it did. One thing is sure. With good pitching, even Astro Turf isn't going to cause a runaway score. Our Turk Farrell pitched nine innings of seven-hit goose egg ball against the Cubs that day, but he still didn't get the win because we couldn't score, either, off lefty Kenny Holtzman of the Cubs. Ron Taylor replaced Farrell in the tenth after Turk was lifted for a pinch hitter in the ninth. Taylor shut down the Cubs one final inning and then picked up the win after I singled off Cubs starter Ken Holtzman, moved up to second base on another play, and then came home with the winning run in the tenth on a two-out single by Bob Aspromonte.

On July 25, 1966, we dropped the home opener of a series against the New York Mets by a score of 6–4. That loss was only special in the sense that it brought our season record down to 48–49, the first time we had fallen below .500 since the last days of April. We wouldn't again see the winning side of the ledger during the 1966 season. Something else was about to happen. For me, although I didn't see it coming in late July, my baseball year also was about to end in great pain and disappointment.

On August 1, 1966, we were playing the Phillies in the first game of a three-game series at Connie Mack Stadium in Philadelphia. The place was once known as Shibe Park, but more recently, it had been renamed for the man who managed the Athletics for a half century. It was the oldest park in the majors at that time, having been built in 1909 as the first concrete stadium of the so-called modern era.

I had played the park often enough by August 1 to have known the special dangers of the place, most notably the lack of good warning on some awfully hard walls and exposed steel girders in certain areas of the outfield fence. But, since baseball is the fast-moving, all-out game that it is, we ballplayers don't just automatically remember all these things when there's a play to be made. I went racing over to my left on a ball that was streaking toward the fence. Today I don't even remember the batter or the game situation. All I still see in my mind's eye is that soaring baseball and me running with everything I've got to try and catch it.

The next thing I knew, everything went dark. I had briefly knocked myself out running into that wall, apparently crunching my left arm and hand into one of those girders that any reasonable person with time to think about it would have stayed clear of, no matter what.

That's just not the life of a baseball player who wants to win.

I broke my left hand, my left wrist, and my left elbow on that play. None of the damage was permanent, but it ended my season for the first and only time in my career due to injury. The emotional disappointment was far greater than any of the physical pain. I just hated to be put out of action for any reason, but especially so during a season in which we still had a shot at our first non–losing record.

We lost, 6–5, to the Phillies on the day of my season-ending injury in 1966, and that dropped our record to 49–55. My contributions tabbed out at 18 home runs and 62 runs batted in, but my final batting average had dropped to .249.

The club would stumble to the finish line in 1966 with a 72–90 mark, good or bad enough for another eighth-place finish in the ten-team National League, but a respectable twenty-three games back of the first-place Dodgers. It could've been worse, but not with the New York Mets and the Chicago Cubs playing their own special brands of losing baseball on the trail behind us.

I ended the season mentally ready to start another year, but still on the physical mend from my wallbanger injury. I could only hope that the fans had not given up on us. I also had a good feeling about what lay ahead for Jimmy Wynn and the Houston Astros in 1967.

CHAPTER 8

Houston's Toy Cannon

"Jim Wynn is Houston's Toy Cannon." That's the way the late *Houston Chronicle* sportswriter John Wilson put it in an article titled "Wynn Packing Cannon on His Spindly Frame" that he did for *The Sporting News* back on August 26, 1967. It was only the six-word opening sentence of a late summer baseball piece that Wilson wrote for that weekly newspaper magazine source we used to think of as "baseball's Bible," but it was that right-tag-at-the-right-time-by-the-right-people call that struck a chord with the fans and launched a two-word nickname for me that would stay with me for the rest of my life: Toy Cannon. Other than Jimmy Wynn, which I've always preferred as my formal name to the Jim Wynn reference used by Wilson, I've been the Toy Cannon in the minds of everyone in baseball from that moment on.

"Did you hear what John Wilson is calling you?"

Teammates who saw the article started bringing me the word on the Toy Cannon. Finally, someone actually showed me the article and I read it quietly in the clubhouse. I couldn't altogether believe that John Wilson was actually writing about me in such flattering terms, but I privately ate it up because of everything my dad always said about nicknames: "You haven't arrived until you have one."

Did becoming the Toy Cannon really mean that I now had it made? I didn't think so. I never thought that way. Even in those younger years of taking so many other things for granted due to my inexperience and youthful naiveté, I never had a moment of false assumption about my major league career. I was just blessed in that regard with the simplest word of wisdom: In major league baseball, you either do the job or you lose the job.

The 1967 season just happened to be my biggest breakout year as a home run hitter and John Wilson just happened to ring the bell that practically everyone in the National League was raising as a question or exclamation point: How is a guy this little, a guy who always weighs in the 166–169 pound range, hitting so many home runs for such incredible distances in places like Crosley Field, Forbes Field, and Sportsman's Park?

We didn't have steroids back in 1967—or any other chemicals that added bulk or power to the body or muscle tissue. Besides, using drugs of any kind was never my style, anyway. The only thing that I ever did that may have helped the natural muscularity of my body back then was lift a few weights. I didn't make a big deal of it because of the attitude that so many older baseball people held about pumping iron back in the 1960s. The majority of baseball people back then held to the old belief that lifting weights would make baseball players too muscle-bound to play the game. All it did for me was to give me a little extra power pop on the balls that I really did pulverize.

I'll always believe that my human ability to actually become baseball's Toy Cannon came only from God. He gave it to me through my genes and the early-and-often instruction on hitting that I received from my dad. It blossomed from my own desire to hit a baseball with great power. If weightlifting contributed to this outcome, it was little more than the icing on the cake.

John Wilson also described me in his article as a bargain pick-up for the Astros when they drafted me for $8,000 from the Reds five years earlier. He also apparently had spoken with manager Grady Hatton and batting instructor Harry Walker about me too. Both of those men agreed that I could probably improve upon my .260-level batting average without harming my home run production, but neither wanted to offer any suggestions that might get in the way of batting progress that I was making on my own.

There were some hints of a problem that I would face later with Harry Walker in the Wilson article. Whereas Grady Hatton told Wilson he was surprised to see me doing this well so soon on the heels of the horrific injury I suffered in 1966, Harry Walker offered that I could become a .300 hitter without falling off in my power numbers, if I could learn to cut down on my strikeouts. (At the time Wilson wrote his article, I had struck out 93 times in 403 times at bat.) Walker would wait for greater authority as manager before he showed all of us on the club the full blowhard spirit of his heavier hand.

If anything, the 1966 injury in Philadelphia had played a big, but humbling part in my new awareness of how fragile the major league dream is for all of us who have ever pursued it. No matter how much talent we possess, no matter how much we learn, no matter how fortunate we may have been during our careers to have been surrounded by the right people and supported by the right organizations, we are still human—and luck can turn from good to bad on a dime.

On August 1, 1966, I could have had sixty home runs and been bearing down on the record of Roger Maris and it still would not have bought me any special consideration once I met up with that wall at Connie Mack Stadium, running hell-bent for leather. Once the wall and I met up, it was all over for good in '66. I'm just grateful that it wasn't over for all time.

If anything, the benefit side of humility is its place as the foundation of all lessons worth keeping. Coming to terms with my own vulnerability as a human being helped me to better appreciate each new day, and each new game that I was well enough to play.

The realization came right away in spring training. The first time I got out there on the field at Cocoa Beach in 1967, I thought, "Man! In what now seems only like a few minutes ago, I was in Philadelphia, getting ready to run into an unforgiving wall. Now here I am with another chance to keep playing the game I love, to keep doing the only thing I ever wanted to do. Thank God! I'm going to try to stay grateful and to never take anything for granted again!"

April 11, 1967, marked our Opening Day at the Astrodome as we took on the Atlanta Braves with future Hall of Famer Eddie Mathews playing first base for the Astros against his former club. Mathews had come over to Houston in a New Year's Eve trade, along with infielder Sandy Alomar and pitcher Arnie Umbach. We gave up pitcher Bob Bruce and outfielder Dave Nicholson to get the greatest third baseman in Braves history during the twilight of his career, but we already had a younger guy named Bob Aspromonte holding down the hot corner, so the elder Mathews moved over to first base for the sake of getting his bat in the lineup.

In case you're wondering, the elder Sandy Alomar never saw an official time at bat with Houston. On March 24, 1967, Astros GM Spec

By 1967, Jimmy had become the "Toy Cannon." His 37 homers in '67 were second in the National League to the 39 hit by Hank Aaron of the Braves (National Baseball Hall of Fame Library, Cooperstown, NY).

Richardson traded Alomar to the New York Mets for somebody named Derrell Griffith.

Eddie Mathews paid immediate dividends in support of starting pitcher Mike Cuellar. He picked up two hits, including a triple, plus he both scored and batted in a run. We won the game, 6–1, and that sort of set the tone for us as an upbeat, win-hungry young club. Except for Mathews at first base, youth gelling on some brief but good major league experience was our calling card on the future.

John Bateman was our catcher. Bateman was a guy with fair defensive skills, some good pop in his bat, and a mind that worked in its own curious and different way. Once, during a night game at old Colt Stadium, Bateman dropped what appeared to be a fairly easy catch of a pop foul in the area behind home plate. After the game, a reporter asked John what had happened on that play. The answer was pure John Bateman.

"I lost it in the moonlight," Bateman explained.

After Mathews at first base, we had my roomie and best friend Joe Morgan at second base. Little Joe, as others, but not me, were now often calling him, was really on the brink of turning from good to great as a second sacker back in 1967. Joe had made the National League All-Star team in 1966, but he had been prevented from playing in the game due to an injury.

The big difference for Joe Morgan seems to have been the presence of a great mentor on the club during the 1964–65 seasons. That playing coach was a future Hall of Fame second baseman named Nellie Fox, who taught his student well—so well, in fact, that both the student and the teacher had dates with destiny as future members of the honored few at Cooperstown.

My belief is that Joe Morgan had the talent and temperament to make the Hall of Fame anyway, but it sure didn't hurt Joe to have a guy like Nellie Fox in his life as a teacher at just the right open moment. Nellie taught Joe how to use the smaller glove, how to handle the footwork on double plays, how to best position himself in the field against different kinds of batters in various situations. In other words, Nellie taught Joe all there was to know about playing second base that Joe was willing to learn. That's all any good teacher can do.

At third base, the 1967 Astros featured the slick-fielding, strong-armed Bob Aspromonte, the same fellow who picked up all those club-first records on the first Opening Day in franchise history back in 1962. I wasn't here at the time, of course, but I soon learned after my 1963 arrival that Bob Aspromonte had the first time at bat, first hit, first base runner experience, and first run scored in franchise history. If I've left anything out, I'll just have to beg Bob's forgiveness.

The 1967 season was Bob Aspromonte's best year at the plate. His .294 batting average and 58 RBI were second and third place on the club in those two departments. His fielding, of course, was often a game-winning difference maker.

Young Sonny Jackson held down the shortstop position with a lot of speed, skill, range, and athleticism. Unfortunately, Sonny's offensive production had fallen hard from a .292 with 49 stolen bases in 1966 to only .237 with 22 steals in 1967. Hopes remained high for a Sonny Jackson rally at the plate, but it never happened. The National League pitchers had adjusted to Sonny Jackson over the off-season and he had not been able to counter their moves. It happens all the time in baseball. Some hitters counter-adjust to flourish again. Others fade and perish because of their inability to make their own changes to the new things that pitchers are doing with them.

Hall of Fame pitcher Warren Spahn once put it this way: "Hitting is timing. Pitching is upsetting timing." I've never heard it said any better. A pitcher will do anything that works to upset your timing as a hitter and it's not always the same thing. If you're unsure of yourself, or show any fear, you will get the Bob Gibson Treatment. Gibson could send you a chin-whiskers pitch that was designed, more than anything else, to plant the idea that your life may end on the next throw.

If a pitcher sees that you have success sitting on fast balls, and that you are dedicated to so doing, no matter what, you will never see another fast ball for 50 pitches or so, if ever again. In the meanwhile, you will see plenty of change-ups and curves.

If you can't stay away from those eyes-wide, unhittable high pitches, watch out, here they come, riding the arc of the pitcher's arm like the 7th Cavalry. If you can't stay away from those outside pitches in the dirt, get ready for an avalanche of wild and wicked sliders. You may as well have ordered them from room service.

It boils down to this: Whatever you can't hit, don't need but will swing at, or duck away from, those generous big league pitchers are going to give you. And they are going to give it to you just as soon as the first one figures out whatever your brand of poison may be. Once that happens, the scouts from other clubs will spread the new word faster than you can call up your mama to tell her that you're homesick.

Anyway, Jackson at shortstop wasn't our only offensive hole in 1967. Aaron Pointer started the season in left field, but after only 27 games and a .157 batting average output over that span, a fellow named Ron Davis took his position for most of the season. Davis batted .256 with 7 homers in 94 games.

Rusty Staub and I had right and center fields covered better than at any other time in the club's brief franchise history. Rusty Staub batted .333 with 10 home runs and 74 RBI on the year.

My 37 home runs on the 1967 season did not come with an increase in my batting average (I hit .249 on the year), but my RBI total climbed to 107 and my slugging average elevated to .495. I was hitting some cannon shots, both at home and on the road, and a lot of people were starting to notice my work for the first time. A lot of that attention spawned in the idea that a guy as small as me, 5' 9" and 170 pounds, shouldn't be hitting home runs at all, let alone blasting drives of Ruthian distance and rainbow arc.

Well, I'm going to ask you to believe me on this one. I wasn't getting the big head from any of this attention, and, as I expressed earlier, I was finished up to my nose with taking anything new for granted because of my accident in 1966.

I was just doing what I've always done by hitting long home runs, but I was getting better at it and doing it more often now on a bigger stage. Like most of my peers from that era, I wasn't really all that involved with statistics or milestones. In fact, much of what I'm reporting here now, I learned about much later. I probably didn't even look at my statistical records until after my retirement. Once I retired, and more and more all the time, ever since the late 1970s, I have met all kinds of people, fans and media alike, who have brought me up to speed on all my various records.

When this happens, my reaction most of time is to say something like, "No kidding? I did that?" I'm amazed to learn these things and I'm as equally surprised that there seem to be so many people out there who know and care about my career accomplishments even more than I do.

Playing baseball was the game to me, not the compiling of statistics. So, when I now bring you up to date here on anything I've done statistically years ago, please read that information in the spirit it is intended. I'm writing for history now, and I'm not reporting from a bunch of ego notes that I've been squirreling away for decades. Most of this data is news to me too.

I did know that the 37 homers I hit in 1967 was a franchise record. I was also completely aware late in the season that Hank Aaron of the Atlanta Braves and I were locked in a battle that would go down to the wire for the National League home run title that year.

Add to all of this statistical adventure the extra twist that my 37 homers and the .333 batting average of Rusty Staub would both stand as club records from 1967 forward until Jeff Bagwell surpassed both by hitting 39 homers and batting .368 during the strike-shortened season of 1994.

In 1967, it didn't take us long to find ourselves in a tailspin. By April 27, we rolled into the last contest of a three-game series in the Dome against the St. Louis Cardinals nursing a ten-game losing streak, with our Larry Dierker set to face the always tough Bob Gibson of the Cardinals. A five-run Astro banger inning in the bottom of the seventh chased Gibson and Cardinal reliever Hal Woodeshick. It took three extra Cardinal pitchers to halt us. Joe Morgan's bases-loaded triple off Woodeshick turned out to be the backbreaker for the Cardinals and the key hit in picking up a win for Larry Dierker, and hanging a rare loss on Bob Gibson.

Anytime you beat Gibson, you had to know too that he would remember what happened and be looking forward to seeing all of you the next time. See what I mean about Gibson? This game was played over four decades ago and those thoughts are still planted firmly in my mind.

What do you want to bet that Bob Gibson still remembers Joe Morgan's triple off Woodeshick with the bases loaded in that game back in 1967? Pitchers have long memories, especially when it comes to home runs and players who beat them late in a game with scratch singles—or any kind of extra-base hit.

As for pitchers, our starters on the '67 club were a pretty darn good cast of talent, character, and characters. In addition to the man who would become one of the icons in Colt .45s/Astros history, Larry Dierker (6–5), we were paced that year by the wonderful Mike Cuellar (16–11), and he was ably assisted by the fiery, up-and-coming Don Wilson (10–9) and the crafty Dave Giusti (11–15). Our fifth man was Bo Belinsky (3–9), who came over to the Astros from the Phillies during the winter to pitch as a one-season Astro.

Two memories of Belinsky stand out: (1) He brought his old adopted street dog with him to spring training; and (2) about the comfortable Astrodome seats, Bo said, "Just wait until the punks with the knives get a load of these things!"

I think Belinsky thought he was still back in Philadelphia. If memory further serves on this minor note, I don't think seat carvings were ever a major problem for the more civilized baseball fans of Houston, Texas.

On May 2, 1967, we hauled our sinking-hard 5–13 record back to the scene of my lost consciousness and Connie Mack–scuttled previous season in Philly. This time, as compared to 1966, the results of our first game there fell on the pleasant side as we rallied from a 3–2 deficit by scoring eight runs in the top of the eighth for an 11–3 win. Bob Aspromonte had a three-run homer in the big inning and I collected hits in both my times at bat in that one frame. Rusty Staub had four RBI on the day and even winning pitcher Mike Cuellar banged a run-producing double in support of his own victory. The Astros win pushed Cuellar to a 2–1 record on his amazing trek in behalf of our going-nowhere good team.

We had some fun moments in '67. Back at the Astrodome on May 18 for a game against the Giants, I led off scoring in the bottom of the first with a two-out, nobody-on-base home run that struck the left field foul pole. At least, that's how home plate umpire Shag Crawford called it.

Before I could even complete my trot around the bases, Giants manager Herman Franks was out there raising Cain with Crawford, claiming in violent terms that the ball had not hit the pole, but was foul. When someone on the Giants club called umpire Crawford a "meathead," Shag turned around and pointed the finger of blame at Ollie Brown, tossing him for the insult, but also starting another explosion as Brown protested his innocence to no avail.

We went on to win the game, 6–2, behind Larry Dierker (4–2). After the game, Giants starting and losing pitcher Gaylord Perry confessed, admitting that he had been the one who threw the "meathead" title out there earlier as another name for umpire Crawford.

More fun times unfolded at Wrigley Field on May 26. With the winds blowing out as well as I've ever seen them blow, back in the all-day-games era at Wrigley, four of us on the Astros club homered off the Chicago Cubs pitching staff as we blasted our way to a 17–4 victory. Rusty Staub led the way with a three-run shot, and Joe Morgan, Ron Davis, and I all kicked in two-run blasts.

The favorable hitting conditions (wind at our backs and facing bad pitching) almost caused the same reaction in our hitters that sharks are known to have to the smell of blood in the water.

Late in the runaway slaughter, when Astros catcher John Bateman was plunked by the latest Cubs pitcher, he begged the umpire to let him forgo the free pass to first so he could keep hitting. The umpire saw through Bateman's forgiving attitude and forced him to abide by the rules of the game. The example set by John Bateman speaks volumes for the way the hitting frenzy tilted some of our loyal members into overkill mode that fine Chicago day, but who could blame them? More often than not, our club found themselves as the ones checking into the slaughterhouse.

The beat went on.

On June 7, 1967, the Astros were in St. Louis for the third contest of a four-game series against the Cardinals. Having taken the first two games, the Astros were hungry for more. We jumped on starter Steve Carlton and five relievers for seventeen runs and twenty-three hits that night, producing a 17–1 victory that was then the biggest winning margin in franchise history. Astros third baseman Bob Aspromonte had five hits; Astros catcher Ron Brand had four hits; and Astros second baseman Julio Gotay and right fielder Rusty Staub each had three safeties on the night. I was two for three, with three runs scored and a steal off lefty Steve Carlton. That was a plenty good enough night for me.

Bo Belinsky (1–1) pitched us to his first Astros victory, with "save" help from reliever Claude Raymond. In spite of the offensive heroics, our record was still only raised to 20–31 on the year, but we hung in there, doing what we could as a team to win for Houston.

By this time, the notions of writer John Wilson must have been building to that article he would write about me for *The Sporting News* later in the summer. In the meantime, I wasn't trying to help him or any other writer toward such a flattering account of my abilities. I was just playing my game as best I could as certain things, not totally explainable, began to happen.

On June 11, 1967, we were in Cincinnati at Crosley Field for a series-closing double-header against the Reds. We had lost single games to the Reds the two previous days and we were hoping to split things by taking both ends of the twin bill. Naturally, as was always the case on our trips into my old home town, my parents, brothers, sisters, aunts and uncles all had turned out to watch me play.

We won the opener of the double bill by 7–4, thanks largely to a two-run homer by Bob Aspromonte and some fine pitching by Mike Cuellar (7–2). The second game found us tied 1–1 when I came to bat against Sammy Ellis with a man on base. Other than the outcome, the rest of what happened next is blurred by the passage of time. Even I have trouble wrapping my mind around the power that came into play in that time at bat.

On the second pitch from Ellis, I took my usual level swing at a ball that ran right into the zone and found the sweet spot of my bat. A hitter always knows the special feel of that crunch. You can barely sense the contact, but you know it was true, landing as it did like the warm, moist kiss on your lips that slips into your life from a woman you really care about.

Kiss it. Kiss it gone.

The ball took off from my bat on a high speeding arc to left field, changing quickly from ball size to pea size to dot size as I watched it disappearing into the afternoon Cincinnati sky. No way has the ballpark held this one, I thought, so I began my trot at a respectful pace around the bases. Before I even reached first base, I heard a moaning rush of ooohs and aaahs, especially from the stadium seats that held a clear view of the area beyond Crosley Field.

What's it all about?

When I got back to the stunned congratulations of my teammates, I saw that even their eyes held onto a look of awe that cried out for explanation.

"What's going on, guys?" I asked. "So I hit a home run, so what?"

"So what?" their silent looks seemed to answer in group chorus.

Then I started to get the story, little by little, from everybody there who either saw it happen, or else survived a first-hand hysterical account of the ball's travels from someone else. The ball not only left the ballpark, apparently, it also left the grounds. It didn't just stop there either. The ball landed on a freeway that once ran parallel to the left field stands beyond the grounds of Crosley Field. By some magical extra power, it then took a high bounce off the freeway and headed on its way down a street beyond that leads directly into a nearby neighborhood.

Here's where the chills I got from this information went far beyond anyone else's. If these accounts were true, that ball I hit found Colerain Avenue, the very street where I grew up, the same street I used to race down as a kid on my way to and from Crosley Field.

No one ever reported finding the ball, but I like to think that it had enough pep left from the corner to travel another three blocks. Wouldn't that have been something if some other baseball-loving kid then living at 1917

Colerain Avenue in 1967 had found the ball I hit that day in Cincinnati?

The long homer in Cincinnati was my tenth on the year. Bob Aspromonte also hit another one in the 4th, his fifth on the year, but we lost the game in the bottom of the ninth when Reds pinch hitter Don Pavletich delivered a grand slam to break up a 4–4 tie.

I left Cincinnati on a long-ball hot streak. The next night, June 12, 1967, we were back in Houston to start a four-game series with the Giants and I hit another one, my eleventh on the year. By the fourth game with the Giants, June 15, 1967, I was ready for the biggest home run game of my career. Even the Grand

In 2004, the Texas Baseball Hall of Fame established the Jimmy Wynn "Toy Cannon" Award as its iconic way of annually recognizing an individual from the baseball community for his or her distinguished community service.

Canyon that was the Astrodome couldn't hold me that day. I hit three solo homers against the Giants in our series finale, two off starter Bobby Bolin and another one off reliever Bill Henry. We won the game, 6–2, as starter Mike Cuellar ran his season record with our then 24–36 club to a personal mark of 8–2 and climbing.

With fourteen long balls on the year after the big three-homer game at the Dome, my personal confidence about the future soared to a new high. I knew that I just had to keep my head about me and keep doing what I knew how to do. The rest would take care of itself. All I wished for was the day we came together as a team of contenders in the National League. We had some good players. We just weren't getting it done on the consistent winning side of the ledger.

The very same day, June 15, 1967, and minutes before the trade deadline slipped by, the Astros made a big deal with the team that was coming to town, the Atlanta Braves. GM Spec Richardson packed away closer Claude Raymond to the Braves in exchange for starting pitcher Wade Blasingame. Less than 24 hours later, on June 16, 1967, I homered off Braves starter Denny

Lemaster. It was my seventh homer of the week and my fifteenth on the year. We still lost the game, 9–8, when our former closer, Claude Raymond, came on to save the game for Atlanta in the ninth.

Two days later, on June 18, 1967, 22-year-old Don Wilson of the Astros pitched the first no-hitter of his career against the Atlanta Braves. It was a 2–0 Father's Day shutout in the Dome that concluded with Wilson having to get the final out in the most difficult way by striking out Hank Aaron for his fifteenth "K" on the day. How tough do things have to be? If they are worth it, plenty tough!

We scored the only runs of the game in Wilson's no-hitter in the third when I doubled off Braves starter Phil Niekro to plate runner Sonny Jackson. I then later scored our second run on a sacrifice fly by Eddie Mathews.

By the time we played our last game prior to the All-Star Break on June 9, 1967, against the Cubs at the Astrodome, I was closing out the first half of the season with twenty-one home runs and battling Hank Aaron of the Atlanta Braves for leadership in that category. Aaron went into the break with twenty-two HR.

In spite of the fact that our 33 wins and 50 losses at the break stood the Astros at seventeen games under .500, three of us were selected for the National League All-Star team that took the field on July 11, 1967, at Anaheim, California. In addition to yours truly, outfielder Rusty Staub and pitcher Mike Cuellar boarded the plane on July 9 for the big game set for two days later in California.

All I can say for sure is that the whole trip felt like a movie, one starring my two teammates and me, plus a few other, better-known stars. Once I got to the ballpark in Anaheim, the descent from those clouds came around like a sliding board at the playground. Here was I, Jimmy Wynn, suiting up to play in the same clubhouse with guys like Willie Mays, Hank Aaron, Roberto Clemente, and Bob Gibson. How in the world did this ever happen? It was a really awesome and humbling experience. No other words come to mind or apply.

I wasn't starting, but I had to be ready. I wanted so much to simply make a contribution if I were called upon at any point to play in the game.

As remains the case today, the managers of our two All-Star clubs in 1967 were the same men who led their teams to the previous year's World Series. Earl Weaver of the Baltimore Orioles was on hand to manage the American League club. Walt Alston, leader of the World Champion Los Angeles Dodgers, was on deck to manage our National League team.

I had no way of knowing back in 1967 that Walt Alston and I would have another shared rendezvous with baseball history down the line a few years, but I already liked the man. How could I not? We both wore uniform number 24.

Hank Aaron and I didn't talk about the home run leadership race. I even wondered if he ever gave it a thought. Obviously, I did. The idea passed through my mind that it just may be that only younger guys, guys who have never won anything in the big leagues, think about things like winning the home run title against one of the best sluggers in the game.

Because I like westerns, the embarrassing thought invaded that maybe I had become like the young gunslinger that had come to town to take on the old pro gunfighter in a street fight, just to see where he stood, or if he stood at all.

Not liking that picture at all, I shut down that silent movie in my brain almost as quickly as it came. Shortly thereafter, Hank Aaron and I had our brief encounter in real time as he walked into the National League clubhouse.

"How are you doing, Jimmy?" Hank Aaron asked with a smile.

"Just fine, Hank, how are you?" I answered, also with a smile.

The 1967 All-Star Game itself was a classic, low-scoring, multiple pitchers' duel. I finally entered the game in the top of the ninth as a pinch hitter for pitcher Bob Gibson and I managed to take an outside pitch from Al Downing the opposite way to right field for a single. I didn't score, but I later learned that my single had been the first All-Star Game hit in history by a Houston batter. Understand too that, up until 1967, pitcher Turk Farrell had been our major representative at the All-Star Games and, as a pitcher, Turk was never a strong candidate for even getting an All-Star time at bat, let alone a legitimate hit in a game of this type.

Rusty Staub also got a pinch-hit single off Catfish Hunter in the eleventh, but he didn't score either, and Mike Cuellar also pitched a couple of scoreless innings along the way, completing the cycle of contributions by our Astros All-Star trio.

The 1967 All-Star Game was finally decided by a Tony Perez solo homer in the fifteenth as the National League then held on to a 2–1 victory over the American League. As for us Houston guys, we all went home happy and feeling good about our Astros participation in the midsummer classic.

On July 14, 1967, we were at Candlestick Park to play the San Francisco Giants when something happened that you don't see every day. Eddie Mathews was the batter in the top of the second inning of a scoreless tie when time had to be called because of something "Mickey Mouse" that was going on in center field. We could see Willie kind of scooting down, watching something small as it moved on the ground around him. Then we saw Willie Mays motioning with both his open and gloved hands, chasing the little creature toward the outfield wall.

A distant cheer arose from the outfield crowd as the little living thing scrambled to safety from the menace that was Willie Mays. It wasn't Mickey Mouse, but it *was* a mouse that ran from Willie. For a few minutes there, the little fellow was big enough to halt both a major league baseball game and a time-at-bat contest between future Hall of Famers, pitcher Juan Marichal of the Giants and batter Eddie Mathews of the Astros. Of course, it took another future Hall of Famer, Willie Mays, to coax the little four-legged guy into either buying a ticket or leaving.

After play resumed, Juan Marichal struck out Eddie Mathews. Two innings later, with no further appearances by the mouse, Mathews took Marichal deep for the 500th home run of his career. As the superstitious natures of ballplayers go, you should be able to figure out how this one broke down for the likes of Eddie and Juan, even though I never asked either of them about it. My guess is that this game planted the idea that the appearance of a mouse in the outfield was either good luck, or bad luck, depending upon what happened next on this first appearance at Candlestick.

For all I know, either Eddie or Juan may have seen a mouse show up on the field in some other previous game. In that case, the strikeout was either a thing that fit or broke the old pattern of good luck or bad, depending on your point of view.

At any rate, this whole train of thought is simply designed to show you how complicated baseball superstitions can get to be. Sometimes it's just hard to know when to step on or over a foul line when you're going back and forth, to and from the field and the dugout. The only thing for sure about this practice is, once you start doing either, stepping on or over foul lines the same way every time, you will never again feel the same about the sight of long lines of chalk.

When I went out to center field in the bottom of the second, I have to admit that I looked around my area, just to see if I was playing the position alone, or with company. The little fellow didn't show up again, but once was enough for the mouse to bring good luck to the Astros, I suppose. We won the game, 8–6.

Elsewhere on July 14, 1967, Hank Aaron hit his 23rd home run of the year at home for the Braves against Rick Wise of the Phillies. That solo shot in Atlanta gave Hank Aaron a two-homer lead over me for the leadership in that category.

Two days later, on June 16, 1967, I finally hit my first home run since the All-Star Game break. Number 22 for me came against Jim Brewer of the Dodgers with one man on base in the top of the sixth inning of the second game we played as a twin bill in Los Angeles. Our 4–1, 8–2 sweep of the double-header at Dodger Stadium pushed our record up to a still bad 36–52 on the year.

My homers suddenly were coming in bunches, spread apart over gaps in time, but going far, whenever they went. On July 23, 1967, at the far and deep outfield graveyard that was Forbes Field, I cranked a couple of long balls, one of which was a monster shot beyond the batting cage in center field and beyond the center field wall. It landed on a Little League field located behind Forbes Field. Those two homers brought me up to 25 on the year and they tied me with Hank Aaron for the league lead. Hank had hit his 25th a day earlier against the Cardinals.

July 23 turned out to be a special day for teammate Rusty Staub and me. Between us, we either held or were tied for the National League lead in all three of the Triple Crown batting categories. In addition to my tie with Aaron for the home run lead, I led the league with 75 RBI and Rusty Staub led the Senior Circuit with a batting average on that date of .358.

On July 30, 1967, I closed out my July homer hitting by posting two more in the second game of a home double-header against Jack Fisher of the New York Mets. One of those was my only career inside-the-park job. That all-the-way run, plus the normal winger, brought me to 27 and one up on Aaron as July closed.

August 17, 1967, proved to be a sad day for the players on the Astros club. Another trade by GM Richardson ended our less-than-one-season association with the great Eddie Mathews, who moved on to Detroit in exchange for pitcher Fred Gladding and cash. It was just another one of those days that once more brought home the point that the baseball life is often like an old boot. As soon as you start getting comfortable with it, the thing rises up and kicks you.

Saying goodbye to Eddie was fast, but tough. As much as we needed relief pitching, we would miss the presence and leadership of a guy who was already bound for a place called Cooperstown.

Meanwhile, August heated up, and the home run race between Aaron and me stayed steady at neck and neck. In a Dome game against Atlanta on August 23, 1967, I became the first Astro to reach 30 homers on a season when I took pitcher Clay Carroll deep in the bottom of the 6th. On the what-really-counts side, we lost that game in a 9–3 rout by the Braves, dropping our record on the '67 season to a miserable 52–74. Back then, I wasn't really thinking of home runs as strongly as I'm reporting them now, but I was bothered by the fact, one more time, that the Houston Astros were shaping up as another bad ball club. That hurt bad.

I didn't have to think of my home run pace. The beat reporters and TV news people were doing it for me. John Wilson of the *Houston Chronicle* gave me my nickname of the Toy Cannon, but the other writers stayed on my heels too in their daily review of the late-season home run race between Hank Aaron and me. We weren't Mantle and Maris in 1961, or Ruth and Gehrig in 1927, but the precedent was already there for the media to keep playing up the home run competition angle.

Everybody else among the fans also talked up the subject as well in letters to the newspapers. I can just imagine what it would have been like for Aaron and me had the Internet and baseball bulletin boards and forums been around back in 1967. I'm also grateful that they were not. Too much free-floating chatter about every little detail in the world on a club can be both very distracting and very tiring to the ballplayers. Not paying attention to all the distraction that goes on around the game isn't always as easy to do as some people would have you think it is.

As the 1967 season moved hard and fast toward September, my homers began to fall like the leaves of an early autumn. On August 29, I hit number 31 off John Hartenstein of the Cubs in support of a 5–3 Don Wilson win in Chicago. On August 31, I crunched number 32 in a Bo Belinsky 9–3 losing cause against the Cardinals in St. Louis. Then, a week later on September 8, I smashed number 33 off Don Sutton and the Dodgers in a 4–2 Astros defeat in Los Angeles. One day later in Dodger Stadium, I reached a plateau that I wasn't even thinking about at the time. Again, people had to tell me about this one much later. I wasn't keeping track of this stuff back in the day.

On September 9, 1967, my two homers off Claude Osteen and Bob Miller of the Dodgers in a 5–3 Astros victory over the Dodgers at Los Angeles boosted my totals on the year to 35 home runs and 100 RBI. I had become the first player in Colt .45/Astro history to reach either of those heights. In fact, another nineteen years would pass before Glenn Davis became only the second different Astro player to break the 30 season homers level. I would do it again in 1969, but that doesn't count on this measurement scale.

The funny thing is, I still feel a little embarrassed talking about these things. I'm not a bragging person who goes around tooting his own horn. I'm just trying to stick to my two major commitments in this book: (1) tell the truth in all things and (2) write for history.

Truth to tell, I had no idea what benchmarks I'd reached on the day I hit the 35 HR/100 RBI levels, but I was aware that these two homers had tied me with Hank Aaron for the National League HR lead in games played through September 9. I was attuned that day to the fact that our victory in support of pitcher Mike Cuellar had boosted his season record to 13–11 on the year. That seemed to be the man and the stat that we needed to celebrate. With a couple of more pitchers like Mike Cuellar and Larry Dierker on our future staff, the Astros stood a chance of becoming a winning ball club! Am I wrong? Wasn't that one the kind of fact and stat we needed to be paying attention to back in 1967?

The next two days proved a little interesting, even to a humble, young guy like me who didn't always like to talk about such things. I was just a 168-pound center fielder with a God-given talent for hitting home runs with a 36-ounce bat.

On September 10, I homered again off Dodger reliever Bob Miller in the top of the 11th to give our guy, Dave Eilers, and the Houston Astros a 1–0 win at Los Angeles. My 36th HR of the 1967 season put me one ahead of Hank Aaron at day's end.

The next day, September 11, we survived the redeye flight back from LA in time to lose to the Chicago Cubs, 2–1, at the Astrodome, but our single tally came as the result of my homer off Ray Culp. I hate to admit this fact, but I've never been happier after a losing game. My home run gave me 37 on the year, a lead of two home runs over Hank Aaron at 35, and a good feeling of confidence with only two weeks to play in the season. I was well on my way to one of Yogi Berra's main lessons. You know the one? It goes, "It ain't over till it's over!"

The rest of the year and off-season contained some sadness and shocks. On September 14, 1967, we received the bad news that former teammate Walt Bond had died that day of leukemia at Methodist Hospital in Houston. Those of us who knew Walt were especially saddened. He was only 29, but he had walked in our midst until only recently as a man with wisdom beyond his years. I will always value Walter Bond as the man who taught me more than any other about how to wear the uniform of a big league ballplayer with dignity, dedication, and pride. Houston lost far more than a ballplayer with his youthful passing. It lost a man who truly belonged in the Hall of Fame for decent human beings.

Pitcher Jim Umbricht of the 1962–63 Colt .45s and Walt Bond, in many ways, were cut from the same cloth. I just had a stronger bond with Mr. Bond. Perhaps that was because we were both black and position players while Jim Umbricht was white and a pitcher, but even saying that takes away from my intent here. I don't mean to slight Jim Umbricht, a very good man who also died of cancer prior to the 1964 season, nor do I ever want to sell Walt Bond short as one who reached out to me only because of our shared racial kinship.

Both Umbricht and Bond were fine human beings who cared about others and died way too soon for any of us to understand God's plan for each. What I fail to understand is simply the answer to this more earth-bound, human question: If the Houston club believed that it was fitting and proper to retire Jim Umbricht's uniform number 32 in his honor, which they did, why couldn't they have done the same for Walt Bond and retired his number too? Bond even played more games as a Colt .45.

The answer to that one again, my friend, is also out there, blowin' in the wind.

There was little time to mourn in late September 1967. The team was playing better and we were mostly pushing to do well, rather than just mailing in the rest of the season. On September 11, our Mike Cuellar bested Jim Bunning, then of the Philadelphia Phillies and Hall of Fame bound (and today a senator from Kentucky), in a 1–0 11-inning pitchers' duel at the Astrodome. It was the kind of game that fans today will probably never get to see because of today's rosy romance with pitch counts, but both men went the distance, and each gave up only six hits. Chuck Harrison finally drove in Rusty Staub with the game-winning run with two outs in the bottom of the eleventh.

Mike Cuellar struck out twelve that day on his way to a season record of 16–11 for our 69–93 overall record which made us the ninth-place club.

How's that for production? In 1967, Mike Cuellar also became the first Astros pitcher to win sixteen games in a season. We were all very proud of him. We were just hopeful that he would be a Houston Astro for years to come.

I never hit another home run that year after I bagged number thirty-seven. No matter what the reason may have been, it was nothing but a homer goose egg for me over the last sixteen games of the '67 season. Meanwhile, my friend and rival, Hank Aaron, was busy dislodging four final homers over the same period to take the 1967 National League Home Run Crown by a 39–37 total home runs edge over my best effort.

Hank Aaron couldn't have been a nicer, better sport about it. He even made the statement to the press that I should be declared the real winner for having played 81 home games in the cavernous Astrodome while he played out his Braves home games in the homer-friendly band box that belonged to Atlanta.

I thanked Hank Aaron for his good sportsmanship and I felt OK about how things turned out. It fit into my belief that all things happen for a reason and that all things just end up being whatever they are. It's up to each of us to learn from whatever happens, and never get stuck on resentments or regrets. I was still pretty young in 1967, but I was picking up on all the things that Mom and Dad always tried to teach me. It's just that now my lessons weren't just coming only from their words. Now the lessons were coming at me harder as those words spilled into my own real-life experiences with other people.

At the end of my greatest year in baseball to date, 1967, there was room left over for humility with no shame. I had lost the 1967 National League home run crown, for sure, but I had lost it to the greatest legitimate career home run hitter of all time, Mr. Henry "Hank" Aaron. For whatever it's worth, I also lost the National League RBI race to another future Hall of Famer in 1967. Orlando Cepeda had 111 RBI to my 107. No shame there either.

It was time to move on to the off-season and to 1968. We played as well as we could for Manager Grady Hatton in 1967 and we closed down the year hoping we could do an even better job for him in the future.

How little we knew what was coming in the year that lay ahead. When a team doesn't improve, sooner or later, that gets the manager fired. Once that happens, the club dips its hand into the box of new managerial candidates in much the same way that Forrest Gump dipped his hand into that famous box of chocolates.

You never know what you're going to get.

Late in 1968, we got Harry Walker.

CHAPTER 9

The Trouble with Harry

The winds of change in 1968 actually started whirling shortly after the end of the 1967 season. On October 8, 1967, General Manager Spec Richardson dealt shortstop Sonny Jackson and first baseman Chuck Harrison to the Atlanta Braves for left-handed pitcher Denny Lemaster and infielder Dennis Menke. The deal turned out as a plus when Denis Menke developed into a two-time All-Star shortstop for the Astros and Denny Lemaster won thirty games and saved another six during his four seasons in Houston.

No fooling. On April 1, 1968, Spec Richardson continued the overhaul by selling the contract of pitcher Bo Belinsky to the Chicago White Sox. The Belinsky deal was not a big surprise. Belinsky already had bolted away from spring training camp to pursue his engagement to former Playmate of the Year Jo Collins after refusing a contract assignment to the Astros' AAA minor league club at Oklahoma City. The White Sox also planned a minor league assignment for Bo, but he much preferred their AAA locale in Honolulu to a tour of duty in the capitol of the former Indian Territory.

Troubled times fell upon us fast in 1968. On April 4, just as the baseball season was about to get underway, the word came blaring over the TV that the Reverend Dr. Martin Luther King Jr. had been assassinated in Memphis. That tragic news made me sick to my stomach and saddened my soul. Most of us players, black and white, didn't feel much like playing baseball after the horrible death of Dr. King. As a result, the start of the 1968 season was delayed for several days out of respect for Dr. King and a grieving nation.

When we finally got going on April 10, the Astros actually jumped out to their best start in history. Beginning at home, we won our first four games and five of the six games played on that original home stand.

Our first home stand success was no thanks to me.

I was now playing left field and apparently taking my trips to the plate with no lumber in my hands. I went 3 for 27 (.111) with no homers in those first six games and I didn't even begin my climb out of the doldrums for quite a while. In fact, I didn't get my first homer of the year until April 27, when

I connected in the 13th game of the season off Rich Nye of the Cubs at Wrigley Field.

No excuses here. Baseball is a funny game. Before the '68 season breathed its last, I would have fewer homers, but a better batting average than I had in '67.

I can't really explain the slow start. What ballplayer ever can? I had a lot of good things going for me, even if I may have seen the move to left field, in favor of Ron Davis taking over in center, as a demotion. I'm not for sure I knew much at all about what manager Grady Hatton was thinking at the time, although it seemed pretty obvious to me then that he must have felt, for a while at least, that Davis or somebody else was a better answer than me in center field.

By April 1968, Ruth and I weren't getting along all that great, but I did what a lot of young baseball ballplayers do when domestic issues become a problem, especially during the season. I just blocked them out of my mind as well as I could and tried to stay focused on what I had to do to take care of myself and get better on the field. As for Ruth, these had to be tough times too. She was married to a ballplayer, and that's a guy who has to be on the road half the time while his wife stays home and takes care of the kids. In our case, that meant Ruth was the only parent on hand, most of the time, to our two little kids: Kimberly, age 2 years, 8 months (born August 4, 1965) and Jimmy Jr., age 1 year, 3 months (born January 20, 1967).

In the meantime, most of my attention at the start of the 1968 season was all focused on dealing with how tough the pitchers were on me as we came out of the gate. As the baseball world would soon enough learn, the '68 major league season would quickly take its place in history as the Year of the Pitcher. The 1968 season would be forever symbolized by St. Louis Cardinals pitcher Bob Gibson and his 1.12 Earned Run Average.

Because the greater height of a pitcher's mound gives advantage to the pitcher, the dominance of pitchers during the 1968 season would result in the lowering of the height of the pitching rubber by four inches at the start of the '69 season. In April 1968, we were just playing our way into the drama of all the reasons that brought us to a change that has lasted through 2010 and counting.

It didn't take the Houston Astros and the New York Mets long to become poster children for the 1–0 shutout game. On April 15, 1968, the Astros and the Mets squared off at the Astrodome in a game that turned out to be one for the ages. Six hours beyond the first pitch, and two outs deep into the bottom of the twenty-fourth inning, Bob Aspromonte hit a little rolling ground ball that found its way under the glove and through the legs of Mets shortstop Al Weis for an error that allowed base runner Norm Miller to trot home with the first and only run of the game.

Tom Seaver of the Mets and Don Wilson of the Astros had both started the long game and pitched admirably. Wilson goose-egged the Mets on six hits over his nine innings of work; Seaver held the Astros to only two hits over his ten innings of labor. Then the bullpens flew into action. Wade Blasingame took the win as the fifth pitcher on the long night for Houston. Les Rohr took the loss as the eighth hurler of the late-show game for New York.

On May 6, 1968, we hosted the San Francisco Giants on the thirty-seventh birthday of the great Willie Mays. Judge Hofheinz was a huge admirer of Willie Mays, as well as a man way ahead of his time when it came to organizing sideline game events that might help pump the gate. The Judge ordered a 569-pound birthday cake for Willie.

As a baseball club, we followed Willie's birthday cake gift from the Judge with a 10–2 Astros thrashing of the Giants. The big damage in this unusual high-scoring game in 1968 was provided by none other than Rusty Staub, who went four for four with a double and six RBI on the day. Our Denny Lemaster was the winning pitcher and future Baseball Hall of Famer Gaylord Perry took the loss for the Giants on Willie's birthday.

It's impossible for me to think about Gaylord Perry without being reminded of the fact that he could have also served as a charter member of the Spitball Pitchers' Hall of Fame. He doesn't even deny the fact these days that his career on the mound was moisturized for success. He's also a good friend and fun guy to be around today, but that wasn't so true back in the day I had to bat against him. He wasn't just wet. He was wily too. He kept everyone guessing as to just how wet the next pitch was going to be.

My old teammate and friend Carl Warwick tells a great story about facing Gaylord Perry in a game played on one hot and steamy night at old Colt Stadium. "I was getting sprayed in the eyes by the spin-off moisture that came whizzing by me with every pitch from old Gaylord that night," Carl says. "Finally, a ball came in low and just rolled away in the dirt from the Giants catcher. I could see the dirt accumulating on the ball along the line of wetness that came with the pitch."

"Hey, ump," Carl called out to home plate umpire Jocko Conlan, "could you please check that ball out for me?" Carl says that umpire Conlan obligingly walked over and picked the ball up, bringing it with him as he looked it over and returned to the plate.

"Damn humidity!" Conlan said with a smile. The old Hall of Fame umpire then threw the ball out of play and shouted, "Get back in there. Let's play ball!"

Sometimes the rules that pertain to spit are ignored. Sometimes they are not, as Rusty Staub soon found out only a short while after Willie's 1968 birthday game. On May 17, 1968, Rusty Staub was playing first base for the Astros during a 6–0 loss to the Dodgers at their park in Chavez Ravine. At one point in the game, Rusty had gone to the mound to try to help pitcher

Larry Dierker settle down during a crucial situation. With Zoilo Versalles of the Dodgers at bat and holding on a 3–0 count, Rusty just absent-mindedly made things worse by spitting on the ball while he was standing on the hill, talking to Dierker. The umpire saw it and called for an automatic ball credit on the count to the batter. That made it ball four for Zoilo Versalles, who took first and then came around to score.

In baseball, the final score sometimes turns far less on the heels of our great expectations, and far more on the wings of how the umpires treat our smallest game-time expectorations.

A couple of days after the Staub spitting incident, on May 19, 1968, Denny Lemaster and Mike Cuellar pitched the Astros to 2–1 and 3–1 wins in a twin-bill sweep of the Dodgers at Dodger Stadium. My most exciting moment came in the second game. On a walk to first base, I spotted what looked like a rope on the base paths that turned out to be a snake, one of God's creatures that I have no stomach for seeing in a ballpark or anyplace else, if I can help it. Well, after I had not too quietly pointed out the presence of the serpent on the field, one of our Astros coaches, Mel McGaha, came rushing to the rescue. After Mel beat the thing to death with a baseball bat, play resumed on the happy task of the Astros taking two from LA.

May 27, 1968, turned out to be a big day for baseball off the field when the National League awarded expansion franchises to San Diego and Montreal, with play to start in 1969. The people up in Dallas–Fort Worth took this decision as a snub of their area and they blamed Astros owner Roy Hofheinz for either blocking the award of a second team to Texas, or else just not working very hard on the support of a new team that would cut into his statewide market area.

One of the Dallas newspapers even published a photo of Judge Hofheinz with the image of a bull's-eye printed over it. At a time that was not five years after the assassination of President John F. Kennedy in Dallas, you might think that any responsible Dallas newspaper would have avoided such a suggestion. I guess the fact that they did run that picture answers any questions about that newspaper's sense of responsibility for putting out a better image of their city.

The American League also announced that the Washington Senators were moving to Minneapolis–St. Paul and that new franchises also were being awarded to Washington, D.C., and Seattle, also starting in 1969. After three seasons in the nation's capitol, the new Washington Senators would also move, this time to the Dallas–Fort Worth area, where they would become the Texas Rangers in 1972.

Even though Dallas–Fort Worth eventually got its major league club, many people from that area would continue to blame Roy Hofheinz for delaying the expansion of baseball into North Texas for as long as possible.

Speaking of the Judge, Roy Hofheinz wasn't exactly allowing any dust to settle over his ambitions in the summer of 1968. Three years after the opening of the Astrodome, Hofheinz was gearing up for the grand new start of an enormous amusement park across the freeway from the domed stadium. It was an event that had been ballyhooed for over a year on TV and radio with a little commercial jingle that played every station with something like, "Astroworld! Astroworld! It's a wonderful world of fun, fun, fun!" I guess it worked in spite of, or because of, its drumming-into-your-head monotonous message as a jingle. By the time Astroworld opened, people were flocking to the place in large zombie herds.

Astroworld, with its entire jam-packed array of thrill rides, carnival games, special exhibits, and musical performances, opened in Houston on Loop 610 South on June 1, 1968. By coincidence, we played a baseball game that same day in the Dome, with Don Wilson losing a humdrum and largely forgettable 3–1 contest to Bill Hands and the Chicago Cubs. I went 0 for four. Our record fell to 21–25 as a result of that loss.

How little we knew back on the day that Astroworld opened. Our ability to string along boring losses in early summer was about to cost us dearly before July rolled around. We were on track for the coming of "King Harry," a small-minded man who would make any troubles we had prior to his arrival pale by comparison. Neither Astroworld, nor any other amusement park in America, held any relief for the kind of trouble that Harry Walker would soon enough bring into our lives.

Most of us woke up on the morning of June 6, 1968, expecting it to be another ordinary summer day in Houston and the twenty-fourth anniversary of the D-Day invasion of France. Those of us who played baseball for the Houston Astros were at home, nursing some bad feelings over having dropped the first three games of a series with the Cardinals, and also, one more time, for having now strung together another five losses in a row. That would all change, just as soon as we picked up the newspaper or turned on the radio or TV news.

We would soon discover that presidential candidate Robert F. Kennedy had been shot in Los Angeles at a late hour of the previous evening and that he had died shortly after midnight of this same date, June 6, 1968. A mere two months after the assassination of Dr. Martin Luther King Jr., and not quite five years after the assassination of President John F. Kennedy, Senator Robert Kennedy had now also fallen as the latest victim of hateful violence.

I remember briefly thinking: What's this all about? How can something this hateful be happening in a place called America? Then I remembered my own bad experience in Palatka, Florida, and my wonder went away. Prejudice and bigotry are blind to reason. They each breed only the hate that gives rise to violence by word and deed. All I could do was weep and repeat for Robert Kennedy what I had done on separate occasions for his brother John and Dr. King: I said a little prayer for his soul.

The pale gloom of grief and disbelief hung over all of us that night as we prepared to play the Cardinals in the fourth game of our series at the Dome. We lost again, this time by 4–0, as I went hitless in three trips and the Cardinals left town with a four-game sweep. Bob Gibson had shut us out on three hits.

Rain, shine, or indoors, Bob Gibson was well on his way in 1968 to that now famous 1.12 ERA on the season. Even in the dark shadows of national grief, Bob Gibson's use of his huge talent shone forth as a beacon of hope for the triumph of good over evil, even on a night that he did it to us "good guys" from Houston.

We lost again to Pittsburgh on June 7, extending our losing streak to make it seven down, or a great big "0-fer-June." We stopped the streak on June 8 by taking the Pirates in the Dome by 3–2, but that game marked the eve of a day that most major leaguers wanted to cancel from the schedule as a day of respect and memorial honor for the late Robert Kennedy, whose funeral was June 9. When the memorial cancellation of games was rejected by the commissioner's office, a handful of players boycotted the games anyway. Bob Aspromonte and Rusty Staub were the only two Astros to boycott play on Sunday, June 9. Neither played, and we lost again.

I don't recall what action, if any, was taken against the players who stayed away that day. I pretty much think that Major League Baseball simply allowed the matter to blow over out of respect for the players who protested, and also to avoid any bad public relations that could have fallen back on MLB for punishing those few who chose to show their respect for RFK by protesting in this way. As for me, I felt no need to join the boycott. Prayer and playing baseball were my ways of showing respect for the life and values of Robert F. Kennedy. At the same time, I held nothing but great respect and admiration for Bob Aspromonte and Rusty Staub because of the stand they each took on behalf of RFK's memory.

On that same June 6 that Bobby Kennedy died, and we merely lost a shutout ball game to Bob Gibson and the Cardinals, the Houston organization was also busy gambling or planning for the future. The Astros drafted catcher Martin Cott of Buffalo, New York, in the first round of the June 1968 draft. With the very next pick, the New York Yankees also chose a catcher, a fellow named Thurman Munson of Canton, Ohio. This example just goes to show you how easy it is for the roots of good scouting and good or bad luck to be lost in the pages of history. Sometimes the biggest wheels of change in the future turn quietly, at first, to the soft sound of some kid signing his first contract to play professional baseball.

At any rate, the beat goes on, every day, no matter whom a club picked, or failed to pick, in some ancient draft, or in which club wins or loses their battles with Bob Gibson. The assassination of Senator Robert F. Kennedy on June 6, 1968, was the big news on that date, as it should have been.

In the smaller world of big league baseball, the Houston Astros were not far away on June 6 from walking into some major, if less earth-shattering, bad news of their own.

On June 15, 1968, we were in Pittsburgh, in the middle of a five-game series with the Pirates that would turn out to be the biggest part of a six-game losing streak. It was here that Spec Richardson made one of his drive-by speed trades, moving outfielder Ron Davis from the Astros to the Cardinals in exchange for outfielder Dick Simpson and a pitcher named Hal Gilson. Gilson got into only three and two-third innings of relief work for the Astros before being shipped out and never heard from again. Dick Simpson was a tall, lanky guy, about a year younger than me, but with no record that came close to mine by comparison.

By the time we lost the fifth game with the Pirates at Forbes Field and had built our total losing streak to six in a row, we got the word on June 17, 1968, that the Astros had fired Grady Hatton and that they had replaced him as manager of the club with Harry Walker.

As a result of his firing, Grady Hatton was flying home to Houston from Pittsburgh. The rest of us, the Astros club, were on our way to New York to meet up with Harry Walker and prepare to take on the Mets in a four-game series that would begin the very next day, June 18, 1968, with a double-header.

Joe Morgan had a lot of accurate things to say about Harry Walker in his own book, *Joe Morgan: A Life in Baseball*, a book that he wrote with David Falkner back in 1993. Everything Joe Morgan wrote about Harry Walker in that book was true. Walker was both a racist and a stupid "people person." When it came down to managing a big league baseball team of grown men, Harry Walker was either the meanest man in the world, or else the most clueless manager in baseball history.

If anything, I had more trouble with Walker's personal style than I did his racism. I had learned how to protect my soul from people who would despise me simply because of my skin color, but I had not yet learned how to keep my mind safe from people who wanted to make me over in their own image.

I had been raised to respect authority. Therefore, when I finally ran into an authority that seemed hell-bent on getting me to play in ways that fit neither my abilities nor my interests, I was mixed up, at first, about what to do. The whole period of Harry Walker's time as manager of the Astros was my longest day in baseball. It only started getting better when I realized that I had to stop letting him tell me what to do. I didn't like his sideways racist comments that implied, as Joe Morgan suggests in his book, that blacks don't work as hard at the game as whites, but I didn't allow his ignorance and prejudice to get in my way of being the best ballplayer I could become. I just resolved that I would have to continue my baseball education with no help from my manager.

My reaction was mild when compared to the more outspoken anger of my best friend, Joe Morgan, but neither of us could match the wild rage that pitcher Don Wilson sometimes felt and acted out toward Harry Walker.

Joe Morgan tells in his book about a time in which Don Wilson carried a two-run, late-inning lead into a game versus the Dodgers in Los Angeles. Anyone who was there will remember it well. It was almost unbelievable, and very much unforgettable. LA was Don's hometown and he really wanted to do well there.

At any rate, Don walked the first man he faced in the bottom of the eighth. That walk suddenly prompted Harry Walker to pull Wilson, even though Don had the ball game under control until that point. The relief staff then proceeded to blow the game, with the winning Dodger run scoring on a bases-loaded walk.

As soon as we got back to the clubhouse, Harry Walker did this big dramatic thing of sweeping the food table clear with his arm. Then he began shouting at everybody as they filed in: "We are a bunch of chicken-shit losers. We get a goddamn lead and can't hold on to it. You wanna know why that is? I'll tell you why: Starting pitchers on this team don't have a damn bit of guts."

Joe Morgan and I both had the same first reaction to hearing these words. We each looked around to see if Don Wilson had yet returned to the clubhouse in time to hear this condemning statement. He apparently wasn't back. Otherwise, there would've likely been long black fingers suddenly wrapping themselves around Harry Walker's bulging red neck in the ten seconds that followed.

Harry Walker then stirred the glass of word arsenic even louder: "I said, I don't think the damn starting pitchers on this ballclub have any guts; they're always looking for help from the bullpen."

No doubt about who heard it this time.

A wood-scraping sound sprang violently into the noise of a stool falling rapidly to the floor over in the area adjacent to Don Wilson's locker. Next came the loud boom of a hand slapping hard against the metal locker door that Don had been using. We all froze and stared over to the place where these sounds had come from. We all knew what was coming.

All of a sudden, like a human tornado, Don Wilson came clattering through all the stools and tables in his way, propelling himself more like an energy force than a human body. He suddenly rushed forward, heading on a pure beeline to the center of the room and the location of Harry Walker.

Joe Morgan acted faster than the rest of us. He slid a table into the path of the charging Don Wilson, slowing him just long enough for some of us to grab Don and hold him back. Meanwhile, Don Wilson was screaming at the top of his lungs: "I'll show you who has the guts! I'll show you who has the guts!"

While this was all going on with Wilson, the now even whiter Harry Walker fled silently on a tiptoe run to his office on the other side of the room. He ran inside his little room, slammed the door, and clicked on the lock. The next few minutes we all spent on one team goal, quieting down Don Wilson from his Incredible Hulk state of rage. We didn't want to lose our friend, and one of our best pitchers, on an LA murder rap.

What happened next is reported in Joe Morgan's book:

> ...A few minutes later, one of the coaches emerged from Harry's office and asked me to go in there with him.
>
> I was ushered into the office, which was locked behind me. Harry was sitting there, visibly upset, but clearly hoping the incident was over.
>
> "Joe, I called you in here because I want to thank you for what could have been an ugly scene out there," he said.
>
> What a farce.
>
> "Harry," I said, "I didn't do that for you. I did that for Don. Don's my friend. If he kills you, he can't play baseball.' I turned and walked out of his office [p. 116].

Walker was a total control freak. That was the biggest trouble I had with Harry Walker. He didn't know anything about helping a man to become the best natural player he could be. Everything he did was about trying to change you into the kind of player he was convinced you should be. Harry tried to turn me into a table-setter, a get-on guy who hit to all fields and used his speed to work himself into scoring position for the real RBI guys, whoever he may have imagined them to be. He even tried to make me stop using my own bats and use his own model.

Harry Walker had been his own kind of Punch-and-Judy hitter during his career in the big leagues. He won the 1947 National League batting championship with an average of .363 while playing for two clubs, the Cardinals and the Phillies, but he collected a lot of hits when they did nothing to help his club. Walker's 186 hits that year included 140 singles, 29 doubles, 16 triples, 1 home run, and they all accounted for only 41 RBI. That's the record of a Punch-and-Judy Hitter Supreme, the guy who get his hits for the benefit of his personal average and not in service to what may have been best for the club.

I couldn't stomach the thought that Harry Walker had tried to make me into the same kind of Harry Walker hitter during much of the time he served as my manager. For the first time in my life, I had met a man that I really didn't like.

No sir! I wouldn't have liked this man if he had come into my life as the reincarnated soul of Dr. Martin Luther King Jr., but a Dr. King with that same Harry Walker personality. That's how strongly I disliked Harry Walker, even though I now forgive him too after his death, and after all these years, for just being who he was, a man who apparently could not rise up to face his own issues during the time his life pathway crossed with mine. I can only trust and pray that Harry finally did make his settlement with the truth eventually, and that his eternal soul now rests in peace.

Back in June 1968, however, the "Trouble with Harry" era was just getting started for a number of the Houston Astros.

In Harry Walker's managerial debut with the Houston Astros, we took a twin bill from the Mets by scores of 3–2 and 6–5. I even got my seventh homer of the year in the opener against Nolan Ryan. That one sure didn't smack of Punch-and-Judy, but maybe Harry wasn't looking at the time. After all, it was only his first game at the Astros helm.

We then dropped the last two games at New York before returning home to take a series from the Phillies by two games to one. After then taking the first two games of another home series against the Cubs by scores of 3–1 and 4–2, we went looking for a sweep on June 26, 1968.

By now, we were making the switch to Harry Walker look pretty good in the early going. In Game Three of this Cubs series, the Astros' Dave Giusti gave up two hits to Don Kessinger and Glenn Beckert in the first inning. Then he shut down the Cubs the rest of the way for a two-hit 2–1 victory. I went three for three that day, with a solo shot homer (my eighth of the year) in the second inning off Cubs starter Bill Hands. Pitcher Dave Giusti provided us with his own winning margin in the fifth inning when he singled in Bob Watson with the run that spelled victory.

We went to the cusp of the All-Star break with a Sunday game against the Braves in Atlanta on July 7, 1968. Everybody in Houston especially looked forward to the game in 1968 because it marked a year of firsts. It would be the first Major League Baseball All-Star Game played in Houston, and, of course, because of the Houston Astrodome, it would be the first All-Star Game ever played indoors.

We beat the Braves on July 7 behind Larry Dierker (9–10) and reliever Tom Dukes. Braves All-Star outfielder Hank Aaron connected for this eighteenth homer of the season in the game, and I posted my tenth long ball for the winning side. Based on the year I had going for me to date, I wasn't selected for the All-Star Game in 1968.

That was OK. I hadn't earned my spot by the All-Star break of 1968. People like Hank Aaron, Willie Mays, and the Alou brothers deserved to start ahead of me and just about everybody else.

The All-Star Game of 1968 played out like a signature on the whole season of pitching domination. Willie Mays led off the bottom of the first with a single to left field. He then went to second base on a failed pickoff attempt by American League pitcher Luis Tiant that flew wildly past first baseman Harmon Killebrew. Mays then ambled over to third base on a wild pitch by Tiant to Curt Flood. After Flood reached first base, Willie McCovey came up and hit into a double play that scored his Giant teammate, Willie Mays, from third with the only run of the game.

Rusty Staub of the Astros got into the game as a sixth-inning pinch hitter for pitcher Steve Carlton and popped out for the only game appearance by the only 1968 All-Star Astro. The final score was National League 1—American League 0, and Willie Mays was named as the Most Valuable Player.

Even though other factors affecting pitching were at play during the 1968 All-Star Game, that televised spectacle gave national exposure to the Astrodome as a place where long fly balls go to die. The stadium's deserved reputation as a pitcher's park was sealed. For as long as my career remained on course with the Astros as the Toy Cannon, the dead ball air and spacious outfield distances of the Astrodome would be with me forever as my personal obstacles to overcome.

In spite of, not because of, new Astros manager Harry Walker and his snide remarks about the intelligence and work ethics of black players, my home run and general hitting production improved after the 1968 All-Star break. I had a total of ten homers at the break, but I added sixteen after play resumed. My 26 homers for 1968 was eleven down from my 1967 top homer year, but my batting average had improved twenty points on the year from .249 in 1967 to .269 in 1968. My RBI total fell by forty from 107 to 67 in 1968, but my on-base percentage had climbed from .331 to .376.

Again, I feel the need to remind you: I was not paying attention to all these stats back in 1968. Pete Rose was the only guy I knew back then who kept up with all the stats he was piling up. The rest of us were just playing baseball. I'm sure I knew that my homers were down and my average was up from 1967, but that would have been about it. I just knew that I was getting to be very comfortable being baseball's little-guy power hitter and Houston's "Toy Cannon." In spite of the fact that I received no spoken support from manager Harry Walker for my achievements in that regard, I knew I was getting the job done, better and better, at bat and in the field. I wasn't yet where I wanted to be, but I had full confidence that I could get there. I hadn't defined my goal as a certain high batting average mark, but as becoming a consistent timely hitter who left few ducks on the pond. That being said, and even though I still saw my real future as a power hitter, I would take a game-winning two-out, two-RBI single in the ninth over a meaningless home run in an already lost-cause game, any day of the week.

The second half of the '68 season bore bittersweet fruit. We played nearer to .500 under Harry Walker than we had under Grady Hatton. That may have sent the wrong message to the man who was now clearly in charge, Spec Richardson, that he had made the right decision in bringing on Walker as our new manager. Oh, I'll grant you this much: Harry may have sparked some early wins that were kindled from our early contempt for him, but those gains would eventually be consumed by the fire of angry rejection that many Astros, including all of us black players, would come to feel about his attitudes and over-the-line methods.

The 1968 Houston Astros finished the season with a 72–90 record, tying our best franchise effort to date for wins in a single year, but placing us in tenth, or last place in the National League, for the first time in our history.

In 1968, the New York Mets finished a game ahead of us in ninth place for the first time in history. Think that was "amazin'"? Imagine how we were going to feel on the Houston Astros team in 1969. While our club would go on to its first non–losing season in 1969, finishing fifth in the new six-club National League West Division, the "Amazin' Mets" of New York would go 100–62 for a first-place berth in the new six-club National League East. That "amazin'" record would precede their victory over the Atlanta Braves for the first national pennant decided by a playoff series between divisional champions and push them forward to a date with destiny in which they then would roll over the Baltimore Orioles American League champions for their first World Series championship!

The Astros and Mets were both born in 1962, but it only took the Mets eight seasons of play to win their first World Series championship in 1969. The Astros would not even reach their only World Series until 2005, and that came after forty-four seasons of play in the National League. By the time the White Sox swept the Astros in the 2005 World Series, our twin brother expansion buddy Mets already had won two of four World Series appearances.

Looking back at our Astros-Mets comparative franchise records with the World Series still hurts. The pain serves as just another reason to look ahead, not behind. I'll keep looking back here for the sake of history, but I will try to stay away from the land of what might have been as much as possible. Sometimes that's easier to say than do.

We could have gotten much better in 1969, I think, but some of the worst trades in Astros history were about to unfold during the 1968–69 off-season. One of these bad deals, if you please, would be made worse by the presence of Harry Walker at the helm of our club. The other bad news is the fact that these awful trades, bad as they were, were not the end of a mindless stream of actions taken by Spec Richardson during his time on the clock as general manager. The worst was yet to come three years later on November 29, 1971, but we'll get to that move in time. All of you ancient and deep-rooted Astros fans already know the deal I'm talking about. For now, we have enough damage to cover in our brief review of Spec Richardson's 1968–69 trading dance cards.

On October 11, 1968, Spec Richardson traded pitcher Dave Giusti and catcher Dave Adlesh to the St. Louis Cardinals in exchange for veteran catcher Johnny Edwards and never-heard-of-again prospect infielder Tommy Smith. The Astros would get six serviceable, but mediocre hitting years out of Edwards. Dave Giusti would go beyond his one year as a Cardinal to seven big years as a vital member of the Pittsburgh Pirates' relief staff.

Three days after the Giusti trade, on October 14, 1968, the Astros would lose hot first base prospect Nate Colbert to San Diego in the 1969 expansion draft. Colbert enjoyed five strong years as a power-hitting RBI man for the Padres. Nate went on to a career that included a now famous double-header explosion against the Cardinals in St. Louis in which he collected five home runs and thirteen runs batted in on the day. Rumor had it among the players that Harry Walker's dislike for Nate Colbert was the reason he was made available to the draft.

On December 4, 1968, the Astros dealt away the last man from their original 1962 Colt .45 roster by sending third baseman Bob Aspromonte to the Atlanta Braves in exchange for infielder Marty Martinez. This deal was not a big surprise. The club had a touted rookie named Doug Rader waiting in the wings as the future of third base. They were also acquiring a player who could help fill in during the transition in the presence of Martinez.

Also on December 4, 1968, came the separate trade that really broke my heart. A few days earlier, I had some business down at the Astros administrative offices and I ran into General Manager Spec Richardson while I was there. Spec called me in to talk with him. He told me he had been considering a trade with Baltimore and that he wanted to know what I thought about it.

"What do you have in mind, Spec?" I asked.

"I'm thinking about trading Mike Cuellar to the Orioles for first baseman Curt Blefary. To my way of thinking, Blefary has the kind of bat that would really help our lineup."

As I took Spec's message all the way in, I almost did something that would have pleased our racist manager, Harry Walker: I almost turned white!

"Please don't make that deal, Spec," I said. "Mike Cuellar is one of our best, most reliable pitchers. We can't afford to lose him."

I said it every way I could think to say it: "Keep Mike Cuellar. Don't deal him away to anybody for anything." All I got back from Spec Richardson in return was a quiet stare off into space as he smoked away on his big old cigar. "Thanks for coming in, Jimmy!" Spec said, as he quickly brushed me away from our brief unscheduled talk. I left there not feeling too good about it at all.

On December 4, I heard the news over the radio: "The Houston Astros announced today that they have traded left-hand pitcher Mike Cuellar to the Baltimore Orioles in exchange for first baseman Curt Blefary."

Thanks, Spec! All we gave away was a guy who would go on to become a consistent 20-wins-per-season pitcher over the next three seasons for the Orioles, a fellow who would win no fewer than 14 games a year over the next seven seasons as a final cog in Baltimore's wheeling march to baseball dominance. In return, we received a first baseman who hit .253 in his one season as an Astro before going over to the Yankees in 1970 in exchange for Joe Pepitone.

Next there came the other horrible trade that occurred during this period of time. On January 22, 1969, the Astros dealt away their poster boy rookie phenom from the Colt .45 days, Rusty Staub, to the expansion club Montreal Expos in exchange for outfielder Jesus Alou and first baseman Donn Clendenon.

Spec felt that Rusty, already age 27, didn't have the kind of legs that would allow him to have a long career in the big leagues. All Rusty did was go on to play another 18 seasons beyond the trade date to Montreal, amassing a career total of 2,716 hits and 296 home runs, while also becoming one of the great pinch hitters in baseball history.

There was another, more immediate problem. Donn Clendenon decided that he would not report to Houston. It didn't come out in the media at the time, but Donn's reason for refusing the assignment of his contract to Houston was as simple as the man who managed the Astros. Clendenon had played for Walker at Pittsburgh and he wanted no further part of him. Donn even explained to several of us by phone that he would love to play with us in Houston, but not if it meant again enduring the racist stupidity of another spin with Harry Walker. Why the true reason for Clendenon's rejection of the trade never came out, I really can't say. I just know what the real reason behind it was all about. And it truly was all about Donn Clendenon's not wanting to play again for any team managed by Harry Walker.

Now, if you are unaware of what happened next, you may be thinking what most of us did back in January of 1969. If one guy won't report, the trade is dead, right?

Wrong!

New baseball Commissioner Bowie Kuhn was under pressure to make sure that the Staub trade survived, no matter what. Major League Baseball was betting that the league would succeed in Canada and they were doing all they could to make sure that Montreal got all the support they needed.

From the moment the Staub trade was announced, and before it hit the skids by Clendenon's refusal to report, the Montreal club had embarked on an immediate marketing plan of selling Rusty Staub to the fans of Montreal as the new face of Expos Baseball. Launching into a major advertising campaign that promoted Rusty Staub to Montreal as *"Le Grand Orange,"* the club already had sold season tickets on that exact image.

It was a trade that hit the point of no return from the moment it was announced and Commissioner Kuhn agreed with that kind of thinking. No matter how Houston may have been hurt by Clendenon's refusal to report, the damage to Montreal from any nullification of the deal was seen as the greater potential harm to organized baseball.

Commissioner Kuhn ruled that the Houston Astros would have to agree upon acceptable substitutes for the now-scratched inclusion of Donn Clendenon.

On April 8, 1969, the rearranged Staub deal was finally settled. In exchange for Staub, the Astros received outfielder Jesus Alou, pitchers Jack Billingham and Skip Guinn, and $100,000 in cash.

The loss of Rusty Staub to Houston over time is impossible to calculate. The Astros gave up an arguably Hall of Fame–quality player, a guy who may very well have been a major difference-maker for the Astros during a bleak period of losing baseball that faced the club well into the late 1970s.

The trouble with King Harry was just beginning its four-year reign, but the combined presence of Harry Walker as manager, and the first major gutting of our talent base by General Manager Spec Richardson, was already ringing bells that could not be un-rung. The future of Houston Astros baseball was on a downhill course that would last another decade.

The bells of fatal action ring loud and hum long. Sometimes we just have to wait for the humming to stop, and for the bell ringers to go away, before we can renew any hopes of being born again. As I see it, that's pretty much where the Houston Astros found themselves in the winter of 1968–69.

We just had to survive long enough to hear that hum of failure fade away.

CHAPTER 10

Mediocre Was as Good as We Got

The 1969 season proved to be the first year in the history of major league baseball that a Houston franchise team won as many games as it lost. Sadly for me, 1969 would also prove to be the only season in my eleven-year Houston baseball history that I played with a club that did not have a losing record.

The constant hum of that losing club bell-ringing I mentioned earlier outlasted me in Houston. I'm just glad that I didn't know that would be the case when the 1969 season got underway. We needed hope back then. The cold splash of reality would have been harder to take, had it not come with a dash of hope for something better, and the sooner the better.

It didn't take too long for the quick new guys from this year and the slow old guys from last year to start getting the picture of manager Harry Walker. He was a genuine *blah-blah* mouth who did all of the lecturing/talking and none of the listening. Harry knew or cared little about pitching, and he believed from his head to his toes that his approach to hitting was the only way to play the game. Worse, he also thought that he knew you better than you knew yourself, even if he couldn't even remember your name half the time.

During games, Harry would be sitting on the bench, making up one of his little charts, and a situation would come up requiring a decision, maybe a change of pitchers or a pinch hitter. He would often seem surprised or startled when it came time for a decision, and he sometimes acted confused, as though he didn't know what to do next.

On pitching, he could always motion to one of the coaches, someone like good old Buddy Hancken, to step in and do something like call the bullpen, warm somebody up, or bring somebody into the game. On pinch-hitting, he just seemed unable to remember anyone's name under the heat of fire. I don't know how many times we saw Harry point at somebody on our bench that he knew quite well and just motion to him with a finger to go get a bat and pinch-hit.

It was a bunch of little things that all added up to a personality and attitude in Harry Walker that made him almost impossible to like or respect as a leader. Of course, we black players also had to endure his sliding comments that suggested we weren't bright enough, or industrious enough, to play the game of baseball in the right way.

Bright enough? Industrious enough? Talented enough? Harry Walker was a total idiot. He had Joe Morgan, a future Hall of Famer, playing second base on his team. Joe played the game hard and with an intelligence and talent that few have matched. Our total boob of a manager couldn't see past his own prejudices to recognize the truth.

New Astros outfielder Jesus Alou, of the one and only famous Alou family of the Dominican Republic, proved himself quickly to fellow players in 1969 as one of the nicest guys we've ever had on the team. Unfortunately, neither that personal quality nor his good production were enough to spare him the wrath of King Harry. Walker always needed to assert his authority and Alou's gentle nature made him an easy target.

You had to understand how Harry worked. By the 1969 season, he was still trying hard to convert me into a Harry Walker–style Punch-and-Judy hitter, but at a harder pace. Meanwhile, he apparently was paying attention to Jesus Alou in the back of his mind. Alou struggled at the plate in his first year as an Astro, finishing the '69 season with 5 homers, 34 RBI, and a .248 batting average for a production level that was way under what we hoped to get from trading Rusty Staub away.

I finally just refused to use the Harry Walker bat and went back to thinking for myself on how I needed to play the game. Harry gave me a little of his prissy fussiness along the way but he finally just gave up and left me alone.

By my 1969 numbers, I pretty much proved to anybody with eyes to see that I just happened to be a smaller guy who hit for a good average with great power. I batted .269 again in '69, but my home run production, using my own Louisville Slugger 36-ounce bats, was back up to 33, with 87 RBI and an amazing (even to me) on-base percentage of .436, the highest level it ever reached during the course of my fifteen-year major league baseball career.

I walked 148 times in 1969. Why does that happen? Is it because a batter has a great batting eye? Was it due to the four-inch-lower mound that pitchers had to get used to? Was it because I never swung at balls out of the zone? Well, while all those factors may have played their part in effecting my walks, the big thing was the fact that other clubs pitched around me, as well they should have.

With the slightest bit of discipline and knowledge of what the pitchers were doing to me in 1969, even a young guy like me could see what it was about. Why couldn't Harry see it? Or, if he did, why couldn't he, at least, acknowledge that he saw it? With no other established power hitter on the Astros ball club to back me up in 1969, enemy pitchers could afford to simply pass me off to the place where potential runs went away to wait and die. For the 1969 Houston Astros, it was a place called the base paths.

I'm really not sure that Harry ever understood why I was getting all those walks, but the evidence of its meaning was right there under his nose to either see or ignore: Pitchers feared giving up the long ball. They would simply rather put me on base than pitch to me.

I was neither Punch nor Judy. I was Pull and Blast. I knew how to use the whole field, if need be, but it wasn't my style to play that way all the time, just for the sake of puffing up my batting average as Harry once did to win the National League batting championship. As a team player, he never won anything in the big leagues as the member of a pennant-winning club. He was always counting what he did for his own season batting average as the most important thing. Now, here he was again, getting the chance to mislead another group of grown men.

The 1969 Astros got off to a slow start, but our five-game losing streak to start the season didn't cause too many eyes to blink in shock. We finally won our first one in the Dome on April 13, 1969, behind the complete game, ten-strikeout, five-hit pitching of good old rambling man Don Wilson. Don Drysdale took the loss in that one, but I got my first home run of the season in the fifth inning off reliever Pete Mikkelsen. Shortstop Denis Menke and new third baseman Doug Rader also homered in the game. Like my own, Menke's homer was a solo shot, but young Doug Rader, the red-haired hot-shot that everybody soon called the Rooster, hit his difference-making dinger in the third inning off Drysdale to jump-start the score at the time from 1–0 to 4–0. The final score was 5–2, but both of the Dodger runs were unearned. No matter. The Astros were off the goose egg seat on wins for the rest of the 1969 season.

The next day, April 14, 1969, we kept up our winning ways against another future Hall of Famer named Don Sutton. Our own Larry "The Icon" Dierker again held off the Dodgers, 11–5, thanks to some good team-produced run support and a successful save appearance in the ninth by Fred "Freddie Flintstone" Gladding, the bear of a man we acquired from the Detroit Tigers the previous August in the Eddie Mathews trade.

No one ever called Larry Dierker "The Icon" back in the day because none of us had any idea back then how important his name and his present and future contributions were going to be to the history of the Houston Astros. I'll take both the credit and the blame for laying it on him now by way of hindsight.

Larry Dierker is the Icon of Houston Colt .45s/Astros baseball history. The man is sufficiently deserving and humble enough to wear that title too. If Larry Dierker were like some other former players, the ones whose egos lead them leaning into everything new by the sheer weight of their heavy egos, a handle like "The Icon" would be like the feather that knocked down the self-centered giant. Fortunately, Larry Dierker is not one of those phony baloney guys. He alone possesses the body of work as a Houston baseball player and manager that earns him the honor I have chosen to attribute to him here.

Back in 1969, however, Larry Dierker was just getting started in that first win against Los Angeles. He was on the road to being the first 20-game winner in the history of the franchise.

On April 30 and May 1 of 1969, the Houston Astros and the Cincinnati Reds were involved in one of the most unusual two-day game strings in baseball history. It all took place in Cincinnati, and appropriately in the last season of play at my old childhood baseball dream factory, in a place called Crosley Field. What came to be there in those two days had happened only once previously between pitchers of opposite teams, and that was in 1968, a season earlier, and it involved pitchers Gaylord Perry of the San Francisco Giants and Ray Washburn of the St. Louis Cardinals. It may never happen again, but I know it happened this second rare time in Cincinnati because I was there as a player in both games.

On April 30, pitcher Jim Maloney shut us down with no hits, striking out thirteen while walking five. The outcome was never in doubt once the Reds scored seven runs in the bottom of the fourth and went on from there to defeat the Astros, 10–0. The very next day, May 1, the Reds would have done better to have stayed home and just mailed in their own May Day call. On Day Two, our magnificent monster man, Don Wilson, came right back and threw a no-hitter for the Houston Astros against the Reds. Wilson struck out thirteen while walking six, or the same number of strikeouts and one more walk than Maloney had allowed a day earlier, but that didn't matter. We had won the contest that is even now best remembered in Houston as our "Revenge No-Hitter."

Don Wilson said it was his revenge for the way the Reds showed us up with Maloney's no-hitter. Whatever else it was, it was sweet for other big reasons. The Maloney no-hitter had capped our Astros April with a gloomy 4–20 record to start the season. Don Wilson then came back the next day, pitching like a baseball monster, breathing fire and giving us new hope. It was a near-miss hope that almost blossomed for us before our season carriage finally turned back into a pumpkin in the twenty-third hour of the day.

As I said, Don Wilson truly was a growing baseball monster by the time the 1969 season rolled around. Still only age 24, Don now had two career no-hitters and no telling how many others left in his tank for future delivery. Among active players, only the great Sandy Koufax stood ahead of him in that department. I can barely think of the late Don Wilson without a whole ton of thoughts, feelings, and memories welling up inside me. Some of those memories are pretty scary, none of the thoughts are easy, and the feelings he inspires, even now, are all over the yard.

This may be as good a time as any to talk about pitcher Don Wilson and my personal relationship with him. It isn't easy because of the tragic way we lost him years ago. If you recall, they found Don Wilson sitting in his car with the motor running inside his garage at his home in Houston on the morning of January 5, 1975. I won't comment further on the cause of his death, except to say that I was shocked and deeply grieved over the loss of my close friend.

It wasn't easy being a close friend to Don Wilson. He didn't make it easy for anyone to like him. In fact, he did his damnedest sometimes to make liking him a complete challenge. He had a violent temper; he drank way too much, as did a lot of us back in those days; and he could foul-mouth you faster than just about anyone else I've ever known.

I told you earlier the story about how he tried to get at Harry Walker. Don didn't just dislike Harry Walker. He hated him. And Joe Morgan was right when he explained to Walker why he got in the way of Don's attempted assault in the LA visiting team clubhouse. Don Wilson very well could have killed Walker. And that would have been the end of his baseball career. As his friends, we had to get in the way and keep that from happening.

Don could also be violent toward his friends. How well I know.

Once, while we were in New York for a series with the Mets, Don Wilson and I were down in the hotel bar, having a few drinks and probably a few too many. As things used to happen back in the day, Don struck up a conversation with an attractive girl who "just happened" to run into us at the bar.

As I'm sure is still true for today's players, you really needed to be wary and careful about strange women back in the day. Back then there was also a whole lot more open drinking to excess and public carousing going on involving players too. Drinking on team buses, going to and from games, was also common. Some players carried their own flask supplies onto buses, and nobody stopped them.

On the road, the idle hours were a time to either watch TV or hit the bars. The big saloons and little watering holes that were known hangouts for major league players on the road attracted women like bug lights. The trouble was, you never knew for sure what these women were selling, beyond the obvious, and you had to be very careful of financial con jobs, blackmail artists, and messy emotional entanglements that just spread pain and suffering like a wildfire.

At any rate, on that night in the New York hotel bar, something happened that almost got me killed. Don was really working to get the phone number of that girl in the bar, while I'm just drinking along with him and watching out for anything that might go wrong. You did that if you knew Don's potential for explosion and also thought of him as a friend. Nobody had to tell you. You just watched out for things that might cause trouble and worked to avoid them, if at all possible.

Because of how much Don had been drinking, and because of the tension I saw building between Don and the girl, I decided to get in the way by getting the number myself, simply to keep him from using it.

I persuaded the girl to give me the number as the safest way to make sure that Don wouldn't lose it. Don didn't see this exchange happen, but I made the mistake of telling him about it after we made our way back to a room we were sharing with Joe Morgan.

I don't recall how I got Don to leave the bar, but Joe was in the shower when we got back to the room. Once I broke the news to Don that I had the girl's number in my pocket, an argument broke out. Don wasn't so much mad over the fact that I had the number now, but he was livid over the knowledge that she had given the number to me and not him.

Don is shouting at me and I am shouting back at him. Bad idea.

The next thing I know, Don is all over me. He's screaming at me and calling me foul names as though I had just committed the most horrible crime in history. Then he's wrestling with me, and pushing me hard toward an open window in our twentieth-floor room. To my amazement, I'm just getting madder by the moment too, but Don is bigger than me and he is winning the physical struggle.

Holy cow! All of a sudden, Don Wilson is holding me by the ankles and pushing me through the window. Now, to my absolute horror, the hands of this very drunk maniac of a teammate and friend are the only things keeping me from dropping to my certain death on the sidewalks of New York.

I can still hear the frantic voice of Joe Morgan spilling out the window into the air. He is trying to talk some sense into the head of our deranged friend as my eyes look around at the shaky, upside down and swaying New York skyline.

"I'M GONNA DROP THE MOTHER!" Don screamed. "I'M GONNA DROP HIM!"

I screamed back, just as loud: "GO ON, DROP ME! I DON'T CARE, DROP ME! I DARE YOU, DROP ME!"

What was I thinking? Obviously, I wasn't thinking too well. That's for sure.

How did I know after that incident that Don Wilson really was my friend? Well, all I have to go on for sure is the fact that he didn't drop me twenty stories up from the street. That would have had a messy effect on our relationship for sure. Don didn't do that. He pulled me back into the room and, with some considerable help from Joe Morgan, we both settled down from our argument.

The meaningless phone number of the hot chick was never used.

As for his actions toward me, Don never apologized, nor did either of us ever tell Joe Morgan what it was all about. To my best recollection, it was a long time before I went out drinking again with Don Wilson after that incident, but we did remain friends on some deep unexplainable level. He felt the same way about me too.

Don once observed that I seemed a little afraid to dig in against Dodger pitcher Bill Singer. When I told Don that it was due to the fact that Singer had once beaned me in the minors, Don took it upon himself to seek out Singer during our next date with the Dodgers, just to deliver a message of his own.

"If Jimmy Wynn so much as gets a dirt mark on the heels of his shoes leaning back from a pitch of yours," Don told Singer, "I'll bust your head open."

Bill Singer never bothered me again.

Joe Morgan knew about the Singer incident and, of course, the hotel room window-dangling business long before he intervened in LA to keep Don Wilson from killing Harry Walker. When Joe told Harry that night that we had stepped into the middle to protect his friend from a murder rap, he wasn't kidding.

It's just too bad that a troubled soul and alcohol won out over such a talented and really good-under-the-surface human being. Don Wilson was a terrific pitcher. His 16–12 record and 235 strikeouts in 225 innings pitched, plus the bagging of his second career no-hitter, marked 1969 as one of his finest years. With a little stability in his life, Don Wilson could have gone on to have become one of the great pitchers in baseball history.

There must have been something magical in the air of all that New York turmoil of so long ago. On July 30, 1969, we took the "amazing" future 1969 champion Mets in a double-header by scoring twenty-seven total runs and doing some pretty "amazing" things on our own dance card time at bat. In Game One, Denis Menke and I led the charge when we both crushed grand slam home runs in the same eleven-run ninth inning of a 16–3 Astros slaughter of the Mets. It was only the second time that any two players had performed that feat in the same game for the same National League club. The Astros also took Game Two by an 11–5 count, with pitcher Larry Dierker doing the improbable by taking Nolan Ryan of the Mets deep for a home run as his hitting contribution to a ten-run Astros third-inning scoring binge.

We just didn't win big often enough, or win close often enough, to get over the invisible hump. Nevertheless, and in spite of our personal problems, and in spite of Harry Walker, the Astros club was looking pretty good for quite a while in 1969.

On September 10, we blasted the Dodgers 8–1 in the Dome, pushing our season record to 75–65. The win pulled us into a tie for fourth place in the new West Division of the National League. The race was tight. In spite of our fourth-place tie, however, we were now only two games out of first place with only twenty-two games left on the schedule.

For the first time in franchise history, Houston fans had a club that was involved in a real pennant race. As a result, the Astros sought and received permission to print World Series tickets for sale to season ticketholders.

Printing those World Series tickets proved to be the kiss of death.

The next day, September 11, the Dodgers took us out 1–0 before we debarked for a crucial series in Atlanta. Then, on September 12, the leading Braves beat us 4–3 in the opener of the big showdown trip. In spite of these setbacks, hope reared its always-appealing head again the next night.

On September 13, Larry Dierker carried a no-hitter into the bottom of the ninth of a scoreless tie game. With two outs, Felix Millan of the Braves broke up Dierker's bid for a no-hitter by singling to left field. Disappointed but undaunted, Dierker hung in there, carrying the shutout through twelve innings.

We broke through for two runs in the top of the thirteenth, but the Braves came right back against reliever Fred Gladding in the bottom of the inning. Led by former Astros Sonny Jackson and Bob Aspromonte, the Braves rallied for three runs to take the game in thirteen innings by a score of 3–2.

That heartbreaking loss in thirteen innings to the Braves did us in. We fell to fifth place as a result and the Braves went on from there to take the division title. We lost the final game of the Braves series, also by 3–2, on September 14, and then we flew on to San Diego, where we dropped two more. Six straight losses and we were hanging at 75–71 on the season and locked into a state of free fall.

Larry Dierker found a little redemption for us on September 17 at San Francisco. Dierker reached his 20th win of the season through a 2–1 victory over the Giants and another future Hall of Famer, Gaylord Perry. Jim Bouton picked up a two-inning relief save for Larry that day.

Larry Dierker would make three more starts in 1969 beyond the Frisco win, but his win total would stick on 20. His overall record of 20–13 helped make up for the loss of Mike Cuellar and it was the primary reason we finished the season at an Even-Steven 81–81.

The 1969 season was the closest I ever came to playing for a winner during my 1963–1973, eleven-season career with Houston. The thought still saddens me that we could not have overcome all obstacles, especially those made by the loss of talent through trades, and just gone out there and won it all for the deserving good fans of Houston. Sorry, Houston fans. It just wasn't meant to be.

As for those printed World Series tickets that seemed to immediately turn everything sour, I say best wishes to those of you who kept them as souvenirs. Those precious ducats today are worth far more as collectors' items than they were worth back then at their 1969 face value ticket prices.

As the mediocre 1969 season wore down, I hit my 33rd and last home run of the season off Gary Nolan of the Reds with nobody on in the top of the fourth inning of a game in Cincinnati played on September 25. It gave us a first score 1–0 lead and it ended up being the difference in a 4–3 victory margin for the Astros' winning pitcher, Denny Lemaster. That win gave us a temporary three-game bulge on our goal of closing with a winning season, but our 79–76 record fell back to .500 ball by year's end. Lemaster would win one more game before he was done at 13–17.

Of course, 1969 was no year for anything associated with the space program, even if it were only connected by name, to be served up in a soup of mediocrity. After all, July 20 marked the date when our Neil Armstrong walked on the surface of the moon for the first time. On that same date, the Houston Astros were sitting on a 48–48 record and waiting for a game to be called because of rain in Cincinnati. The good news was that the bad weather gave us a chance to watch the first moon walk on television.

We went into the 1969–70 off-season feeling OK about reaching .500, but not so OK about watching our expansion club brothers, the New York Mets, jump way ahead of us by winning the National League pennant during the first scheduled playoff year and then going on from there to capture both the World Series and the hearts of the national media. That's ground we've already covered.

What did the Astros do during the off-season to make up for all the talent balance we lost to the Amazin' Mets in 1969? Well, on December 4, 1969, Spec traded first baseman Curt Blefary to the New York Yankees in exchange for first baseman Joe Pepitone.

Get my drift?

Oh yeah. We still had Harry Walker on board as our manager in 1970. Amazing!

CHAPTER 11

Stormy Monday

Some rainy days last longer than others. And so it was with the 1970–1971 and 1971–1972 seasons. It started to rain all over my life in those years. And even when the rain slowed to a trickling stop in 1972–1973, I still wouldn't see the sunshine again until I found it further west, but let's not get ahead of ourselves here.

Spec Richardson peeled way back on the trading solution to our problem during the 1969–1970 off-season winter, although, as we would learn painfully enough a year later, the Houston general manager was definitely not cured of tearing up the ship because he needed the materials for fuel.

On December 4, 1969, Spec traded one-season first baseman Curt Blefary to the New York Yankees in exchange for first baseman Joe Pepitone. The real meaning of this trade was clear: Blefary had not been the answer that Spec hoped for. But the trade couldn't make up for the harm already done to our ball club by the loss of pitcher Mike Cuellar to the Baltimore Orioles a year earlier.

Blefary had not been worth what we lost. As a 1969 Astro, Curt had batted .253 with 12 homers and 67 runs batted in. Meanwhile, over in the American League, Mike Cuellar had posted a record of 23–11 with an ERA of 2.38 for the Orioles. For Mike, it would be the first of four twenty-plus win seasons and also the first of seven seasons in which he won no fewer than 14 games. I never told Spec "I told you so" in the Cuellar matter. What would've been the point? The man didn't listen when it really counted, and that was before the trade.

Now he was trading Blefary for a veteran Yankee who had hit .242 with 27 homers and 70 RBI in 1969. The new trade turned out to be pretty much a wash on Blefary-for-Pepitone, if you don't count Joe's special grooming needs and his introduction of the hair dryer into the Astros clubhouse as standard equipment.

Spring training wasn't too bad in 1970. Our new third baseman, Doug Rader, was really asserting himself more strongly as both a player and a character. Every active member of the Astros roster soon enough learned fast that having Rader on the club meant you had to stay on your toes when you opened your locker door. Unless you kept it locked, there was a good chance you might reach in there and pick up a snake, a rabbit, a rat, or a spider, or whatever else Doug may have found that he thought would work funnier in life if he gave it a place among your personal items.

Also, you didn't want to leave your shoes out in the open. Doug Rader had a bad habit of nailing shoes to the clubhouse floor. I came to believe that Doug Rader felt that peace of mind was something no one should have.

Don't get me wrong. Doug was a good guy. He was just a little bit goofy when it came to his ideas about what any good friendship should include. I also came to think that Doug believed that any friendship worth having was also one which included a lot of built-in irritation.

Personality aside, the Rooster, as the crowing redheaded Rader came to be called, was shaping up as a pretty slick-fielding third baseman. Doug had excellent reflexes, great instincts, a powerful arm, and a powerful bat that could have been even better had Doug ever developed his pitch-selectivity skills.

Headed into the regular season, Doug Rader and I marched into a mutual rendezvous with destiny at the Astrodome. On April 3, 1970, as we played in an exhibition game against the New York Yankees, Doug Rader did something that no other player had ever done in the Astrodome. He belted a monster home run that landed all the way up in the fourth-level gold seat section in high up and far away left field, down the line.

People were stunned. Nobody thought it could ever happen. Few thought it would ever happen again, but it did.

Nine days later, on April 12, 1970, and this time in a regular season game the Astros were playing against the Atlanta Braves, I hit a ball that took off on a high arc to deepest left field. My blow also landed in the gold seat section of the fourth-level Dome stands, just a few seats back of where Doug's homer had made its home.

The crowd and my teammates went wild. I was so mobbed by everyone at the plate after I rounded the bases that I almost feared personal injury from all the joyous slaps of congratulations. I felt good about the fact that my home run to that farthest-away area was the first to take place in an official game and that I got it off another future Hall of Fame pitcher, the great knuckleballing artist Phil Niekro. It also turned out to be the last home run an Astro player ever hit into that nearest part of indoor heavenly space.

In the thirty-five years that the Astrodome served as Houston's home to Major League Baseball, home runs to the gold section in high left field took place only twice, and they both happened nine days apart in April 1970, thanks to a couple of everyday regular guys named Doug Rader and Jimmy Wynn.

Doug and I were further honored by the club's decision to paint symbols for each of us on the two seats we touched with our local-record home runs. On the seat that Doug Rader hit, they painted a red rooster. On my target seat, of course, they painted (what else?) a toy cannon.

After the club moved from the Dome following the 1999 season, I received the seat that had been decorated in my honor as a gift from the Houston Astros. I still have it at home today as one of the few symbols of any home run I ever hit. As I've now said repeatedly here, I was a ballplayer back then, not a statistician, and definitely not a stadium seat collector.

Our 81–81 best-ever record from 1969 carried us into the 1970 season with the blessing or curse of greater expectations from the Astros fans. It was a blessing because a winning club always stirs the pot of hope for next year. It was a curse because the fans were now a lot more impatient with failure. The 1970 season probably was the first year that we started hearing boos for Astro players who choked in the clutch.

Houston fans weren't horrible, as they were and still are in places like Philadelphia and New York, but they were baseball-smart enough to pretty well know what it took to win in the National League, and they knew when we weren't doing it.

While we're on that subject, I do have to speak up for our Houston people. Our fans do know baseball. A lot of people think of Houston as a football town that never heard of baseball until the city entered the National League in 1962, but nothing could be further from the truth.

The city of Houston was founded in 1836 by the Allen Brothers, a couple of real estate speculators from New York. Many of the first Houstonians were from New York and other eastern states that already knew about "base ball" as a game. On April 16, 1861, the first Houston Base Ball Club was formed, just weeks after Texas had seceded from the Union to join the Confederacy. It was a little hard for the original Houston club to recruit players under those circumstances, but they got started in earnest just as soon as the Civil War ended in 1865.

After years of developing amateur play in the area, Houston joined the new Texas (Minor) League during its 1888 first year. The first Houston professional "base ball" club played its first game in the city at a downtown site called the Houston Base Ball Park on March 6, 1888, in an exhibition match against the mighty big league club from my old home town, the Cincinnati Red Stockings.

Houston lost, 22–3, committing 13 errors that helped the visitors to no good end. Six of those errors were committed in various ways by a fellow named Tim Flood, the first man to ever pitch and also go all the way as a starting pitcher for Houston in a professional base ball game.

Except for some odd years over the first fifteen seasons of the Texas League, Houston was a member in good standing of the circuit under several different nicknames. The city rejoined the Texas League as the Houston Buffalos in 1907 and never looked back, playing through 1958 as such, and then they played three final seasons as the Houston Buffs of the American Association before giving way to the major league Colt .45s in 1962. Yes sir. Baseball had a long ride in Houston prior to the big league years. In fact, baseball was king in Houston long before football, I'm told.

Football didn't really get big in Texas until rural electrification brought the Friday Night Lights spotlight onto high school play during the 1930s.

Today, Texas pretty much is a football state because of the pros and the big state universities, but our fans didn't start that way, and our core baseball people have not abandoned our national pastime to jump on the football bandwagon.

We are a family! A Houston baseball family! Our core Houston fans can hold their own in baseball knowledge with Boston, St. Louis, Cincinnati, or any other great baseball-wise town you may care to list. We may not have as many of these blue-chippers as some of those other cities, but the ones we do have are knee-deep steeped in small ball facts about how you play the game and about the history of organized baseball itself.

Enough said. Just thought I'd let you know how I see the fans of Houston, while also sharing with you too some of the facts about how ancient a baseball town this city really is. Now I'd better get back to the subject close at hand: the stormiest every-day-is-Monday season that I ever lived through long enough to be telling about it now. The Harry Walker Era in Houston lasted from 1968 to 1972.

Harry Walker was starting his second full season as manager of the Astros in 1970 after taking over for Grady Hatton at mid–season in 1968. Our love affair had not heated up. By now I had just taken to ignoring him as much as possible, as had most others who had problems with him, and that mainly included all of our black players, but Harry never gave up looking for new souls to torture with his mindless advice.

In 1970, Jesus Alou became Harry's new big target. Jesus was a gentle soul of a man who didn't seem to have an angry thought about anyone else in the world. He had not done as well at the plate as he had hoped in 1969, but he had really turned that around on his own during the off-season and was well on his way in 1970 to a batting average of .306 and an on-base percentage of .335, just the kind of performance we needed from a table-setter at the top of the batting order.

Harry Walker never heard of "If it ain't broke, don't fix it." Maybe he just remembered Alou's struggles from 1969, or maybe he just needed someone else who seemed willing to put up with his crap, I don't know. All I know is that Harry decided that he was going to fix any batting problems that Jesus Alou may have been having. Whether those problems existed in 1969 or 1970 didn't seem to matter to Harry.

Harry also failed to understand quite a few things about "Mr. J. Alou," as he usually referred to himself in the third person. Mr. J. Alou wasn't taking crap from Harry, or anybody. He was just one of those guys who truly had the ability to let unpleasant words roll away like the water off a duck's back. He also had a sense of humor that allowed him to kid about qualities that we all knew he did not own.

For example, and as Joe Morgan also points out in his own book, Alou once came up to a large group of us in the clubhouse before a game at Dodger Stadium and offered this tongue-in-cheek comment of self-confidence: "How come the J. Alou don't hit fourth? Nobody in this league can get the J. Alou out! Give him a chance! The J. Alou drives in as many runs as anybody!"

Everybody on hand but Harry Walker seemed to understand and get a kick out of Jesus Alou's sense of humor about himself. Harry, on the other hand, saw it as a chance to tell Alou that he wanted him to stop using his own bats and to start using his Harry Walker model. And remember, Alou was already batting in the neighborhood of .300 when this suggestion came down from the mountaintop.

J. Alou politely declined Harry's offer, explaining that "J. Alou's bat is fine" and that it has plenty of hits left inside it. Alou proceeded to use his own bat in the top of the first that night, flying out to left field. On his second trip to the plate, however, Alou noticed that his favorite bat was missing.

"What happened to my bat?" Alou shouted out.

Somebody pulled it out for Jesus. It had been found halfway up the runway, broken in two.

"Who did this to my bat?" a now uncharacteristically angry Alou shouted.

Harry Walker admitted to breaking the bat, dismissing the action with the throwaway comment, "If you don't use my bat, you don't play at all." Alou simply turned away, ignored Walker, and used one of his other bats. Walker did nothing in response. He neither removed Alou from the game, nor fined him, nor apologized or offered to pay for Alou's destroyed personal property.

The damage had been done. Harry Walker had made the gentle Jesus Alou incredibly angry. We just didn't know the depth of his anger for a few days, but it all came to light when Harry launched into one of his now regularly predictable clubhouse lecture attacks on how certain players on the Astros team (all of them black) didn't seem to have it in them to play smart baseball.

You could really cut the atmosphere with the proverbial knife this time. The silence seethed with rage. Only one voice, speaking only two words, at first, began to answer the allegations by Harry Walker. "Be consistent!" were the words that rose from a quiet whisper to several growing levels of the spoken statement.

Finally, even Harry Walker could no longer ignore the words of Don Wilson.

"What did you say, Don?" Harry asked.

"I said, 'BE CONSISTENT!' " Don raged as he simultaneously rose to his feet and leapt into another attack path upon Harry Walker.

Doug Rader tackled Don Wilson before he could get to Walker. Then four or five others of us held him down to keep him from his appointment with mayhem. All the while, Don continues screaming at the top of his lungs that we can't hold him down on the floor forever and that, whenever he does get free, he's "going to kill the mother!"

By this time, it's déjà vu all over again. We players are left with the job of restraining and calming the fires of Don Wilson, our Houston Astros version of the Wolf Man, but it sure wasn't easy. Nobody brought any silver bullets to a job that had put us all in danger of getting our own throats slashed, but, somehow, we got it done. And the very real threat of losing our good friend and valuable teammate to death row passed away, one more time.

Meanwhile, the real shock was that now we had another teammate riled in ways we had never seen. Just about the time we got Don Wilson settled, the usually kind and sweet-tempered Jesus Alou kicks in like a raging bull. Days later, his anger over the favorite bat that Harry Walker had broken was now kicking in like the last fast-burning straw. It had been smoldering ever since the bat incident, but now it had burst into roaring flames of rage that none of us had ever witnessed in the man.

"I'm sick of you, Harry Walker. I'm sick of you!"

Jesus Alou sprang to his feet, yelling at Harry Walker. In his own book, Joe Morgan recounts Jesus Alou's words in this way: "The J. Alou don't bother nobody ... nobody! I just wanna play baseball. You don't let me play baseball! You're always picking on the J. Alou. You don't mess with these other guys. You don't mess with Morgan, you don't mess with Rader, you mess with the J. Alou. Well, the J. Alou is going home. I go to the Dominican. I can't stand this anymore! The J. Alou is going home!"

With two guys still hanging onto Don Wilson, the rest of us are now trying to hold back our laughter as we work to calm down Jesus Alou. We for sure aren't laughing at Alou; we are laughing in shock over the discovery that he is capable of anger at this level. And as we so work on his state of mind, Alou keeps repeating: "I go to the Dominican; I can't stand this anymore! The J. Alou is going home!"

Restraining Wilson! Calming Alou! Team upset!

Harry Walker had won the day, at least, in his own mind: Two black players had lost their cool, proving once more that Harry Walker was in control and that they were not. And everyone else was left to clean up the mess as the manager retreated again to the locked-door safety of his office.

The man had no right or good reason for baiting the temperamental

Don Wilson! The man had no business breaking the bat of Jesus Alou! The man had no good heart about him when he kept referring to the blacks on his team as "you people" or "these people"! I have learned to forgive him for not being able to rise above the errors of his own ignorant hate and spite, but that will never mean that I shall ever be OK with him, or anyone else, who acts in cruelty toward another human being because his skin color is different.

White hate for black; black hate for white: it's all racism to me. In my mind, nobody in this world has a pass that allows them to blindly hate another human being simply because of his race, color, creed, sex, or country of origin. Racism is simply the tip of an even broader ignorance and it is the epitome of evil. I was not old enough and wise enough to say all these things to Harry Walker years ago.

I only wish I had been able to tell Harry these things during his lifetime, but that's not how things worked out. Wisdom is like a tool that you only get from the pain of your own experience, and you only receive this tool, through the Grace of God, when you are mature enough to use it.

Deeper wisdom about racism wasn't the only tool I could have used back in the time of Stormy Monday. I could have used a few pearl-handled instruments on the art of having a healthy relationship with a woman too. Those would come in time, but not in time to help me with the trials I would soon face in my personal life. It would be from these trials that the form of new wisdom would begin to take shape. I said, *begin* to take shape. Back in 1970, I still had so much to learn about the world and so many years of hard-knocks school still lay ahead of me.

The man on our 1970 club who seemed wise beyond his years on worldly things, wiser than the rest of us, was my best friend, Joe Morgan. Joe had good intelligence and an instinctive way of handling things in this difficult atmosphere that went way beyond the rest of us, but that just made him Harry's main target.

Harry may have been dumb in some ways, but he was smart and conniving too. He was smart enough to see how the rest of us black players looked up to Joe Morgan as a leader. He seemed to sense that breaking down Joe Morgan, as he had done with Don Wilson and Jesus Alou, was the key to really separating the rest of us from any hope of a better deal. Harry wanted to take the fight out of us.

The problem for Harry was that Joe knew what he was doing too and he wouldn't allow it to happen. I'm not sure that Harry really understood that Joe was onto him, but, either way, it didn't stop Harry from pulling out the kitchen sink and trying everything he could to break the spirit of Joe Morgan.

Harry Walker finally came up with a way to try to get to Joe Morgan by using me as a pawn in his plan. It was the sort of the thing that only the devil could have devised for its sheer evil character. It involved a managerial decision that affected both Joe and me in a way that could have busted wide open our friendship, had our relationship been as weak as Harry assumed.

Harry was wrong. He was wrong about Joe. He was wrong about me. And he was wrong about us.

The issue all came to a head in the third game of a series we were playing against the Mets at the Dome on August 29, 1970. I wasn't playing that day, but Joe Morgan had gone four for four at the plate with two doubles and a critical RBI.

It was the bottom of the tenth. Joe Morgan was coming to bat with two men out and the tying run standing on second base. Lefty Tug McGraw was pitching and the Mets were leading, 7–6.

With Joe out there in the on-deck circle, out of ear shot, Harry Walker came up to me suddenly and says, "Get a bat, Jimmy, you're hitting for Morgan!"

"I won't do it!" I protested. "Joe's four for four and he's the best hitter we've got! I will not embarrass him or myself in this situation!"

"You will pinch-hit, Jimmy," Walker stated. "If you refuse, consider yourself fined and under immediate suspension! I am the manager of this club, not you, and not Joe Morgan!"

About this time, Joe was walking back into the dugout, having gotten the callback news.

Harry right away turned his wrath upon Joe. He started yelling at him: "You tell your friend he hits or he gets fined and suspended—and believe me, I'll make it stick."

I could tell that Joe wanted to bash Harry. So did I, but neither of us did.

"Go up and hit for me," Joe told me.

"I'm not doing it," I answered.

"You've got to," Joe added. "Don't let him do that to you."

"He's doing it to you, man," I told Joe. "If he wants to do a number on you, let him get somebody else."

"Jimmy, you just go up there and win the game for us," Joe said. "Believe me, I can take care of myself. Don't do it for him. Do it for the rest of us. Win us a game."

My memory of what happened next is aided by the fact that box scores are now readily available on the Internet in ways they weren't around for everybody back in the early 1990s when Joe Morgan wrote his book.

Joe's memory of the game is that we lost. We actually won, 8–7, but that doesn't vindicate Harry Walker from what he was trying to do. I didn't get a hit in that game, but, based on the box score, I must have either walked or been hit by a pitch because I later scored what probably was the winning run.

Maybe you had to be there; maybe you even had to be either Joe Morgan or Jimmy Wynn to completely understand why Harry Walker did what he did that day. Sure, he was the manager and, as such, he had every right to send in a pinch hitter for anybody at any time for any reason. Harry's story on that one occasion would have been the old righty/lefty match up featuring Wynn/McGraw that he preferred over the lefty/lefty contest starring Morgan/McGraw.

So what! Joe Morgan was our best hitter against lefties or righties! He was already four for four on the day! You don't send in anybody, least of all his best friend, to bat for Joe Morgan in the tenth inning with the game on the line.

But Harry did.

Joe and I talked later that night. He told me about passing Harry Walker on his way to the clubhouse while I was heading up to bat. He told me about telling Harry, in passing, "You know, you're not trying to win."

Walker had said nothing to acknowledge the comment, according to Joe.

Joe and I both had a bad feeling about where this was all going. Soon, or sometime after the season, there was now a big chance that one or both of us would be gone from the Houston Astros. Harry Walker had pulled out all the stops to break our bond and to get Joe Morgan or myself to knuckle under. Neither of us would react by making the stupid violent moves that would prove Harry's point that we were nutcases.

Something else would have to give. In the meanwhile, the dark clouds of Stormy Monday just turned a blacker shade of blue.

On June 20, 1970, a personnel call-up from our AAA farm club in Oklahoma City would set in motion a change that had short-range and long-term importance to the careers of several Astro regulars and probably most of all, to me. The club called up a 19-year-old Dominican kid named Cesar Cedeno from our Oklahoma City farm team.

This kid was a five-tool guy who could do it all. In the short time he was down there at Oklahoma City in 1970, Cedeno had compiled a .373 batting average that also included 14 home runs and 61 runs batted in. The kid was already earning alternate comparisons from the media bandwagon as either the next Roberto Clemente or the future Willie Mays. All he had to do was put on a major league uniform, play about fifteen years, and then sit around and wait for his call from the Hall of Fame. As a lot of us soon enough learned, it doesn't work that way, no matter how talented you are when you first sit down at the big league banquet table.

When Cesar Cedeno played his first big league game for the Astros against the Braves in Atlanta on June 20, 1970, he played center field. Meanwhile I took what started out as a day of rest, before entering the game late to play center while Cedeno moved to right. I had watched enough to see what Cedeno could do in the field. I knew right away that I was looking at the Astros' center fielder of the future, if not sooner, but that was really OK. The way things had been going for me under Harry Walker lately, I really expected a change soon, anyway, and quite frankly, I was more concerned at the time with just hoping that Harry might take a pass on screwing with Cedeno's head as he had the rest of us blacks and Hispanics.

Not wanting to come off as a clubhouse poison guy, I didn't say a whole lot to Cesar Cedeno about Harry Walker once he joined the club, but I kept my eye on the situation as best I could, and I know that Joe Morgan did too.

Cedeno's bat stayed hot at the big league level from Day One. He quickly took over as the starting center fielder, but I didn't mind the shift to left field. Other things, like Harry Walker and a marriage that seemed to be getting worse by the day, were taking up most of my spare energy by then. Ruth and I just reached a point where we bickered and fought over everything. I found it harder and harder to go home, knowing pretty much that it was guaranteed we were going to get into another screaming match.

I hated it. It wasn't right for our two little kids and it wasn't good for either of us, Ruth or me, to live that way either. Joe Morgan and his wife Gloria would invite us over to their place for dinner on those rare moments we were home and had the time, but that had a way of turning into me going alone because of some fight that came up between Ruth and me at the last minute.

Life was getting to be no fun, no fun at all.

In the meantime, other things stirred the pot in the Astros clubhouse. One of our newer players, veteran pitcher Jim Bouton, had just published a landmark baseball "tell all" book called *Ball Four* that really shocked the baseball world. In the book, Bouton had gone into detail about the drinking, carousing, and childish pranks played out by such star former teammates as Mickey Mantle and Whitey Ford.

Whoa! Authors didn't write baseball books of that kind until Bouton came along! To put it mildly, the major leaguers of 1970 were not ready for this level of honesty at all. It would have been one thing had Bouton been writing only about his own behavior. People didn't write that honestly about themselves either back then, but Bouton's book was about the personal behavior of his teammates. Jim had broken one of the great codes of secrecy. And now nobody felt safe being himself around him.

As an Astro, none of us liked it at all, and it didn't matter if you felt you had nothing to hide. Just the knowledge that you are working with someone who may later write something about you that is your own personal business made for a lot of fear, tension, and anger. Frankly, that condition didn't improve until Bouton left the team, and it never really went away at all after *Ball Four*.

Ball Four was the atomic bomb of baseball books. Once you knew that one writer could drop one on you, you also knew that anyone else could do the same. Given all the other stuff that we were going through individually and as a team in 1970, Jim Bouton had become just another outer band squall line on the path of Stormy Monday.

On the field, the 1970 Astros were anchored in the pitching department by Larry Dierker (16–12, 3.87), Jack Billingham (13–9, 3.98), and Don Wilson (11–6, 3.91). Those three winning margins weren't enough to keep us from slipping to an overall season record of 79–83. That count was good enough for two less wins than we had in 1969, and good enough for fourth place in 1970, but it was twenty-three games off the pace in the West Division of the National League behind the Cincinnati Reds.

Our hitting was up by nineteen points on our team batting average. In fact, my .282 batting average on the season was the highest in my career. In spite of the ongoing turmoil in every direction, I also managed to maintain my power numbers with 27 homers and 88 runs batted in on the season.

Shortstop Denis Menke paced the '70 Astros with 92 RBI, while also hitting .304 and banging out 13 home runs. "The J. Alou" hung around for a season BA of .306, using his own bats, and Doug "the Rooster" Rader clocked in with 25 HR and 87 RBI. Rookie Cedeno also hit .310 in just under a hundred games, and another good friend, Bob Watson, perched on establishing himself as a regular in the Astros batting order. Watson batted .272 with 11 HR and 61 RBI in 1970; his versatility at several positions, including first base, and the addition of Cedeno's promising bat had pretty much made the very unhappy Houston misfit Joe Pepitone expendable by mid-to-late summer. On July 29, 1970, the Astros sold the contract of "New York Joe" to the Chicago Cubs in a straight cash deal.

On a little noted and lesser remembered deal back on June 23, 1970, the Astros traded away a 27-year-old right-handed relief pitcher to the Montreal Expos for an outfielder named Don Bosch and, I guess, the proverbial bag of practice balls. The fellow we gave up only got a shot in four games for the Astros, but after watching him give up five runs and eight hits in five and one-third innings, good old Manager Harry Walker and General Manager Spec Richardson had seen all they needed to see. They saw no point in keeping Mike Marshall around as an Astro any longer.

On the trading block, you win some, you lose some. On October 12, 1970, the Astros traded away infielder Hector Torres to the Chicago Cubs in exchange for a prospect rookie shortstop named Roger Metzger. Now that one turned out pretty good. In Roger Metzger, the Astros acquired their shortstop of the future. Metzger's defense placed him near the top with all the great fielding shortstops of his era, and it was good enough in Houston to outweigh the lightness of his bat.

We will give Spec Richardson certain credit for Metzger, but we also need to remember an old saying that seems to apply here: Even a blind squirrel finds an acorn every now and then.

Joe Morgan and I spent the early 1970–71 off-season waiting for the other shoe to fall in the matter of Harry Walker. Joe was convinced that Harry was now going to do everything he could to get rid of him, or me, or both of us. I was just hoping we'd done badly enough as a team on the field to get Harry fired.

Neither of those things happened, but that didn't convince either of us that our hopes and fears were all imaginary. Inaction on the firing/trade front just said that Harry was still on the clock. He needed to be a little more disappointing for a little while longer to get fired. Also, it told us that Harry had not yet convinced Spec Richardson to pull the trigger on a deal to get rid of either of us. We already knew that Spec was the key domino that had to fall here.

As we already had seen with Mike Cuellar and Rusty Staub, nothing, not even logic or common sense, was going to get in his way once Spec Richardson made the call to trade somebody.

Inaction during the 1970–71 off-season on the Harry Walker issue also said another couple of disturbing things. It said that the Astros executive management group beyond the clubhouse either misunderstood how bad things had become on the team morale front, or else they simply didn't give a flip. Either way was disturbing, but that thought even worsened once it dawned upon each of us that both possibilities might have been true. Remember that old teacher-student joke?

Teacher: "What's your problem, Johnny? Is it ignorance or apathy?"

Johnny: "I don't know and I don't care."

Applying that same question to the Astros about the racist Harry Walker wasn't quite as funny. We had reached a point in which we sometimes had to step in just to keep one of our own from snuffing him out. That's pretty bad.

Could we have gone over Harry's head and complained all the way up to Judge Hofheinz, if need be? Sure, we could have, but that's not how you did things back in our day, or at least, that's not how Joe Morgan and I operated.

The issue had been noisy enough to have been well known to Spec and his people. We expected Spec and his crew to do their job as hard as we tried to do ours. In fact, our waiting for something to happen from above was pretty much a test of our own. Could we believe in management? Naively, it was important to us that the answer came in the form of how management chose to recognize and handle this very tough situation with one Harry Walker.

Fortunately, baseball is a game of seasons, allowing all those who play the game every spring and summer to get away from each other during the fall and winter or, at least, far enough away to escape the everyday tensions of working for or playing with people you don't like. A bad marriage, on the other hand, has no built-in escape plan. You can run, but you can't hide.

Sooner or later, you have to go home and either face the music or get wiped out by the percussion section.

The latter was my fate in late December 1970. I was away from the nagging problem of Harry Walker until spring training. Only an out-of-the-blue big trade or a managerial firing could spare me that reunion, but at least I had a break from that problem for now as we headed into Christmas.

I went home from a round of golf on December 21, thinking as I usually did during the holiday season that Houston never felt like home at Christmastime. As much as I had come to love the people of Houston and the town itself, I missed the snow and all the "white Christmas" feelings that still connected my soul to my family and the city of Cincinnati at that special time of the year.

Driving home in the car near twilight time, my thoughts of Mom and Dad, of my original family, of Cincinnati—they all sort of lulled me into temporarily forgetting that Ruth and I had been on the brink of another big fight before I left the house. When I walked in the door, it didn't take long for all the reminders to kick in. Ruth and I picked up on the same argument we were starting to have earlier. Our unhappiness covered every subject in the world that could go wrong between a young couple. We were just totally lost and mightily struggling.

Then it got worse than ever before that night. As I followed Ruth into the kitchen, our voices kept building in anger. I came up right behind Ruth as she retreated to the kitchen sink. Suddenly she turned around to face me and I felt a sudden sharp pain in my stomach.

We both looked down in horror. In her anger, Ruth had picked up a kitchen knife and plunged it into my stomach.

"Oh, my God!" I cried out.

"I'm so sorry!" Ruth exclaimed.

I grabbed my bleeding belly and sat down as Ruth called for emergency medical help. Lucky for me, help came quick, taking me to Riverside Hospital for emergency surgery. Somehow, Spec Richardson was notified and he met us at the hospital to make sure that I got all the help I needed.

Lucky for me again, the wound turned out to be fairly superficial. If Ruth had pushed a little deeper, or a little more to the side, I might have been killed on the spot by an ordinary kitchen knife, but the Good Lord intervened in my behalf.

It wasn't my time to go, but it was time for my marriage to end. I filed no criminal charges against Ruth, but I did file for a divorce. The marriage that had started for the wrong reason was now coming to an end. I forgave Ruth for what she did and I wanted her to have what she needed to take care of our two kids. I also tried to provide help on the material side. I simply could not continue to live the lie that I cared about making our marriage work after the stabbing incident.

I still cared with everything in my heart for the kids after their mom and I split up. I just had trouble being around them more often because it meant going through their mother. Once somebody stabs you, you need to forgive them, and I did forgive Ruth, but even forgiveness doesn't erase the memory of what might have happened, and it sure doesn't make you want to see them any more often than you have to.

Ruth died of cancer several years after our divorce and after the kids were grown. I can only hope that she somehow found a way during her own lifetime to forgive me too for not being the kind of husband and partner she both needed and deserved so many years ago. I also most actively hope and pray that my two wonderful natural-born kids, Kimberly and Jimmy Jr., can find it in their hearts to forgive their very imperfect father for the way he handled this early part of his life.

I wasn't a bad man, kids; I just made some very bad personal decisions. I hope to God you will forgive me because I've got only one place to go with my feelings for each of you, and that is to love you both with all my heart and soul for as long as the God Lord sees fit to let me keep breathing, in and out, the sweet air of His good earth.

As I physically recovered through the loneliest, most tortured Christmas of my life in 1970, I had no idea what lay ahead for me in the season to come. All I was doing was getting physically well, getting back on the golf course as soon as possible, turning the divorce wheel over to my lawyer, and generally doing what ballplayers are trained to do with yesterday's bad game and big loss. I just wanted to put it behind me and move on. Now I see that I most probably could have been better served by spending some time talking with a doctor, or a counselor, or a minister, somebody—somebody qualified and capable of helping me sort out my emotions and the lessons of my failed marriage to Ruth. I just didn't do it.

I have since learned that the big crises in life we don't sort out are filled with negative forces that drive what we do next. If we don't learn the lessons of a bad marriage, for example, the odds are strong that we will repeat the same basic mistakes with our next partner. We also increase our chances of carrying forward some bad feelings about ourselves and other people that may bring us down and keep us from being productive at work.

I will never use the violent end to my first marriage as an excuse for the bad year I had on the field during the 1971 season, but I can say honestly that I never before felt less like playing ball or doing anything good for myself than I did that year. In plain English, I now know that the terrible ending of my marriage to Ruth left me feeling distrustful of other people and a whole lot less confident in myself. It may not have shown up right away in spring training, I'm not sure, but it soon enough showed its head for everyone to see on the playing field.

As "Jimmy Wynn," I was becoming a hermit in my own house.

I just did my thing on the field, even if I did do it worse than at any other time in my career. I didn't hang out with anybody; I didn't go out with anybody; I didn't respond to invitations; I didn't do anything but play the game and go back to my room and mope around in my own misery. It wasn't pretty.

Joe Morgan reached out to me, but I pushed Joe back with a limitless wave of "some other time" excuses. The only thing that may have improved was the pain I felt from my daily contact with Harry Walker. In 1971, I wasn't feeling much of anything.

Of course, I had given up some time earlier on doing anything to comply with a request or order from Harry, but now I was just flat-out ignoring him.

My feelings about Harry had not gone away. They had just been deadened to sensitivity, along with every other feeling, good or bad, that I was capable of having.

My on-field performance in 1971 was terrible. If they made a movie about my life based only on the 1971 season, they could have easily named it something like *I Was a Zombie Outfielder for the 1971 Astros!* I was that bad but, at the time, I neither knew nor cared why it was true.

I had shut down my feelings about Ruth, the kids, the stabbing, the divorce, Harry Walker, and baseball in general. There was no place for my performance to go from there, but down, down, down. Stormy Monday had fully kicked in.

Sometimes you find personal lows of the spirit that you never knew you had in you, but you fight back inside that deep hole with all that your folks once tried to teach you about what God wants for you. I didn't know much at this point. I just knew I had to get some things right in my life and that those things started with working out my divorce from Ruth.

Ruth and I worked out our agreements OK and, I hate to say it, but it wasn't that I wanted to be back with her either, because I didn't. I just did not have any place outside of me to put down the load of all the sadness I carried with me. It was just easier to feel as little as possible about anything.

The one exception to my blunted feelings was the kids. I felt sad about all the stuff that Kimberly and little Jimmy were going through because of Ruth and me. I felt sad for them. And I missed them. But I couldn't do anything about it.

I tried to plug in my baseball mentality about tough losses: Put the tough losses to bed and turn the page on yesterday. Do something about today's game. The only chance we have for a better tomorrow is how we handle today.

Sounds good; didn't work this time. May have worked on double-header losses; did not work for me in 1971 on divorce and separation from my two little kids.

My batting average fell all the way to .203 in 1971. Over the course of

404 official times at bat in 123 games, I collected only 82 hits, and only 7 of them were home runs. My 63 runs batted in were about half what I had only two years earlier and my .302 on-base percentage and .295 slugging average were the worst of my career. By season's end, I wasn't even playing on a regular basis. That's how bad it was on paper.

In the flesh, it was worse. The only thing that seemed to penetrate that wall of deadness I felt was the changing fan reaction, and that pain came through loud and clear on its own channel. For the first time in my career, Houston fans were booing me. They booed me when I struck out; they booed me when I came up to hit in crucial game situations; they booed me when my name was announced as part of the starting lineup; and, they screamed, at times, that I should be pulled for a pinch hitter.

That reaction from Houston fans was the cruelest pain I ever suffered as a professional baseball player. I didn't want to let the fans down, and even though I understood that most of them had no idea what I was going through at that time in my personal life, it still hurt bad. The disapproval from Astros fans cut all the way through me and my general deadness of feeling like a second knife.

I wanted to do something to regain fan confidence in me. I guess I felt that, if I could, it might be a way to regain confidence in myself. I had those two things backwards in my mind back in 1971; I just didn't realize it at the time. The fact is, if we want others to believe in us, we first have to show them that we believe in ourselves. I couldn't do that trick of the truth back in 1971 because, the truth is, I had lost faith in myself. It just was not happening for me because I was looking for God in all the wrong places back then and relying way too much on my own ego to solve the problem. I wasn't asking for the spiritual help that I so sorely needed.

As a ballplayer in 1971, I was headed for Mendoza Land as a batter, at least, for one season.

In case you've never heard that expression in baseball, Mendoza Land is named for a former player named Mario Mendoza. Mario was famous for hitting right at .200 for his career. That .200 level of bad and terrible hitting came to be known as the Mendoza Line. Any batting average in the neighborhood of .200 is living in what I now think of as Mendoza Land.

Got that one? Good. Let's move on.

The 1971 season, in general, was not much to write home about. Some of that booing directed at me was spawned from the general unrest among Houston fans over the fact that we had just finished our tenth season in the big leagues with no major hint beyond that brief tease in 1969 that we would ever become competitive for a league championship.

For the second year in a row, the Astros finished at 79–83, good enough for a tie for fourth place with Cincinnati in the National League West, but eleven games back of the division-leading Giants from San Francisco.

Something had to give somewhere after the '71 season played out. It did give, all right, but when it did, we, the members of the team, were all whirling in total shock and absolute disbelief. As far as I was concerned, it turned out to be the biggest turkey ever browned and served on a date near Thanksgiving. No one I knew could find any room for gratitude. It was a trade that stirred up the whole team and its legion of fans, but it wasn't just any trade. Most of us thought the separate trades of Mike Cuellar and Rusty Staub were horrible enough by themselves, but this one was the bomb of all bombs.

On November 29, 1971, Houston Astros General Manager Spec Richardson traded second baseman Joe Morgan, shortstop Denis Menke, starting pitcher Jack Billingham, plus outfielders Ed Armbrister and Cesar Geronimo, to the Cincinnati Reds in exchange for first baseman Lee May, second baseman Tommy Helms, and infielder Jimmy Stewart.

I called Joe Morgan right away. He was as shocked and saddened as me, but neither of us was surprised. There is a difference between shock and surprise. It comes down to this: It still hurts and amazes, even if you knew it was coming.

Joe was being forced away from his original organization and the city in which he had made his married-life home with Gloria and also all his early career commitments to community service. Houston, the baseball team and the city, was also the same place where the two of us had met and grown comfortable with each other over the years as best friends, roommates, teammates in the heat of battle, and fellow warriors in the ongoing struggle against the stupidity of Harry Walker.

Now I would have to go yet another course of my life alone. Now I deeply regretted that I had pushed my old roomie away during the time of my personal crisis over the span of this past miserable season.

Regret is a miserable condition in the human experience. It always adds up to a three-word bottom line of pain that spells itself out as "too late now."

What's that you said about "Stormy Monday," Mr. Lou Rawls?

For me, the year 1971 had started with deep regret. Now it was also ending with "too late now." Pure and simple, there was no more room in my sponge of emotional experience for any extra sadness. If it was going to keep coming at me at this same rate, it was just going to have to roll off my heart and go someplace else. I could either take up residence in self-pity from here on, or I could just start learning from my pain and try moving on with my life in gratitude for all the gifts that God had given me. In a small way, I made a turn in the direction of gratitude around the time I was saying goodbye to Joe Morgan over the Christmas season of 1971.

Funny how that works, isn't it? Letting go of Joe Morgan as an everyday friend and teammate in my life taught me to be grateful for the fact that he had even been there in the first place. I still count the ways that knowing Joe Morgan made me both a better ballplayer and a better person.

Joe Morgan and I faced our separation as teammates with many shared memories of our time together on the Houston Astros. I will always think of Joe as one of the smartest, most hard-working ballplayers that I ever knew. The total combination of his intelligence, his work ethic, his team concept, his talent, and his results on the field are together the sum of what convincingly took him to the Baseball Hall of Fame in 1990.

During our teammate days, Joe and I had this "ant and the grasshopper" thing going on. If you remember that old Aesop's Fable, you will have the picture of what I'm talking about. Remember? The ant was always stockpiling food during the warm months in preparation for winter. The grasshopper always spent his summer days and nights playing. When the snows of winter came, the ant did just fine because he had stored up all that food, but the grasshopper got wiped out because he had spent all that time having fun and not getting ready for the hard times ahead.

Joe and I weren't really as extreme in this regard as he might somehow want you to believe, but he was definitely more like the ant and I was definitely more like the grasshopper.

On the road, we had a lot of conversations that boiled down to this fairly simple exchange between roommates:

Joe Morgan: "Are you going out again tonight?"

Jimmy Wynn: "Don't you ever want to have any fun?"

If you've read Joe Morgan's autobiography, you already know that Joe pretty much believes that our "ant versus grasshopper" differences were the big reason why he made it to the Hall of Fame at Cooperstown and I did not.

I can't argue the point. I did a lot of things as well as or better than many of the other outfielders who have made it to Cooperstown, but I never hit for the kind of high batting average that most Hall of Famers achieve. As long as voters place more value on your percentage of hits and fail to look at how important it was that you got your hits in critical situations, while getting on base in all kinds of ways far more often than most, I have no chance of consideration, anyway.

In my own view, I don't think staying in the room on the road and watching more TV would have made any big difference in my batting average, but I have to say this too: I did stay in the room more often than my old roomie gives me credit for doing. I just sure didn't prefer it to a little night life and clubbing.

As I look back upon it now, I have no regrets about wanting to explore and enjoy the cities we were privileged to visit on a regular basis as major league baseball players. Even Joe admits that I made a choice that many talented (and untalented) players make. I just didn't want to remember New York as the same generic hotel room that I stayed in during our last trip to Los Angeles.

Besides, I am not today living the grasshopper's fate here in the winter of my life, so I must have been doing something right along the way. With a little planning and luck, it is possible to have fun now and also later. And sometimes it's just plain funny how this equation works out.

Joe Morgan and I both recall a time in Pittsburgh in which staying home in the room for Joe and running and gunning on the town for me produced opposite results on the field the next day from those you might ordinarily expect from the efforts of a real ant or grasshopper.

Joe remembered this incident as one that took place on July 3, 1966, the night before a 4th of July double-header between the Astros and Pirates at Forbes Field in Pittsburgh. Memories are fragile. When we looked it up in our research for this book, we learned that the Astros weren't even in Pittsburgh on those dates in 1966. The club was in Cincinnati for a game with the Reds on July 3, and we flew from there to Atlanta for a July 4 game against the Braves.

The time that Joe Morgan had in mind actually took place about a month earlier on June 4 and 5 of 1966, the night before and the day of the last game of three in Pittsburgh, but it still stands strong as an illustration of the same point.

The Astros already had lost the first two games to the Pirates on June 3 and 4. Now we headed into the last game of the series with a chance to socialize with some of our close Pirate friends before leaving town.

Willie Stargell and Jesse Gonder of the Pirates were both from the Bay Area, as was Joe Morgan. After an afternoon Astros loss to the Pirates on June 4, Willie Stargell invited Jesse Gonder, Joe Morgan, and me to his house for some barbeque ribs and a little relaxation. We were having a great time.

Around nine o'clock, Willie suggested that we all go out to a club. Well, Jesse and I thought that was a great idea and Joe went quietly along with the plan, even though I knew that he really would have preferred to just go back to the hotel. He even kidded that Willie may just be setting us up for a sweep by keeping us up late and trying to get us drunk.

Joe Morgan didn't really drink. After going to a couple of night clubs, Willie Stargell suggested another one about midnight, but Joe Morgan opted to catch a cab and go back to the hotel. I chose to keep up the night flight with my Pirate night owl buddies. Joe gave me one of those famous-to-me Morgan judgment-questioning looks and then made his departure.

I have to admit, on this particular occasion, we made a real oil-burning night of it. The three of us rolled into Forbes Field with no sleep and with barely enough time to suit up for the game. Once he saw me, Joe Morgan didn't say much, but he made sure that I knew that he had been there at the ballpark on time and that he was fully rested to play the game. I didn't have time to field his flack. I had to hurry and get dressed before I drew a fine from then Manager Grady Hatton.

Based upon how we each spent the previous evening, what are the odds against these results from our June 5, 1966, afternoon game at Forbes Field in Pittsburgh between the Astros and the Pirates?

Of course, the Pirates won 10–5 to preserve their sweep of the series. No big surprise there. Given the different paths taken by our party company from the night before, however, the individual results proved quite interesting.

The sober man with the good night's sleep (Joe Morgan) collected a single in four trips to the plate. One of the party boys with no sleep (Jesse Gonder) did not play. Maybe he got caught up on his sleep during the game. The other two partygoers (Willie Stargell and Jimmy Wynn) each enjoyed perfect days at the plate. For the Pirates, Willie Stargell went five for five with two home runs, three runs scored, and five runs batted in. For the Astros, I, Jimmy Wynn, went four for four, also with two home runs, one double, three runs scored, and three RBI.

After the game, and right before I crashed asleep on the team plane leaving Pittsburgh, I had looked at Joe Morgan in the clubhouse at Forbes Field and said nothing. I didn't have to say anything. We both just about busted a gut laughing over the irony of it all.

Hello, Mr. Ant! Goodbye, Mr. Grasshopper!

When Joe and I reprised that story during the time of our last goodbye recollections in December 1971, we laughed again. And then we almost cried.

Saying goodbye to Joe Morgan was tough.

One good thing came out of my personal "Stormy Monday." I learned that I had to get my head up again and look beyond the bad times to something better. I had to start believing in myself again. Otherwise, life peels on like an old T-Bone Walker song: One bad day just follows another and the next bad one just seems worse than the last bad one that passed a day earlier. Pretty soon, it's just one long stream of blues days, making it easier to slip into self-pity than it does to stand up and look for hope. Well, I'm going to tell you here and now. I'd had enough of that stuff by this point in time.

I was ready to be Jimmy Wynn again, or maybe for the first time to even become all the real Jimmy Wynn I knew I could be. With Almighty God's help, I knew I could do it. I just had to stay humble and use the talents I had been given at birth. If I could do that much, and if I could ask and allow God to help me, I knew I could find my way again in baseball, no matter who was managing the Astros, and even if my old friend Joe Morgan was no longer around to watch my back.

"Go away, doom and gloom," I said to myself: "I'm lookin' for the sunshine!"

CHAPTER 12

Leo the Lip

The first day of Spring Training 1972 at Cocoa Beach rang in like a reunion. The first guy I laid eyes upon when I got to camp was this great big guy with the wide sweeping smile and crinkling happy eyes and a voice that took me all the way back to my baseball kindergarten days in Tampa.

"Well, Jimmy, my man," the familiar strange voice boomed loudly, "here we are, together again! Are you as ready as I am to start getting this job done as the teammates we once might have been on the Reds?"

They didn't call him "The Big Bopper" simply because of his home run touch, his massive muscles, and his *tall-in-the-saddle* appearance. Lee May had a way with his words that just came at you right over the top and landed exactly on what he was thinking at the time. You never had to guess what Lee was thinking. He would bop it right out there for you. That's why, years ago, when Lee pulled that joke on me about the Reds cutting me in my rookie minor league year that I sank so fast. I just assumed that it had to be true because of who was saying it.

"Are you sure I'm still on the team, Lee?" I asked with an arms-open smile.

We gave each other a dancing bear hug. Lee got a big kick out of the fact that I still remembered his "joke" after all these years.

Lee then introduced me to my other two new teammates from the Reds, Tommy Helms and Jimmy Stewart. It's not as though I was seeing them for the first time. After all, we had been playing against each other for a little while now. It's just that when somebody from another club joins your team in a trade, you want to do what you can to make them feel welcome and to help them move all of their loyalties over to your side of the action. It occurred to me too that Joe Morgan and the others were going through that same transfer of allegiance over in the Reds camp, and very probably at the same time we were dealing with it in Houston.

In the case of our guys who went over to the Reds, two were veterans who had already been through the trading rip on emotions (Billingham and

Menke) and two were rookies (Geronimo and Armbrister). Joe Morgan was the fifth guy and the only career Astro that faced the full blast of all the things that getting traded makes you feel. Joe did get to carry with him the knowledge that he was "The Man" as far as the Reds were concerned in this deal. God had doubly blessed Joe Morgan. He was going away to join a surefire contender, and going away from Harry Walker. When all was said and done, I was happy for him.

Coming at us were two career Reds, May and Helms, and one journeyman, Stewart. Helms had to be the guy in the trade feeling the most unwanted because everybody knew that Joe Morgan was going over to Cincinnati to take his place at second base. Lee May, on the other hand, came over to the Astros knowing flat-out that he was the main guy we gave up Joe Morgan and all these other players to get. We needed a guy who could hit with some pop at first base.

When we greeted the three new Astros on the first morning of spring training 1972, it was all about encouraging a new loyalty together as a team playing for Houston. Nobody, and especially me, said anything around Tommy Helms along the lines of, "We sure are going to miss Joe Morgan this year!" Regardless of my friendship with Joe Morgan, I had to hope as an Astro that Tommy Helms would make us forget all about Joe Morgan as a second baseman in 1972.

We were about to start Harry Walker's fourth full season as manager of the Houston Astros. Counting the half season of time he also worked in 1968 as Grady Hatton's replacement, 1972 would mark his fifth year as the club's field boss.

What made it bearable for a lot of us was simply the knowledge that Harry was now sure to be on his last legs as skipper. We had not progressed in the standings during his time on duty and the hope existed that relief was on the way.

When that kind of attitude exists on a ball club with a number of players, it always raises a serious question: How can a team expect to get better when half the team is hoping that another bad year will get an unpopular manager fired? All I can do is answer that question for myself.

Number one, I never played to lose. I had a very bad year in 1971, but I wasn't playing that way to get Harry Walker fired. I played that way because I was going through an awful time with myself over a divorce and split life from my kids.

Number two, as a player, you have to play to win at your highest level. You only hurt yourself if you do not. A bad club may, as the old saying goes, "fire the manager because it can't fire the players," but that's only temporary. If a club thinks that your bad performance was one of the reasons they had to fire their old manager, you're going to get fired too, eventually, either by trade or by an outright release.

Number three, as my health and age allowed, I always played at the highest level possible for me at that moment in time. That was one of my dad's lessons and another big reason why 1971 was so hard for me to take. I came into the 1972 season totally dedicated to becoming the old Jimmy Wynn again.

I wouldn't mind seeing Harry Walker fired by the Astros, but I wasn't going to help him get there by tanking my performance on the field. That would have been dishonest and it would have only hurt me in the long run. If I played so well in '72 that it helped Harry Walker keep his job, I'd just have to learn to live with it.

Number four, a lot us felt that time was running short on management's patience with Harry's biased and controlling way of doing things, and we were hoping that they also had tired of all the reports that had come leaking back to them of near riots in the clubhouse over Harry's critical words to the team.

Number five, we weren't sinking Harry Walker. Given all the time he had to make the Astros ship sail straight and true, Harry was doing a fine enough job of sinking himself. That's really all I meant by my original comment that some of us had hope in 1972 that Harry's days as manager of the club were now numbered.

If my spirits were lifted during the time of spring training, they were also helped by the fact that I had met a woman through some friends, prior to going down to Florida, who had quickly stolen my heart with her sparkling personality and beautiful green eyes. She was a Creole lady from Louisiana named Joanne Cousin.

The only point I missed back around this time is that you can't really fix the pain of a divorce or loneliness by falling in love with someone else that fast. I'd have been better off first giving myself more healing time from the pain of my broken marriage, but that's just what all the textbooks in all the libraries say. The way we handle things as everyday human beings often works a little differently. Before 1972 was done, I followed my divorce from Ruth by getting married to Joanne and buying a new house in Houston.

I couldn't see how things wouldn't work out for Joanne and me. This one felt so different. I was head over heels in love; I wanted to get married; and we just had such a great time being together. How could it miss?

I had forgotten about all the long-haul issues, the ones that any woman faces once she chooses to marry a big league ballplayer. These are all the things that happen to a baseball couple once they get past the early, easy part of happy dating and hot romancing. These things are so strong, and so tough, as obstacles to long-term good feelings. Finding a woman who is special enough to handle all she faces in her life with a ballplayer over time is anything but easy. In fact, I will go this far with it: Any woman who marries a ballplayer and doesn't live to regret it eventually is a very special lady.

When she's married to a ballplayer, a woman has to be able to tolerate long periods of separation while her husband travels half his time to most of the major cities in North America. It takes a very special woman to be married to a ballplayer. On the road, the arms of temptation surround him at every turn. A woman has to trust that her ballplayer husband has the strength and loyalty to stay faithful, and that he possesses the honesty to shoot straight with her about what's happening on the road.

Some, but not all, ballplayers have a code of fidelity that disappears when they go out of town. On page 360 of her biography *Sal Maglie: Baseball's Demon Barber*, author Judith Testa expressed an extremely dim view when she quoted Vern Stephens of the 1940s-era St. Louis Browns and Boston Red Sox as crudely but accurately defining infidelity for ballplayers as "getting laid in the same town where your wife is."

Be clear on what I'm saying here. Not all baseball players are like the ones described by Stephens, and not all traveling men are unfaithfully hiding behind a selective code of ethics that says what you do when you're out of town doesn't count. Where fidelity is concerned, it all counts, no matter where you are, and regardless of whether you realize it or not.

Another problem on the road for some players used to be drinking. That problem hasn't gone away, but I do think it was a lot more prevalent back in my playing days, as it was a very public problem all over America, and not just for ballplayers. There isn't a bad decision out there that can't be made a whole lot faster and considerably easier once you've downed a few drinks of your favorite alcoholic beverage.

Marital relationships and excessive drinking are serious subjects, but we've all got to keep our senses of humor about us too. Those who don't, don't survive. On cue, that reminds me of a story attributed most often to old New York Yankee and Hall of Fame pitcher Lefty Gomez. Lefty put it something like this: "I never can remember for sure what my wife told me, but having a bad memory sure got me in trouble. She says she told me before I went out with the guys to have only one drink and be home by twelve. I thought she said go ahead and have twelve drinks, but be home by one!"

We ballplayers are not the same as the baseball cards that fans collect. We are human beings. As such, we are capable of both great and terrible things, but we are neither perfect nor exempt from human error—nor do we get a pass on what it takes to have an honest loyal relationship with a woman. Like all other men, we ballplayers either have to learn and apply what it takes to have a good relationship with a woman, or we get to suffer the consequences of refusing the lessons of our previous experience.

That being said, I was married again in 1972. And even if these were two different women that I married in each of my first two marriages, one thing was the same in both instances: One more time, I was going to have to get to know my new wife (this time, Joanne) after we were already married, and she, in turn, was going to have to learn all about living life with a ballplayer from her own lonely personal experience.

I see it now. I didn't then.

On the field, the 1972 Astros came across a lot stronger than many people predicted they would after the Joe Morgan trade. The main man we got in return for Joe, Lee May, had solved our first base problem big time with his 29 homers, his .284 batting average, and his 98 runs batted in. The two-time All-Star first baseman for the Reds kept that streak going with the Houston Astros too as our representative in the 1972 game.

In fact, it didn't take the Big Bopper long to establish himself as the new big troublesome wrinkle in the 1972 Astros lineup. After dropping our first two games of the season, we ran off a nine-game winning streak that was decidedly helped by the presence of Lee May in our lineup. On April 23, we were in San Francisco, working on win number six in that streak. It just didn't look as though we were moving in the right direction for most of the time. We went into the top of the ninth, trailing the Giants, 7–3. Then, with some big help from a three-run long tater by May, we rallied for ten runs in that one inning to take the game, 13–7.

With an early season, two-to-six-hole lineup that rang out as Cedeno, Wynn, May, Watson, and Rader, the opposition had to respect that we were perfectly capable of popping them with the long ball at just about any time. I didn't mind having that wall of May, Watson, and Rader hitting behind me in the number three spot. For the first time in my big league career, nobody could really afford to pitch around me. Getting good pitches to hit, along with my new and revived positive outlook, were the big reasons for my statistical comeback in 1972. As much as I hated the loss of Joe Morgan personally, our acquisition of Lee May, combined with the gelling of Cedeno, Watson, and Rader in the lineup, stood tall as a big favor to me as a hitter, at least for this one year.

Johnny Edwards anchored the catching position with a savvy touch and a very respectable .268 BA. Tommy Helms played a capable second base and batted an acceptable .259. Doug Rader's good reputation as one the best defensive third basemen in the league continued to grow too and, even though Rader's average dropped to .237, he still hammered 22 home runs and batted in 90 tallies on the year. One of the great defensive artists in the game also showed up at shortstop in 1972 in the form of Roger Metzger, the kid we got for a song from the Cubs prior to the 1971 season. Metzger's average fell to .222 in 1972, but he and Rader together gave the Astros a pretty airtight defense on the left side.

With young Cesar Cedeno taking over in center field, my position was now in right field, while Bob Watson anchored things in left. We became a three-man outfield wrecking crew at the plate. I ended my dive to the bottom in 1971 by bouncing back to a .273 BA with 24 home runs, while tying Rader for second place in RBI with 90. Bob Watson hit .312 with 16 home runs and 86 RBI, and Mr. Cesar Cedeno crashed the gate hard with a club-best BA of .320, while adding 22 homers and 82 RBI of his own to our offense.

Cesar Cedeno also began to show up with an accidental touch for comedy, too. As his 1972 year began to unfold for what it was, which was pretty darn impressive, "CC" began to start talking it up in the clubhouse about the commercials and product endorsements he expected to get as a result of his newfound success. When all of these offers didn't suddenly fall in his lap, Cedeno began to grumble.

When someone suggested to Cedeno that his thick Latin accent may be holding him back, he fielded the comment as though it were a serious fly ball. "Why should my way of speaking hold me back?" Cesar Cedeno shot back. "Sure, I know I have an accent, but so does that actor, Ricardo Montalban, and look at all the commercials he gets!"

There was nothing funny to other clubs about Cedeno's performance on the field in 1972. Cesar began to make some amazing catches in center field and he also tore up the base paths with 55 steals on the year. His impressive first half performance also earned Cedeno his first of four All-Star Game appearances and, on August 2, 1972, he became the first Astro to hit for the cycle as we crushed the Reds in Cincinnati, 10–1.

As the 1972 Astros went deeper into the color orange as their predominant visual signal to the rest of the baseball world, the nicknames "Orange Crush" and "Orange Crushers" began to find their ways into media stories about big offensive wins by the club. Even as we began to win with greater regularity, the club played loose, but hard, and there was a lot of humor and kidding that went on to keep everybody's feet in contact with the earth.

Even Harry Walker couldn't spoil it as, more and more, the club played ball around their manager as though he were the little loudmouth who wasn't there. As one of our club comedians and primary pranksters, Doug Rader also added some quirky spoken humor to his bag of tricks in 1972. When asked by a reporter for his advice to Little Leaguers, Rader offered this jewel of wisdom to the youth of America, and he did it with a serious straight face: "Eat bubble gum cards. Not the bubble gum, just the cards. They have lots of good information on them about hitting and pitching."

There were few jokers in the five-card hand of Houston's 1972 starting pitcher rotation. Old anchors Don Wilson (15–10, 2.68) and Larry Dierker (15–8, 3.40) continued to do their jobs better than most and they were ably aided by Jerry Reuss (9–13, 4.17), Dave Roberts (12–7, 4.50), and Ken Forsch (6–8, 3.91).

For quite a while, the club that ended up as the biggest run-producer in the league in 1972, the Houston Astros, also challenged for the pennant. Although we soon enough fell behind the Reds in the NL West, and stayed there, we did make a few other clubs nervous in the early going.

On May 10, 1972, in a game we won over Bob Gibson and the Cardinals at Busch Stadium in St. Louis by a 10–7 count, Lee May went four for five at the plate with his fifth home run of the season as young Roger Metzger even drove his first career homer off the great future Hall of Fame right-hander to help seal the deal. The victory pushed us into first place, if only for a day.

On June 18 and 19, Jerry Reuss and Larry Dierker showed how important pitching was to the new fire-breathing Astros. Reuss and Dierker teamed up to tie a major league record by pitching back-to-back 1-hit shutouts in the Astrodome against the visiting Phillies and Mets.

Reuss had been obtained in a trade with the St. Louis Cardinals on the first day of the 1972 season in exchange for Scipio Spinks and Lance Clemons. Pitcher Dave Roberts had been acquired from San Diego back on December 3, 1971, for three minor leaguers. Both had turned the Astros 1972 starting rotation into a force to be reckoned with in the National League West.

I was just happy to feel like my old self one more time and happy with just about everything else in 1972 too. I was finding the sunshine again.

A lot of people assumed, wrongly so, that I resented Cesar Cedeno for "taking my job" in center field. They were far off the mark with that idea, but you probably had to be walking around in my skin, going through what I had been going through, to really understand why Cedeno's success was no threat to me.

I've tried over the years to put it in other words, but allow me to use these here. It's like this: You see, Jimmy Wynn was never stopped by another player from being all he could be. Jimmy Wynn was only stopped temporarily by the pressures he put on himself through his own life choices. Once I figured that part out and began making the changes that transformed my life, everything started working out fine.

Not perfect, but humanly fine.

I never said I had to play center field. Remember? I came to the Astros as a shortstop. It was the club that put me in center field, once upon a time. Now they had somebody else in mind for that particular job, someone who was younger, faster, talented, and better suited for the future than me. I had no problem with that decision. I saw it coming as early as the first time I saw young Cesar Cedeno playing the outfield in late 1970.

I was good to go with my own aspirations and abilities at age 30. As long as my level of play was sharp enough to earn me a spot anywhere in the starting lineup, I could still be the best Jimmy Wynn I knew how to be, no matter where I played on the field.

What mattered to me in 1972 was simply that I was back. I was still the Toy Cannon. I could still fire at the opposition from any location on the diamond on defense with my still very strong arm. And on offense, it didn't matter where they played me in the field. On offense, we all fire from one or the other side of the same two left or right spots in the batter's box when we go up to hit. As hitters, it's what we do most often when it really counts that matters, and, in 1972, the Toy Cannon was back on track as a mattering hitter.

By the time we rang up our ninth win in a row on April 26 to run our season record to 9–2 with a 5–4 win over the Chicago Cubs in the Dome, I had slammed my third home run of the 1972 season. More than I can say now, that mattered to my confidence back then. When a player has a lost season, no matter what else he tells you later, believe me: He has to do it well again to know that he's really back.

I was back. And I was lucky to find it out early in the season.

In spite of our good team start for the Houston Astros, the 1972 season did not exactly start trouble-free in general. For the first time in history, the new Major League Baseball Players Union used a work stoppage against the owners to gain more money for the pension plan and to establish player rights to salary arbitration.

Right behind Curt Flood's legal fight for free agency, the first strong stand by the players' union really started the pendulum of total control by the owners moving in the opposite direction toward a greater balance of power in baseball between management and labor. Many would argue today that now the balance of power has shifted way too far to the labor side of things in organized baseball, but others whose bread is buttered by the players' union would argue the opposite.

It's still the same old struggle. The owners kept battling for control and the players keep fighting for freedom. The funny thing about it is that the owners also want freedom from the players and the players also want control of the owners. That contest will never improve in baseball unless we shall all, management and labor alike, really look for answers that serve the best interests of the game, even if both sides have to give up some freedom and control for the sake of what best serves the interests of the fans who support the game.

We don't have to look far to see how the short-sighted struggle for control and freedom between owners and players has hurt, and even come close to killing fan belief in the motives of professional baseball.

The 1972 work stoppage, as it was called, cost baseball every game on the schedule from April 1 to April 12, when a new collective bargaining agreement was reached between the owners and the union. After a lot of sweat and threat, the owners agreed to pay an additional $500,000 into the players' pension fund. The players' union agreed to forfeit player salaries for the games missed due to the strike, but they made this rather small concession in exchange for something far more powerful and far-reaching: The players' union gained the right to salary arbitration.

In the short term, both sides agreed to play out the 1972 season with the uneven schedule of unplayed games that remained for each team.

Wouldn't you know it? That short-range solution to the 1972 season would be the very thing that immediately came back to bite baseball, and smack dab in the deep down dimple of their American League East pennant race. Because the Detroit Tigers had a 156-game schedule facing them based on the strike solution, they used that extra game advantage to edge the Boston Red Sox and their 155-game schedule by a half game for the American League East first-place playoff spot. Detroit ended the season with an 86–70 record; Boston was stuck in second place with an 85–70 mark.

The work stoppage wiped out nine games at the start of the Houston Astros schedule, but we finished with our best record in history through that year. We finished the 1972 season with a record of 84–69, good enough for second place in the National League West, but still ten and one-half games behind the now-rolling "Big Red Machine," the Cincinnati Reds.

In case you've forgotten, the American League West Champion Oakland A's headed off having insult added to injury by defeating the half-game American League East Champion Detroit Tigers in the playoff series for the 1972 American League pennant. The A's then slammed the brakes on the National League Champion Cincinnati Reds in the World Series.

The 1972 season also brought home to roost one of baseball's favorite little ironies and placed it in the office of Harry Walker. In the three-plus years of his previous service as manager of the Astros (1968–1971), the best Harry had done was the 81–81 break-even season of 1969.

That's only fair. Nobody expected any manager, Harry Walker or anybody else, to pull out a miracle cure and lead the 1968 Astros to a championship anytime soon from that point in time. Now it was 1972. We were winning on the field and looking competitive, but the questions above Harry's head had shifted to "Why are we winning?" and "How much does Harry Walker have to do with it?"

Near the end of the season, General Manager Spec Richardson and, most probably, Judge Hofheinz decided that Harry Walker had to go as manager of the Houston Astros. In other words, Harry Walker's job was safe while we were losing, but now that we were winning, he was about to get fired.

How did this happen? I could be wrong, but these are my thoughts on why the Astros fired Harry Walker at a point late in the '72 season with the club riding home on a 67–54 record in the stretch:

1. By August 1972, Spec Richardson knew very well that the club's black players had no respect for Harry Walker and his racist attitudes;
2. Spec also knew by then that Harry Walker was terrible in general handling people and that several of his team talks had led to near riots in the clubhouse;
3. Spec and his management team also knew that the team was winning on their own and in spite of Harry Walker's presence at the helm;

4. The club needed an action that would further help take the fans' minds off the Morgan, Staub, and Cuellar trades as the reasons why the Astros still would not win a pennant in 1972;
5. Spec wanted a manager that could inspire hope and sell a few more tickets during the last dog days of another lost season;
6. And, finally, an available manager was out there and he was the kind of guy who could pump a gate with curiosity seekers in spite of the fact that the club wasn't going anywhere. Baseball is a little bit like the circus in that regard. If a show isn't good enough to attract customers to the Big Top, sometimes clubs do what they can to draw people to the freak show.

It all added up to the firing of Harry Walker as manager of the Houston Astros on August 25, 1972. Coach Salty Parker took over the interim helm for one winning game on August 26, 1972, and then the new man took over for the last game in a series we played against the Montreal Expos on August 27, 1972.

The new manager of the Houston Astros was a fellow named Leo Durocher, one of the fieriest, most colorful characters in baseball history. Ironically (and déjà vu all over again), Leo had only been out of work as a major league manager for about a month. On July 23, 1972, he had been fired as manager of the Chicago Cubs after dropping two straight games to the Astros here at the Dome. Now, here he was again on August 27, 1972, taking over the helm of the very club that helped separate him from his most recent job.

The hiring of Leo Durocher fooled nobody. Astro players and fans weren't stupid. Nobody I remember shed any tears over the departure of Harry Walker, but neither did we misunderstand the hiring of Leo Durocher. We knew it was a short-term publicity stunt pulled off by Spec Richardson because of Durocher's well-known name and his Hollywood celebrity personality.

No way did Spec Richardson fire Harry Walker to save his players. He fired Harry Walker to help save himself from criticism for his own other bad moves. The hiring of Leo Durocher provided Spec with something he hoped would be both an attraction to the gate and a distraction from the truth about what was wrong with the Astros!

Gee-Ma-Nee Crickets! Leo Durocher? In Houston? That managerial fit seemed about as out of whack as the Houston Symphony hiring Spike Jones as their conductor. I'm sorry if you're too young to recall Spikes Jones. In case you are, try this one on: Hiring Leo Durocher in Houston was about like hiring Snoop Dogg as director of the Mormon Tabernacle Choir!

Besides, the guy was exactly 67 years and 1 month old on the day he first took the field as our new manager. How much future could he possibly have had left in either his baseball or lifespan tanks?

Leo Durocher is famous for the quote: "Nice guys finish last." He didn't actually say it that way, but he said something close enough to it and that's the way a New York writer wrote it down. We could spend hours on that subject, but that would be a long and winding distraction here. Suffice to say, for now, players have to learn that there are just some writers out there who are going to write whatever they think best stirs the pot of controversy and sells newspapers.

It's 2010 as I write these words. With the way television and the Internet are coming together, maybe we won't have to worry about getting misquoted in newspapers for very much longer. We'll just have to deal with the Internet, where nobody writes anything unless they know it's the absolute truth.

Right? Yeah, right.

Anyway, the subject here is Leo Durocher.

Leo had been a pretty fair defensive shortstop in his day, a fairly typical "good field/no hit" guy, except that he supposedly played the game like a fire-breathing dragon. I can't swear to the accuracy of those accounts because his playing days came and went long before my time. I'm just giving you information here that you may already know or could just as easily look up as background for what was left of the man by the time he took over as manager of the Astros.

Leo broke into the major leagues with the New York Yankees in the late 1920s. The Yankees dealt him to the Reds in 1930; the Reds dealt him to the Cardinals in 1933. He reached St. Louis just in time to anchor shortstop for the famous "Gas House Gang" club that took the 1934 World Series in seven games from the Detroit Tigers. At St. Louis, Leo had rubbed noses and shoulders with one of the fieriest playing managers of all time, Hall of Fame second baseman Frankie Frisch. At the same time, he also came under the influence of one of baseball's greatest minds, Cardinals General Manager, and another future Hall of Famer, Branch Rickey.

The Cardinals traded Leo to the Brooklyn Dodgers in 1938. The very next year, Brooklyn General Manager Larry MacPhail installed him as playing manager of the Dodgers, where he remained, even after Branch Rickey came over from the Cardinals to take the Brooklyn GM post in 1943. Leo stayed with Brooklyn until he was removed, shortly into the 1948 season. Days after his termination with the Dodgers, Leo Durocher resurfaced across the East River in upper Manhattan as manager of the hated arch-rival New York Giants.

Taking the Giants job proved itself as a typical Leo move. If you hurt Leo in any public form, he would look for a way to get revenge. The Giants just opened the door for Leo on that one. Nothing spelled revenge against Brooklyn quite like throwing himself into the fray as the new brains behind the evil enemy Giants. Nothing, that is, until October 3, 1951, when the Leo-led Giants came from way behind late in the season to force a three-game pennant playoff series with the Brooklyn Dodgers and set up Bobby Thomson's "Shot Heard Round The World" that won the deciding Game Three by 5–4 in the bottom of the ninth inning.

When Giants radio man Russ Hodges shouted forth his now famously loud and repeated call that the "THE GIANTS WIN THE PENNANT!," he may as well have been screaming, "LEO GETS REVENGE! LEO GETS REVENGE!"

Leo and his New York Giants would lose the 1951 World Series to the New York Yankees, but they would come right back and sweep the vaunted Cleveland Indians, 4 games to 0, in the 1954 Fall Classic. That 1954 World Series was the one in which Willie Mays made "The Catch" off that long drive to center field in the Polo Grounds by Vic Wertz.

While Leo was managing the Brooklyn Dodgers, he led his 1941 club in a losing effort against the Yankees in the World Series. He was slated for a big historical moment as Jackie Robinson's first big league manager in 1947, but that opportunity died when Commissioner Happy Chandler suspended Leo from baseball for a whole year for consorting in the company of known mobsters and gamblers. The stench and scandal of the suspension was the last straw for Rickey. It led to Leo's firing by the Dodgers and his quick move to the Giants in 1948.

Leo left the New York Giants after the 1955 season. He spent the next few years hobnobbing with celebrities away from any big part in the game.

In 1966, Leo was hired to manage the Chicago Cubs. It was a decision that led Leo straight back to the land of controversy as his 1969 Cubs became famous for choking up a big lead that led to the first National League pennant for the "Amazin'" New York Mets. To throw in another reverse twist, the Mets were then managed in 1969 by Gil Hodges, one of the great Brooklyn Dodger stars that Leo had abandoned when he threw in with the Giants back in 1948.

Wherever Leo went, controversy and questions about his personal integrity followed like fresh water seeking the ocean. Sometimes he seemed to also carry a little magical dust for creating special moments in baseball history. Just as often, the winds of fickle fate seemed to blow that dust back into the faces of Leo and everyone else around him, creating some uncomfortable and embarrassing sneezes.

What were the Houston Astros going to get from their new, but not-so-young celebrity manager? The real test didn't come until 1973, but it didn't take long to harvest the preliminary results.

When Leo showed up and took over, he didn't disappoint. Allow me to rephrase that comment: Leo didn't disappoint his commitment to trendy style of dress and image. Always known as a snappy dresser, Leo had adjusted over the years. He was a master at trying to look younger, sexy, and stylish. He just seemed to have no idea how obvious his moves were to the rest of us.

Leo showed up on his first day wearing some nicely tailored and crisply unwrinkled dark pants and a light beige jacket. He wore a bright flowery red, *unbuttoned-at-the-top* sport shirt under his coat so that his hairy chest could be immediately revealed as the center of attention for one and all. When he finally sat down to talk with us, Leo made sure to cross his legs in a manly way so that we all could see that he was wearing a beautiful pair of Florsheim loafers, with no socks, as was the style among younger men back in that era.

Leo Durocher was no Harry Walker on the personality side of things, and he was Northeast, as opposed to Deep South, when it came to racial issues, but he offered his own brand of arrogance free of charge. If you listened to Leo long enough at face value, you might get the idea that Willie Mays never could have made it in the big leagues without Durocher's special guidance.

Maybe Willie Mays gives Leo all the credit too. I can't say for sure. I just know that it sounded very much like a self-serving, self-adoring brag when you heard Leo talk about it. As an old center fielder myself, I also knew darn well that Willie Mays did a lot of things out there on the field that no bowlegged blowhard from the Commonwealth of Massachusetts ever taught him to do.

We went 16–15 over the last month of the '72 season with Leo. We were pretty much running on autopilot and likely to have finished the season in about the same manner, regardless of who was "managing" us over the last four weeks.

About the only detailed thing we learned for sure in that last brief stretch was how to play cards with Leo. What we should have learned, and I'm especially talking about me now, was how *not* to play cards with Leo!

I lost what amounted to a ton of money for me, just playing poker with Leo Durocher over that last month of 1972 and all of 1973. I should have learned to trust my gut feeling that he was cheating and just bailed out on trying to bet back to even by continuing to play.

Among many other things, Leo Durocher was a card shark who didn't mind serving as a predator on the pocketbooks of his own players. Leo was really good at it too. He knew how to bait the hook on "Here's your chance to win it all back, Jimmy" faster than anybody I had ever met.

Ripping suckers off in a card game came as natural to Leo Durocher as catching a long fly ball or hitting a monster long home run did to either Willie Mays or me. When it came to winning at cards, Leo Durocher was like Robert Redford in that movie, *The Natural*. The difference was simple. When Redford hit the big one as Roy Hobbs, it was lights out, sparks flying, and everybody got to celebrate. When Leo won the big card game, sparks just flew because Leo had turned out the lights on everybody else—and he was the only one left standing with anything to celebrate.

I was happy to see the '72 season end. I was happy we had done so much better as a team; happy that we had been freed from Harry Walker; happy that I had recovered my offensive touch; happy with the fact that I now had a different-feeling marriage going in my life; and OK with the fact that I knew Leo Durocher was coming back as our manager in 1973.

Based upon my experience through this point in my career, I had just about given up on the idea of again having a manager who could actually do anything to help me improve my abilities. I was willing to learn. I just hadn't met anyone since Grady Hatton who was willing to teach. Walker and Durocher just wanted to ego trip in their own separate ways. With Leo, at least, all you had to do was learn to stay clear of his poker games.

That being said, 1973 did not work out as well for the Astros, for Leo, or for me as we had all hoped. Leo was the first to have his cage rattled too.

After a fairly uneventful spring training period in Cocoa Beach, Florida, we got off to a mediocre 5–7 start. Sad to say, but being honest as I know how to be, the Astros still measured progress by the achievement of mediocrity back in 1973. As a result of that mindset, our record the first few games looked acceptable to a lot of our people. I didn't like it at all, and I wasn't alone in my unhappiness over the organization's level of comfort with just playing closer to .500 level ball in the early going.

It was April 17. We were in Los Angeles for the middle contest of a three-game series against the Dodgers. We had just taken a 7–2 drubbing at the hands of the Dodgers, a game in which starter Don Wilson had taken a beating for all 7 runs and 10 hits over six innings before Leo pulled him in favor of Fred Gladding over the seventh and eighth.

We were piling into the team bus to go back to the hotel as other players continued to walk out of the stadium singly and in small groups. I took a seat on the aisle, about midway back on the bus, as I recall, and very near our wonderful radio announcer, Gene Elston. Gene heard the whole thing I'm about to tell you, too. Those of us who witnessed what I'm going to describe here will never forget it, but you really had to be close enough to the front of the bus to know the whole story, first-hand, from quiet start to loud middle to whispering finish. Leo had taken his manager's seat in the far left side front row, right behind the bus driver. From that place, Leo was in position to speak directly to anyone getting on the bus.

"Uh, oh," I thought to myself. "Here comes Don [Wilson]! I've seen that look before and is he ever pissed. I hope nobody says anything to him." Then I looked over at Leo as Don put his foot on the first step of the bus door. It was almost like watching a bomb that's about to go off, but knowing there's nothing you can do about it.

"Hello, Wilson!" Leo said in a flat and unfriendly way.

"Shut up, [and here Don used the same maternal insult word that he used on me that night he dangled me by the ankles from the New York hotel window]!" As soon as he spoke to Leo, Don headed directly to the back of the bus.

Leo was stunned. He looked back at the still-moving-away Wilson and then across the aisle to Grady Hatton, who was now one of his coaches in 1973. For the longest time, Leo said nothing and there was a hush that rippled from the middle to the front of the bus, roughly covering all who heard what Don Wilson had just said to Leo Durocher.

We hadn't heard anything like this from Wilson since, well, since the last time we had a different manager of the Houston Astros. Nobody ever blamed Harry Walker for the mouth of Don Wilson or for the violent ways he sometimes reacted to the world around him.

It seemed clear to me that Leo was both stunned, and maybe also a little fearful about what to do next. His ego told him that he had to do something. Too many of us had heard the Wilson show of disrespect for Leo to let it pass, but he really didn't want to deal with it either.

Leo decided to play dumb.

Looking again across the aisle to Grady Hatton, Leo quietly asked in a tone of dumbfounded innocence: "What did he just say to me?"

Grady Hatton gave it right back to Leo. Throwing his open hands up in the air, as if to say, "Don't look at me. I didn't hear him." Grady threw in the extra touch of a stupefied face and just smiled.

"What do you do now, Leo?" I wondered.

Leo just stared to the back in silence for a few more minutes.

"I guess I'd better go ask him," Leo finally offered to all of us in general and to no one in particular.

"Uh, oh," I thought again. "This should be good."

With Joe Morgan no longer around, no one had been selected as the new Chief of the Don Wilson Homicide Prevention Squad. Maybe we should've warned Leo that Don Wilson doesn't need a full moon to turn into the Wolf Man. He just needs a manager to rub him the wrong way at the wrong time.

I craned to the left as Leo passed, just to have a better view of the next act.

By the time Leo reached Wilson in his seat, Don was already busy talking and joking with some of the guys around him, apparently on his way to mellowing out. A hornet's nest can look pretty peaceful too.

Out of the blue, and with his hands braced on the seats on either side of him in the aisle, Leo spoke: "Wilson, what was that you said to me when you got on the bus a few minutes ago?"

Leo had his back to me now as he spoke to Don. As soon as he established that position as my view of things, I watched the much taller figure of Don Wilson rising to face him, but standing high enough to even look me in the eye as he very deliberately and very loudly answered Leo's question:

"I said to you, 'SHUT UP, [here's that mother insult word again]!' Did you hear me that time?"

A brief scuffle followed that amounted mostly to players jamming the space between the two men and preventing the fight that neither wanted. Don didn't really want to kill Leo, and Leo really didn't want to get killed. He had saved his honor by going back there, but now there was the unsettled account of what to do about the inescapable fact that Don Wilson had shown him up to everybody on the bus.

Leo sometimes took his revenge quietly. Once he returned to his seat, he spoke to Grady Hatton again in a hushed voice that those of us nearby, but not Don Wilson, could hear: "Fine that man $500.00!"

As far as I know, that was the last of it between Leo and Don Wilson. Leo was no fool. He gave Don a wider berth in the future. Anybody with any common sense soon enough learned to handle Don Wilson during his bad mood times as though he were a six-foot bottle of nitro, all decked out in an Astros uniform.

As a team, the 1973 Astros held their own in the region of mediocrity. We fell back to a near split over the full season, but our 82–80 record was strongly affected by the effective loss of Larry Dierker for most of the season with the sore arm problem that would soon cut his career short. Tom Griffin also had an arm problem that limited his availability and effectiveness.

J.R. Richard and Ken Forsch both filled in to help offset the losses of Dierker and Griffin. I didn't play much with J.R., but anyone could see that he had future greatness written all over him. On August 1, I entered a game as a pinch runner and stayed in to play center field, hit a double, and score two runs in J.R.'s first career shutout, a 3–0 win over the Dodgers at the Dome. Richard gave up only five hits in that game, while walking two and striking out nine. J.R. would finish with a 6–2 record in 1973 while posting an ERA of 4.00 and, foretelling the future, striking out 75 batters in his 73 innings of work.

Jerry Reuss (16–13, 3.74) and Dave Roberts (17–11, 2.85) were the anchors of our '73 rotation, with Don Wilson (11–16, 3.20) catching few of the breaks on wins that rolled his partners' ways. Ken Forsch (9–12, 4.20) and Tom Griffin (4–6, 4.15) handled most of the other starts.

Cesar Cedeno continued to soar in 1973, hitting .320 with 25 homers, 70 RBI, and a club record 56 stolen bases. Bob Watson checked in with a .312 batting mark, 16 home runs, and 94 RBI, and Lee May reigned again as the Big Bopper, bashing 28 home runs, 105 RBI, and a .270 batting average. Doug Rader chipped in another 21 HR and 89 RBI, as his BA hovered at .254. My 1973 marks disappointed me. I had 20 homers and 55 RBI, but my batting average slumped all year, settling finally at the .220 spot, too close to Mendoza and too far away from where I wanted to be—and knew I could be.

I had no excuses or explanations. I just wasn't where I wanted or needed to be at this point in my career and, on the team side, it wasn't really clear to any of us where the franchise was going. We had built the kind of team that was capable of breaking .500 almost any time now, but we still seemed to lack that something special that all winners possess.

If it was leadership we needed, we weren't getting that from the top; we weren't getting it from ourselves; and we sure as heck weren't getting it from Leo.

As the year wore on, Leo seemed to be increasing the "lippy" flow of his complaints about the selfishness and self-centeredness of the modern ballplayer. We had to quietly laugh. Leo griping about the self-centeredness of others was right in there with some of the biggest jokes in the world. What it really said was that Leo was getting too old and set in his ways to adjust to the modern ballplayer culture. We didn't realize it during the season, but Leo was moving toward a decision of his own.

Leo's unhappiness with the modern ballplayer may have anchored in that big unpleasant confrontation he had early in the season with Don Wilson, but he also took ill during the year with some kind of age-related issue. It all added up for Leo as a sign that it was time for him to retire.

September 30, 1973, would turn out to be Leo Durocher's last official day in baseball. It happened in Atlanta and the stands were packed that final day of the season. The fans, however, had not come to Atlanta to see Leo Durocher in his last managerial hurrah for the Houston Astros. The crowd of 40,517 fans, which included Georgia Governor Jimmy Carter, had come to see if Atlanta's own Henry "Hammerin' Hank" Aaron could send the Braves happily into the off-season by breaking Babe Ruth's career home run record. Hank Aaron had tied Ruth at 714 home runs the night before with a home run off our Jerry Reuss.

The Atlanta and Aaron fans went home disappointed. Our Dave Roberts held Aaron to three singles, putting off his magic moment to a special night in April 1974.

I would be there, again as part of the opposition, when Hank Aaron finally did break Babe Ruth's career home run mark the next spring. I just wouldn't be playing ball for the Houston Astros.

As we closed the door on the 1973 season, my career went rocketing in a brand new direction—and it was to a place far west of Houston, but still very much a big part of the National League galaxy.

I was about to have some baseball experiences that brought me back to life and carried me forth to some baseball accomplishments that most likely would never have happened, had I remained in Houston.

Yes indeed. The Lord does move in some mighty mysterious ways.

CHAPTER 13

Born Again in Dodger Blue!

The fall of 1973 began uneventfully, with nothing out of the ordinary. I had some time for family and we took a few vacation trips to relax and unwind from baseball. I had no idea that anything like a trade was in the works, but I wasn't surprised when I got a call from Astros General Manager Spec Richardson about four days prior to Thanksgiving Day. He had called to tell me that both the Dodgers and Cubs were interested in me. Spec wanted to know how I felt about a trade in general and about those two clubs in particular.

I thanked Spec for calling to ask me about these possibilities, but we both knew that he really had no choice. As I was a 10/5 man (ten years in the majors and five with my present club), the Astros needed my approval on any trade they made. If a 10/5 man rejects the idea of a trade out of hand, the club is left with only two choices: (1) keep the player; or (2) release the player and lose the right to compensation that only a trade or sale could bring.

The more that Spec and I talked, the more I realized that he and I were just hashing over a club move that probably had been a long time coming. For the past three seasons, things had not been right for me in Houston. Oh, sure, I had rallied for a little bump-stat production in 1972, but that quickly had washed away this past 1973 season when my numbers fell again.

Funny thing is, and I don't mean "funny" in the happy sense of the word, I mean "the funny thing is," I could hear the booing of the Houston fans for me from this past season replaying, even as I talked to Spec over the phone. The fans were ready for me to go and, hard as it was to admit, I was ready to go too. You can't play this game just to be loved by the fans, but I don't mind telling you, for a guy who feels as deeply as I do about everything in life, that booing by many of the Houston fans in 1971–73 really hurt bad.

I don't blame the fans who did boo. For the two book-end years of those three seasons, I flat-out deserved it. I wasn't hitting home runs at the old rate; I wasn't knocking in runs; and I wasn't hitting for average. On the other hand, I am also grateful to those other loyal fans who simply allowed me to pass through my personal valley of hard times without booing. I didn't need the extra volume on the boo meter to get the picture that the fans were unhappy with me. It was time for me to go.

Spec was just doing his job by looking to deal me. The Astros already had Cesar Cedeno on deck and they also had some other talented young outfielders like Greg Gross in the pipeline. It was time to move the veteran Jimmy Wynn someplace else while he still had some trade value. You hate to feel like a side of going-out-of-date beef in a butcher shop at times like this, but when you're a veteran player on the trading block, that's pretty much how it feels.

Spec asked if I had a preference for either the Dodgers or Cubs. He was going to do all he could to make this the best deal for me too. I appreciated his efforts. And again, I also knew that Spec didn't want to come up with a deal that I might veto.

Jimmy Wynn bled "Dodger Blue" in 1974 and 1975. His 32 homers led the Los Angeles Dodgers to the National League Pennant in 1974 (National Baseball Hall of Fame Library, Cooperstown, NY).

The choice for me was a pick between two of baseball's storied franchises and two of the country's major cities. I had no problem either way with the idea of the two organizations or the two cities. Chicago and Los Angeles were both cities I enjoyed.

The difference-maker for me came down to the two separate potentials. In Chicago, my chances of hitting more home runs went way up playing at Wrigley Field, but I would also be playing for a club that probably wasn't going to win the pennant anytime soon. At least, that's what Cubs history told us back then.

Dodger Stadium in Los Angeles, on the other hand, was a much tougher home run park, no better than the Astrodome, but I would be playing for a club that had a real good chance of reaching the World Series.

So, I had to ask myself: What's really most important to me? Playing for the losing Cubs in Wrigley Field, where I had a real good shot of pushing my career home run total over 300? Or playing for the Dodgers in another park where home runs go to die as long fly-ball outs, but for a team that had a shot at winning it all?

I chose the team potential of Los Angeles over the individual potential that awaited me in Chicago. When Spec came up with a deal that made sense to him for the Astros and Dodgers, I said, "Go for it, Spec, it makes sense to me too."

On December 6, 1973, the Houston Astros traded my contract to the Los Angeles Dodgers in exchange for the contracts of left-handed starting pitcher Claude Osteen and minor league pitcher Dave Culpepper. The Astros had traded starting pitcher Jerry Reuss to Pittsburgh on Halloween in exchange for catcher Milt May and they were looking for another lefty to take his spot in the rotation.

Maybe all position players feel this way about being traded for a couple of pitchers, especially when one them is only a prospect, but I felt the Astros could have gotten more for me. After all, outfielders play every day. Starting pitchers only work one day in five.

Oh, well, that was a lot of water-over-the-bridge time ago, and I feel certain that someone like my former teammate Larry Dierker might have a real different take on the straight-up trade value of Jimmy Wynn for Claude Osteen in 1973. I wasn't Babe Ruth back then, but neither was Claude Osteen anywhere close to being a Sandy Koufax either.

It was what it was, at any rate, and I was gone from Houston for only my second stop in the major leagues. At least, I was still in the National League, where I knew the pitchers and the tendencies of the other players. I was just trading Astro Orange for Dodger Blue.

As much as possible, I tried to make myself believe that it was time to go and that my life in Houston was done and finished forever. Orange to Blue was a good enough way to summarize the change without stirring up a lot of emotions during the Christmas season of 1973. How different could life in Los Angeles really be? After all, it doesn't snow there during the holidays either.

When I went to spring training in 1974 at the Dodger compound in Vero Beach, Florida, before I even personally met any of the players, I right away ran into and met outside with two of the greatest owners in baseball—other than Roy Hofheinz, that is—Walter O'Malley and his son, Peter O'Malley.

The O'Malleys made their interest in me very clear from the start.

"We got you for one reason, Jimmy, and that reason is to be a leader in helping this young ball club win a National League pennant and go to the World Series," Walter O'Malley said. "We came close last year, but we haven't won a pennant or a World Series since 1966. In the Dodger organization, eight years is far too long a victory drought.

"Look," O'Malley continued, "we know what you can do as a player. We know you can hit home runs; we know you can play center field; and we know you have the speed and smarts to steal bases, but those are not the things that matter most here. I don't care if you only hit ten home runs and drive in only fifty runs. What we need here is a leader."

I smiled. And I looked the elder O'Malley straight in the eye.

"Mr. O'Malley, in all due respects," I said, "if I only hit ten homers and drive in fifty runs, no matter what the club does, I'll be gone at the end of the year!"

Walter O'Malley sort of chuckled.

"Sorry I said that, Jimmy!" he amended. "I didn't really mean it. Of course, your personal production is important. I was just overstating the point on your personal numbers to help get across the fact that our big need for you on the morale side is not just talk. We need you to be the veteran leader of this team. The absence of a team leader last year, we've decided, was the difference that allowed the Reds to beat us out in the NL West and then go on to take the NL pennant. Now, what we need to know is, can we count on you?"

Again I made eye contact, and this time with Peter O'Malley first before turning back to his father in steady brief silence.

"Mr. O'Malley," I said to the elder man, "we *will* win the National League pennant in 1974!"

I almost immediately couldn't believe that I said what I had just said. Both of the O'Malleys looked back at me with expressions I can only describe today as stunned appreciation for my words of confidence.

They both reached out to shake my hand as Walter O'Malley added, "Of course, Jimmy, you know we're going to hold you to your word now, don't you?"

I just smiled broadly and continued shaking hands. By the time I walked away from the spot of our conversation near one of the practice fields to my bungalow, I was shaking all over, from my head to my toes.

"What did you just say out there, Jimmy?" I asked myself as I took a long look in the bathroom mirror. "Are you crazy or what? Now I've not only got to deal with proving myself to my new club, I also have to live up to my word to the owners of the club that I will do something that I've never done before, and that is to lead any team to a National League pennant!

"Thank you! Thank you! Thank you! Open mouth! Increase pressure!"

Fortunately for me, I picked a great moment to so publicly place myself on the line. Three years prior to the release of the first *Star Wars* movie in 1977, the Force was about to be with me. My light saber of choice in 1974 was going to be a 31-ounce Louisville Slugger bat.

Seriously, the real energy laser that I found in Vero Beach was all wrapped up and oozing from the souls of Dodger people themselves. From the O'Malleys through Manager Walt Alston to the players, and extending out to the coaches, trainers, and other support personnel, the blanket attitude that "we are all in this together" just rolled over me like a Dodger-Blue tide.

On my very first day in the spring training facility clubhouse, Dodger players Davy Lopes, Bill Russell, Ron Cey, Joe Ferguson, and Steve Yeager all came over to welcome me in the first five minutes. Their message was unanimous: "Welcome to the Dodger organization. We are looking forward to working with you. And here is what we want you to do for us: help us; guide us; do whatever you need to do to make us a good ball club so that we can go to the World Series."

Had the players also been talking with the O'Malleys recently? This team dedication to the ideas of leadership and winning rose above the more common talk of individual goals I was more used to hearing from a lot of the ballplayers in Houston. It felt good for a change to hear players talking about their shared goal of winning the pennant. It also made me glad that I had put myself on the line with the O'Malleys, although I was just as fine with the idea of not spreading my promise to anyone else in the Dodger organization.

Not long after I met my first welcome wagon of new teammates, Dodger Manager Walter Alston slipped quietly into the clubhouse, already dressed for our work in the field on this first day. He gave me a little hand motion that said, "Let's go talk." My directions were obvious. I followed Mr. Alston to his office.

Unlike any of my previous major league managers, I was immediately at ease with the laid-back, quiet-spoken field leader of my new club. I also went into my first meeting with my new boss well aware of what he had accomplished for the Dodgers, both in Brooklyn prior to 1958 and in Los Angeles ever since.

The 1974 season was to be Alston's twenty-first year as the Dodger manager. One season after his 1954 rookie manager year, Walter Alston had led the Brooklyn Dodgers to their only World Series victory in history.

The Brooklyn Dodgers won a second National League pennant under Walt in 1956, but this time they lost the World Series to the same arch-rival American League team they had defeated a year earlier, the dreaded New York Yankees.

After moving to southern California in 1958, Walter Alston took the Los Angeles Dodgers back to the World Series for victories in 1959, 1963, and 1965, before finally losing as a west coast Dodger club to the 1966 Baltimore Orioles. After twenty years as Dodger manager, six National League pennants and four World Series victories through 1973, what else did the man have to say?

Walter Alston must have been doing a lot of things right over time to get that much done. Now, as I sat down with the man for the first time as one of his new players, my already existing respect for Walter Alston just spread though my veins like some strange gift of new life to Jimmy Wynn the ballplayer.

"Jimmy," Walter said in his droll way, "I know you've been wearing uniform number 24 for quite a few years in Houston, but you do understand who holds the clear claim on that number here on the Dodger club, don't you?"

I nodded agreeably. Everyone knew that the Dodger skipper wore number 24 in this house. I was just trying to communicate in my own way, without words, that I was cool with wearing whatever one- or two-digit number the Dodgers chose to give me.

"I want you to be as close to number 24 as you can be, Jimmy," Walt added. "I'm assigning you to uniform number 23."

"Thank you, Mr. Alston," I said.

"It's Walt," he answered, with a firm handshake and a broad smile.

Maybe I read more into it than Walt Alston intended, but I sort of took that close number assignment of my 23 to his 24 as just another, more subtle message that my own manager also wanted me to step up strong and be a club leader on the Dodger team.

No harm done. A good team leader only helps a good manager get his job done. Only an insecure, power-driven, control freak manager would be afraid of a team leader, and that wasn't Walt Alston. He was as about as secure in his own skin as any man I've ever met.

As for the Dodger starting lineup itself, I couldn't wait for the season to begin. We had Steve Yeager and Joe Ferguson at catcher, Steve Garvey at first base, Davy Lopes at second base, Ron Cey at third base, and Bill Russell at shortstop. No other club in the big leagues had that kind of quality infield playing together for as long as the Dodgers had these guys with them in L.A. The four infield spots were about as well-manned and as set as they could be.

Bill Buckner was our left fielder; I was back in center field again; and Willie Crawford platooned with catcher Joe Ferguson and others in right field. We also had the versatile Von Joshua as another outfielder.

The pitching staff was anything but shabby. We had future Hall of Famer Don Sutton, Andy Messersmith, Doug Rau, Al Downing, Charlie Hough, Tommy John, and the great reliever, Mike Marshall. Yes, that was the same Mike Marshall the Astros once tossed away in a bag-of-balls deal.

Walt Alston began spring training camp like no manager I'd ever known in Houston. He just got up there and basically said, "Most of you men know what I expect of you. The rest of you new guys will figure it out soon enough by paying close attention. Now let's get out there and get it done."

Walt Alston only had one rule about spring training practices, and it applied to one and all, from future Hall of Famers to new guys coming over to the club in trades, as well as to wet-behind-the-ears rookies: At the end of every practice, all players had to run, jog, walk, or crawl a mile before hitting the showers. It didn't matter to Alston how they did it, as long as they did it.

With the Dodgers, the players who got the job done best right now got to play. On the Dodgers, people didn't start on the basis of their past reputations or their future promises. You either got it done now or you didn't play.

Having said that, look at the history that some of these guys had for playing together as a team. That Dodger infield wasn't out there year-in, year-out, as a social club. Those guys were out there together all those years because nobody else came along who could do the job better.

The length of time in seasons that the four famous Dodger infielders played together productively is simply the strongest testimony of how seriously the Dodger players took the "I'm leaving it up to you guys to show me" message of their longtime manager Walt Alston to heart.

It's too bad that Bill Buckner will always be remembered by most fans as the guy who let the ball roll between his legs during the 1986 World Series when he was playing first base for the Boston Red Sox, but that's baseball, and that's how fans are going to be. A lot people even think that was the play that ended the World Series and gave the game to the Mets. It wasn't. It was only the end of Game Six. The Red Sox could've won it all in Game Seven, but they did not, and it was through no fault of Bill Buckner. Unfortunately, what happens in baseball a lot of times, and in everyday life too, is that people only remember things the way they want to remember them, and they refuse to let contrary facts get in the way.

A big fact about Bill Buckner is that he had an injury prior to being put in the big game back in 1986 that made it hard for him to flexibly bend over and go get a ground ball, but he also happened to be the kind of ballclub-minded guy who was going to give any playing opportunity his best shot without complaint. That was his work ethic during our time as teammates too. Nobody gave it more effort without lodging a complaint than Buckner. Twelve years after we became Dodger teammates, it cost Bill Buckner big time for being the all-out effort guy he naturally was.

A bright early spot for me was meeting Tommy Lasorda. Tommy was the third base coach for Alston when I joined the team, but he was well on his Dodger Blue way to taking over the helm of the team after I left the club in 1976.

Tommy was an outgoing, happy-go-lucky guy who really did bleed Dodger Blue. He never worked for another club, either before or after I met him, and he would take on Walt Alston-like status over his own time as field manager of the Dodgers, even as he varied from Alston in personality and style in just about every way you may imagine.

Whereas Alston was tall, quiet, and serious, Lasorda was short, loud, and comical. Tommy wanted his players to relax. He would tell you whatever he felt might help you play loose and alert.

In the spring of 1974, the Los Angeles Dodgers seemed primed for a big year. I sure hoped we were. I had come into the House of Dodger Blue as a veteran newcomer, and I had made some pretty big promises to the owners. A pennant wasn't really something I could deliver on my own, obviously, but I was dedicated to the goal of becoming the leader the O'Malleys, Walt Alston, and my teammates had asked me to be. To my way of thinking, leading meant setting an example by the way I played the game itself. All I had to do was play the game the way my dad always taught me to play.

The magic started on Opening Day at Dodger Stadium against the San Diego Padres. We won, 8–0, as I went three for five with two runs scored and three runs batted in. I also slammed my first home run as a Dodger. It came off Mike Corkins, with one on and nobody out in the bottom of the sixth. I was flying hard and low as I rounded third base for the best smile and handshake I ever received from a third base coach, from the man who forever bleeds Dodger Blue, the one and only Tommy Lasorda.

Put that home run in the glad bag of other goodies that came with my first game in Los Angeles and I felt anointed for a season ticket on Cloud Number Nine!

Before my first Dodger game, I had met and shaken hands with Jack Benny and Milton Berle, two of the greatest radio and television comedians of all time. I also had been given a roaring welcome by the fans upon my introduction to the Opening Day crowd.

Now came the icing on the cake, a home run that helped my new team win in their very first rattle out of the 1974 schedule box! How good and sweet could things possibly get? As I was about to learn, the answer was a whole lot better, sweeter, and faster than I ever could have imagined possible.

We swept the Padres in our opening three-game series at home and I homered once in each of my first three appearances as the starting center fielder for the Los Angeles Dodgers. Sometimes in the outfield during that first series, I would even sneak a look down at my uniform jersey chest, just to see that name "Dodgers" scrolling in deep royal blue script across me, Jimmy Wynn.

How many men in baseball history have homered in their first three games with the Dodgers, or any other club, for that matter? I didn't know the answer to that question then and I still don't know. I just know that those first three homers for Los Angeles have a very special place in my memories among the 291 long balls I hit in my career that I do remember. And I sure don't remember them all.

That third home run in Game Three off Vicente Romo had me wondering about how long this string could possibly last. Even Babe Ruth never came close to hitting one in every game of the season. Well, I got my answer soon enough. Right after our third game sweep of the Padres, we flew to Atlanta that same night for a four-game series with the Braves, starting the very next day.

No homers in Game Four of the 1974 season!

I went one for four with two more runs batted in against Atlanta on April 9th, but with no homers in a 7–4 first team loss of the season. We won the next two from the Braves to up our record to 5 and 1 on the year. I was still looking for my fourth homer after six games, but I had managed to string together another streak of having tallied at least one run batted in for each of our first six games.

In fact, and I mean this far more humbly than it may sound to those of you who really don't know me, my numbers over those first six games had sounded the trumpet! Jimmy Wynn was back as himself in 1974 and ready to play some serious baseball. I had collected nine hits in twenty-two trips for a .409 batting average. Throw in the other inflated figures of seven runs scored, twelve runs batted in, and three home runs and I was quite happy to have been a part of a very hot Dodger start.

If this was leadership, this was fun!

After splitting the four-game series in Atlanta, we flew to Houston for our first meeting of the new season with my old club, the Astros, and wouldn't you know it? The Astros cooled me down, and they did it with the very guy they gave me up to acquire. I went nothing for four as former Dodger Claude Osteen went seven and one-third innings to beat us, 5–3. We took the series from the Astros by winning the next two games to extend our record over the first ten games to seven wins and three losses.

I hit my first enemy homer against the Houston Astros on April 14, 1974. It came off a reliever named Fred Scherman. I'd like to tell you that I did the job batting against either Larry Dierker or Don Wilson, but their abilities and baseball luck got in the way of my wishes. That's OK. What really mattered to me was the fact that my new club, the Dodgers, was off to a great start on the promise that I had made to the O'Malleys.

Through ten games, I was hitting .305 (11 for 36) with eleven runs scored, thirteen runs batted in, and four home runs. I was starting to get the hang of what Tommy Lasorda meant when he said that he "bled Dodger Blue."

Lasorda's love and enthusiasm for the Dodgers was infectious, but it wasn't as though he went around putting pressure on the players. As Alston's right-hand man, Tommy just had a knack for helping people take pressure off themselves so they could play their best game at crunch time. He was such an upbeat, constant talker that he always seemed to find something to hash around that distracted or amused people and took them away from the worries that got in the way of their best games. When he took over from Alston as manager of the Dodgers during the 1976 season, I was gone by then, but the Dodgers hardly missed a beat. By 1977–78, Tommy had the club back in the World Series for each of the first two full years of his new administration. In 1974, I was just glad that we had him as a coach. He was that good and that important to our team attitude about winning.

All of the early '74 winning played into a code that is probably stronger in "Hollywoodland" than it is anyplace else. With most of the movie and television industries centered there, Los Angeles is a place that plays the celebrity game better than most and, as part of the entertainment business, professional sports teams have a straight shot into the same spotlight. All one has to do in L.A. to find celebrity is either be a winner or do something outrageous.

The Dodgers weren't outrageous, but we were winners, and I was getting a lot of credit as the missing ingredient who had brought winning back to Dodger Stadium, even though all that praise never really went to my head. I was just most grateful to be back on track personally as part of "the great Dodger comeback of 1974." From early spring forward, we Dodgers were conceding nothing to the Big Red Machine of Cincinnati.

As the new kid on the block, however, I could neither avoid nor did I try to shun the celebrity that was now flowing from my personal comeback on the field. It was fun and I enjoyed it. I didn't confuse it with deep-rooted friendship, but, I have to admit, I liked knowing that so many people I had watched on the big and small screens were now either coming to Dodger Stadium to watch me, or else viewing the Dodger games at home on television. In addition to Jack Benny and Milton Berle, some of my other handshake friends included Ed Sullivan, The Fifth Dimension, Desi Arnaz, and Cary Grant. Telly Savalas even went so far as to take me with him to the studio where he was filming the *Kojak* series so I could watch them film an episode of that popular detective show.

Of course, you didn't have to leave the ballpark to run into a home-grown celebrity. Vin Scully, our legendary Dodger play-by-play man on the radio, was as big as they come. Like Gene Elston back in Houston, Scully had a way of turning the game into a real picture over the air. Even those of us who only got to hear games when we were out of the lineup or on the DL got to hear enough Scully and Elston to know these so-called radio men really knew their baseball. I've liked all types of broadcasters in my time. In later years, I came to appreciate the work of Milo Hamilton in Houston. That man leaned into a game with enough enthusiasm to bring a dead armadillo back to life, if need be. In my own work as an analyst in recent times, I've tried to learn from all the best ones. Vin Scully was second to none in that respect. He was no homer, but the fans loved him. If Dodger Blue had a sound, it was the voice of Vin Scully. We players knew it too.

As the year wore on, the Dodger winning record began to scream out loud and clear, "A World Series in L.A. is possible!" I started to receive invitations to appear on television shows. On the first of two appearances I made with Johnny Carson on *The Tonight Show*, they had me on the air with a young woman named Susan Black, who was then regarded as one of the best female fast pitch softball hurlers in the country.

They also had the stage set up so that Johnny Carson and I could both take some whacks at legitimate pitches from Susan at the regulation distance. Well, Johnny struck at three of them and missed completely; didn't even come close.

"Come on, Jimmy," Johnny Carson cried out in frustration. "It's your turn now. It's up to you to bail us out and get us off the hook here. Get in there and show America how it's done!"

"Whoa!" said my rolling-eyes grin. "So this is what I've bought into!"

It was all good fun, but I'd be lying if I told you I felt no pressure. The best way to bait a ballplayer is to put him in a competitive situation that's a little out of the ordinary and then tell him, "It's all up to you!"

Be that as it may, this was *The Tonight Show*, the late-night program that the whole country watched back in the day prior to cable and Internet, and I had just been baited by America's greatest TV host, the late and wonderfully funny Johnny Carson.

I stepped in to hit against Susan Black with all the confidence of a rookie with a three-digit pin-on number. This wasn't 60 feet, 6 inches baseball pitching I faced in this moment of dare. This was a softball that was going to be coming at me full speed from a distance of only 40 feet. That makes for some big differences in the challenge.

The first pitch shot by like a cannonball. I swung at it, but my bat moved through the plane of contact after the ball already had passed. The second pitch came into me over the plate in the same way and my bat chased after it with the same failed result.

It was time to adjust. I didn't much care for the mocking laughter I was beginning to hear from the audience. I choked up on the bat. I decided to swing earlier, at the point of release in the throw that the ball still looks as though it is still being held by the pitcher's hand.

Fortunately, Ms. Black made no changes in the speed or location of her third pitch. If she had thrown a change-up, I would have been dead in the water.

WHACK! I nailed the third pitch for what would have been a clean single, were it not for the net that they set up to protect the audience. She wanted me to have another go at it, but I politely declined. I had nothing to gain from thereby stretching my luck. I settled for the celebrity applause of my late-night fans and a handshake from a grinning Johnny Carson.

On another occasion, I accepted an invitation to appear on *The Sonny & Cher Show*, which was then a pretty big TV prime-time variety hour program back in 1974. Although it probably would have led to nothing anyway, I may have blown my chances at an acting career by the way I handled my role in a skit that I did with Sonny and Cher.

Fortunately for me, we were taping the skit. Had it been live TV, I might have just croaked from the embarrassment of what happened at the taping.

Get this: I had one lousy line to deliver. All my character had to say was,

"Here comes Henshaw!" Get those three words said on tape, and I'm home free—probably with no Emmy nomination in sight, but done, nonetheless!

When the taping started, we reached my big moment, but nothing came out on cue. I froze. I couldn't say anything. A crowbar could not have loosened those slightly less than immortal three words from my mouth. I'm just standing there goofy-like, looking at the camera.

"CUT!" The director cried.

"I'm sorry," I said, "I just couldn't get the words to come out on time."

"That's OK, Jimmy," the director assured me. "Let's rehearse it one more time. Then I think we'll be able to get it on tape OK."

Without the tape running, I was able to deliver my line with no problem.

"OK," I said, "I think I'm ready now!"

"Won't even be necessary now, Jimmy," the director said. "We let the tape roll through your rehearsal. Without the pressure of you knowing what was going on, I figured you'd do just fine, and you just did. Thank you for coming."

For once in my life, I appreciated being conned. It took a lot of pressure off me then, and it makes for a great story now. It also helped me to remember that I needed to keep my day job. I wasn't in Hollywood to become the next Clark Gable or Sidney Poitier, but I had a lot of fun playing the celebrity game.

I had even more fun on the deeper level of bonding with the real fans of baseball that supported the club at Dodger Stadium. Los Angeles gets a bad rap as a town where the fans supposedly come late and leave early. We had some fans like that, but so does every club. That type, however, wasn't likely to be found in the outfield bleacher seats near my defensive position in center. These fans were rabid Dodger supporters and, as they got to know me better, they even found a way to honor me in a form that touched my heart as much as anything that's ever come my way in baseball.

One day I showed up at Dodger Stadium and I noticed something sort of gleaming in the sunlight on the left center field wall. As I jogged out to my center field position, I saw that it was a plaque that the regular fans of that area had put in place against the fence.

The plaque simply read: "WELCOME TO CANNON COUNTRY!"

What a tribute! I almost got teary-eyed over it. The fans had taken my Toy Cannon nickname from Houston to heart as now belonging to them as well. Since a lot of my home runs went into the stands in that left center field area, the fans had taken it upon themselves to name that area of Dodger Stadium in my honor.

I really was blown away. I blew kisses and hand salutes for quite some time to anyone who would make eye contact with me. If I could have gone into the stands and thanked each of them individually, I most definitely would have. They got the message anyway. We formed a bond that day that was forever. It never died, just as my bond with the real core fans of Houston never died. A ballplayer never forgets the fans who really care about him. He just moves on a lot of times because that's the way baseball plays out, but he doesn't forget the real fans.

You get sold or traded. You get released or you retire. But no matter what, you never forget the fans who care about you. If it was not for these fans, and I'm not talking about money here, the game wouldn't be worth playing. Anyone worth his salt as a baseball player needs to feel that there are some fans in the ballpark who care as much as he does about the outcome of the game. Those sweet people in the left center field bleachers at Dodger Stadium in 1974 were that kind of fan.

One of these L.A. fans deserves special mention. We all knew her as "Miss Frances," and she was an older Latin American lady who pretty well organized everything that happened among the fans out there. She was the fans' leader on putting up individual game signs and organizing special cheering section activities, and whatever else the fans chose to do. She made it happen right.

I got into the habit of going out to center field every day during batting practice when we were home, just to say hello, especially to Miss Frances, and to take her baseballs. She was just wonderful. Miss Frances, wherever you may now be, I just want you to know I have never forgotten you for all your support and many kindnesses while I was a member of the Los Angeles Dodgers. God bless you!

My own blessings spread in great abundance. By the time the All-Star voting had closed, I learned that I had been selected by my peers to go to Three Rivers Stadium in Pittsburgh for the game on July 23, 1974, as the starting center fielder for the National League.

What an awesome honor! I cannot totally put the feelings into words, but I will try. To be chosen as an All-Star at all is wonderful, but to be chosen also as the starting All-Star center fielder for the National League simply soared my spirit into a lofty elevation that I knew only briefly during my career. Believe me, I was equally humbled and appreciative of all those people who played any part in selecting me for this role.

I was also going to the 1974 All-Star Game in the good company of three Dodger teammates. Steve Garvey also had been named as the starting first baseman. In addition, starter Andy Messersmith and ace reliever Mike Marshall had been picked as members of the pitching staff.

Dodger Blue would be well represented on the Senior Circuit side of the annual contest, and well we should have been. Going into the break at the close of games played on Sunday, July 21, the Dodgers had posted a 63–34 record in the NL West, good enough for a five and one-half game lead over second-place Cincinnati and a far-leap lead of twelve games over third-place Houston. In sweet Dodger Land, we had every reason to feel good about both the All-Star Game and our prospects for an eventual pennant in 1974.

The 1974 Dodgers were about winning it all in the National League and nothing less. In that sense, our individual selections for the All-Star Game simply reinforced the point in a way that goes far beyond spoken words.

For me, little Jimmy Wynn from Cincinnati, Ohio, I had not forgotten my roots at the All-Star Game. Here I was, starting for the same team that featured one of my oldest rivals from high school, Pete Rose, and my very closest friend in the whole world, Joe Morgan. Two of my childhood heroes would also be playing in the game. Hank Aaron would be starting in the outfield for the National League. Frank Robinson was now on the outfield roster for the American League.

Former Astro teammate Cesar Cedeno would also be on my side again and another favorite former Astro teammate, Mike Cuellar, who was now pitching for Baltimore, would be playing, of course, for the American League.

It was all shaping up to be a combination of Thanksgiving and Christmas, rolled into one hot summer night in Pittsburgh. The only damper on total joy was our awareness of who was missing, the great and late Roberto Clemente. He also must have been the guy that Major League Baseball had in mind when they first scheduled the summer classic for this specific location a few years earlier.

God rest your big heart and immortal soul, Roberto Clemente! As you most probably remember, the great Pittsburgh Pirate right fielder lost his life in a mercy supply plane that crashed as it attempted to take off on a flight from Puerto Rico to South America to help earthquake victims on December 31, 1972.

The game itself turned out grand. Most importantly, the National League won, 7–2, and two of my teammates took top credit honors for the victory.

Steve Garvey went two for four with one run scored and one run batted in as the Game's Most Valuable Player. Andy Messersmith also started for the National League. Combining with Mike Marshall, Andy and Mike pitched five of the nine innings played against the American League.

I did OK too. I went one for three with a run scored while playing both center and right fields on defense.

National League field manager Yogi Berra batted me fifth in the order. I felt good about that decision too.

After the All-Star break, the season heated up. We stayed hot, but the Reds got hotter. Late in the September twilight of the 1974 season, Cincinnati came to our place looking for a three-game sweep that would have pulled them to a mere half game back of us in the race for the NL West division crown. It got a little hairy over those three days.

When the Reds took the games of September 13 and 14 by scores of 6–

3 and 4–2, things started to get a little quiet around Tinseltown, especially in the Dodger clubhouse. We all knew that another Dodger loss could give the Reds a tremendous emotional edge down the stretch of our few remaining games.

After the Reds, we had another ten straight games at Dodger Stadium, but that was it for home cooking during the '74 season. We had to play our last six games on the road against a couple of spoiler clubs, the Padres and the Astros. The Reds had a softer schedule at home during that last week, playing only their final two games at Atlanta on the road.

We needed a win in Game Three of the last home series against the Reds.

Walt Alston sent Don Sutton out there for us in the game of September 15. Sparky Anderson sent out Fred Norman to pitch for the Reds.

There was no score in the game until the top of the fifth inning when Reds pitcher Norman singled in Cesar Geronimo with the first run of the game. Lucky for us, it would be the only Reds run of the night. We pushed across a couple of runs in the bottom of the sixth inning to take the lead and chase Norman, but we really cranked it up in the bottom of the seventh with Pedro Borbon now pitching for the Reds. I came up to bat with the bases loaded and the score hanging too tight at 2–1, Dodgers.

I caught a Borbon fastball that came in with too much white napkin space resting under it. The ball took off for Cannon Country with "no doubt about it" written all over its high arching flight to the Land of Miss Frances. That grand slam was my thirty-first home run of the '74 season and it may have been the most important one I hit all that year, or any other season. My blast made it 6–1, L.A., and Steve Garvey followed me with a solo shot homer off Borbon to make it 7–1.

As I once told writer Al Doyle, this was the one big game of my career that I am least likely to ever forget. I hit a number of home runs over the years that all meant something unique to me, but this one carried a special importance to my team. It was about seeing my efforts contribute to a pennant, the very reason I had chosen L.A. over Chicago as my preferred trade destination from Houston.

Cincinnati never recovered from the new and eventually final tab of Dodgers 7, Reds 1. With sixteen games remaining on our schedule, we sent the Big Red Machine sputtering away with a two and one-half game deficit to make up on us somewhere down the line. It was still far too close for comfort, but a heckuva lot better than the wolf's-breath heat of seeing them leave L.A. with only a half-game Dodger lead to overcome, had they managed to have won our series finale.

We celebrated that night, but not for long. There was work to be done.

I got my thirty-second and last regular season home run for the 1974 Dodgers as a ninth-inning losing-cause solo shot off Dan Spillner of the San

Diego Padres on September 21 at Dodger Stadium. It was to be, of course, my last regular season deposit downrange in Cannon Country, as it also lowered our losing margin that night to 4–3.

Going into our last series of the year at Houston on September 30, the Dodgers still led the Reds by that two and one-half game margin we had established back on September 15. We had three games left to play with the Houston Astros from September 30 through October 2. The Reds had a day off on September 30 before closing with two games against the Braves at Atlanta on October 1 and 2.

All eyes were on the Astrodome on September 30. When our Doug Rau dropped a 4–1 decision to Larry Dierker of the Astros that night, we could almost sense the heat of rope-burn around our necks from the words that writers were committing to print. I'm paraphrasing here the way I recall several writers' leads on this closing weekend of the '74 pennant race: "The Dodger lead has now shrunk to two games. Another two losses here in Houston, along with a Reds two-game sweep in Atlanta, and the incredible Red Machine will have earned themselves the redemption of a playoff for the National League West Division title!" Stuff like that made us sick at a time we needed to be as well as possible.

Walt Alston didn't say much prior to our next game of October 1. He just told us to take it easy and to go out there and do what we knew how to do.

Don Sutton again took the mound for us October 1. The Astros sent their young mountain monster, the 6'8" J.R. Richard, out to oppose us, and what a game that turned out to be. We pecked away for three scoring innings and a 5–0 lead through the top of the fifth, but Sutton had to leave the game for a pinch hitter in that same two-run scoring frame.

Enter Mike Marshall and some unexpected erroneous play in the field by the Dodgers. Shoddy defense and a weak Marshall outing allowed the Astros to climb back into the game. By the end of the fifth inning, the Astros trailed by only 5–4. We managed to scrap back, outscoring the Astros by 3–1 the rest of the way for an 8–5 division-clinching win. Even J.R. Richard's nine blazing strikeouts and the scariest inside fastball in the world could not stop us that day.

As it turns out, the Reds lost 7–1 to the Braves in Atlanta on October 1, rendering our victory in Houston almost, but not quite, meaningless. It would have felt better to have clinched the title with a game win on the field than to have backed into the division crown with a Reds loss, but that's not how it worked out.

At any rate, what spontaneously happened after the game became more important historically than even our National League West Division title. What happened at the Astrodome after the game on October 1, 1974, was even bigger than baseball itself in the sense that it marked the date of a great social change in sports coverage by female members of the media.

Enter Anita Martini. In 1974, Anita Martini was a 35-year-old female sports anchor for KPRC-TV in Houston. During the early 1960s, Anita had started out as the first female radio call-in host for another landmark sports program on radio station KTRH-AM. I came to know and respect Anita from my early days in Houston. This bright lady knew her baseball.

Let me put it this way: Anita Martini was not just a bright woman looking to make headlines for her personal gain in the wide world of sports journalism. Anita Martini was an intelligent sports journalist who already knew what the heck she was talking about; Anita was a journalist who just happened to also be a woman. As such, she didn't want anything to stand in the way of her doing a job that she already knew how to do.

Something did stand in the way, however, until Anita Martini challenged it on the night of October 1, 1974. Some of us who knew her well also answered the call after the game at the Astrodome to stand up with Anita for what was right.

The old rule about women sports journalists had always closed one door tight against them. After games, male reporters were allowed into the dressing areas of the clubhouses for their interviews, while women were expected to wait outside the clubhouse until the players had showered, changed, and departed for their own questioning of the athletes and managers.

This meant that the male reporters got their stories first and freshest while the female reporters had to settle for whoever had not ducked out a side door in the meanwhile, or whoever remained after the others had begged off having to go through the same questions again outside the clubhouse.

On October 1, Anita Martini challenged the old rule. She approached the Dodger clubhouse and announced that she wanted to go in and talk to Jimmy Wynn about the game, the division title, and the Dodgers' chances against the Pirates in the playoffs.

She got the expected message from the clubhouse door attendant: "I'm sorry, Miss Martini, but ladies are not allowed access to the clubhouse area. You will have to wait until Mr. Wynn dresses and comes out here to talk with you."

Somehow, Anita convinced the man to take a message inside to me about what she was trying to do. When I got it, there was no question in my mind about how I would handle it. I first got the backing of manager Walt Alston, and then I came back out to the dressing area and said something like this: "Listen up, you guys! A very bright lady reporter, who knows baseball better than most men do, is coming in here to interview me. So, get some pants on or wrap a towel around yourselves! Anita Martini has as much right to be here as any of these guys already present who don't even know the history of the game as well as this lady does!" All I got was a roar of support and cooperation from my fellow Dodgers. The male reporters couldn't argue against me because they knew what I had just said about Anita was true.

Everything was different for female reporters from that day forward. The word had spread like wildfire too about Anita Martini. In a short while, players made the dressing adjustments after games and female reporters were going into the clubhouses of all sports teams as though it was as natural as breathing.

Score another "W" in the war on "isms"!

When Anita Martini passed away from cancer in 1993, the world of sports, especially baseball, lost one of its best, most honest reporters. Anita Martini loved baseball above all other sports. Because of her many contributions to intelligent reporting of our game, and also because of her historical role as a groundbreaking unintentional leader against sexist practices in the sports reporting industry, the Texas Baseball Hall of Fame inducted the late Anita Martini into their membership in 2007. I was proud to be a part of that vote as well.

Anita was all business in her interview with me after the division clincher. She wanted me to explain my regenerated productivity in Los Angeles; she wanted to know how I saw our chances against the strengths and weaknesses of the NL East Pirates; and she wanted to know who I preferred as an opponent, if we got to the World Series, Baltimore or Oakland?

As best I could, I tried to palm off all of Anita's questions with the same stock cliché answers that we ballplayers have been handing to male sports writers since the Fall in Eden, but she was too smart for that. I don't remember how we got through the interview, but we did.

In the grander scheme of all things, the fact that we even had the interview where we did was a whole lot more important to history back on October 1, 1974, than anything I had to say. I'm just happy to have been a small part of a very big change in the way baseball treats female reporters.

October 2 turned out to be a day of anticlimax. We won our last game of the season against the Astros as I rested. Since the Reds also lost their last game at Atlanta on the same date, the Dodgers finished the year with a 4-game bulge over the second-place Reds. Our 102–60 mark in the NL West also far surpassed the 88–74 record of the NL East Champion Pittsburgh Pirates.

A couple of Dodgers walked off with the two most coveted individual player awards in the National League in 1974: First baseman Steve Garvey (.312 BA, 21 HR, 111 RBI) was named the Most Valuable Player and pitcher Mike Marshall (83 games pitched, 15 wins and 12 losses, 2.42 ERA, 21 saves) won the Cy Young Award.

As for me, I was as happy as I could be with my final season marks for 1974. I hit for a .271 batting average with 32 home runs and 108 runs batted in. That RBI mark was my personal career season high, besting my previous record of 107 RBI at Houston in 1967.

A cheering crowd awaited us at the Los Angeles airport once we arrived home. We weren't taking the Pirates lightly, but we thought our pitching gave us a far superior chance in a best-three-of-five-games series. Lo and behold, that turned out to be true. We defeated the Pirates, three games to one, for the National League pennant as our American League opponents, the Oakland Athletics, were doing the same to the Baltimore Orioles.

Once the chesty West Coast had knocked out the East Coast in the league championship playoffs, the country headed toward an all-California World Series, featuring the Los Angeles Dodgers of the National League going up against the Oakland Athletics of the American League.

As we headed toward our World Series with the A's, I was moved to curious thoughts of gratitude for one man above all others. "Thank you, Spec Richardson," I thought. "Had you not traded me to the Los Angeles Dodgers during the off-season, about now, I'd just be headed out the same door for a round of golf in Houston. Instead, I'm getting ready for my first World Series! Little Jimmy Wynn, once of 1917 Colerain Avenue in Cincinnati near Crosley Field, is finally and at last headed for the biggest show that baseball has to offer. I will always be grateful to you for opening the door on opportunity, regardless of your motives for trading me away."

Golf could wait for now.

The 1974 World Series opened in Los Angeles at Dodger Stadium as a best-four-games-won-out-of-seven played contest, the formula used by Major League Baseball since the early 20th century. The home/away schedule formula in place, with Los Angeles starting as the home team, was 2–3–2 (two at home; three away; two at home). The Series would be over whenever either team had won four games, but 2–3–2 determined the home team status for Los Angeles, if the full seven games were required for determining our winner.

A day off from any games played would be allowed for travel from one city to another, with a potential for two scheduled off days in the Series, if it took six or seven games to determine a winner. Rainouts or other acts of nature that made any game unplayable simply pushed the schedule back to the next day in which adequate playing conditions were again available.

Those of you who know baseball inside out will hopefully forgive me here. I threw in those last two paragraphs for all my friends and new readers who may not understand the basic wheels that determine how a World Series is scheduled.

Things have changed in recent years in the system for determining "home field advantage." All that means is that the team that starts as home team owns the potential for playing four home games to their opponents' three. Back in my day, the "home field advantage" simply rotated from one league to the other each passing season. In odd-numbered years, the World Series would start in the American League city. In even-numbered years, the World Series would begin in the National League city.

Commissioner Bud Selig changed the rotation system for World Series starts a few years ago. In an attempt to make the annual All-Star Game more "meaningful" to the players, the commissioner attached HFA in the current year's World Series as the league prize for winning the midsummer classic. As a result of American League dominance in recent All-Star Games, all the World Series starts in recent memory have now taken place in the home of the American League champions.

As for me, I prefer the old rotation system. If baseball wants to assign home field advantage to anything, giving it to the team that finished the regular season with the best team record for wins and losses would be a fairer way to go.

At any rate, back in the fall of 1974, we league champion players didn't have to waste energy on such subjects. We had a World Series to play and Game One was about to take place in our Dodger crib.

Game One unfolded on the real Columbus Day that we celebrated in school as kids. That would be October 12 for those of you who may be young enough to think that Columbus was sent here in 1492 with instructions to make landfall on the second Monday in October.

Andy Messersmith took the mound for the Dodgers in Game One. Lefty Ken Holtzman drew the nod as the starter for Oakland before an overflow crowd of 55,974 screaming LA fans. There was nothing laid back and blasé about L.A. fans on that particular night of long ago.

The A's drew first blood when Reggie Jackson led off the bottom of the second inning with a towering shot to right center off Andy. The A's added another run in the top of the fifth when pitcher Ken Holtzman doubled, advanced to third base, and then came home on a squeeze bunt by A's short-stop Bert Campaneris.

Davy Lopes scored our first run in the bottom of the fifth inning with the help of some sloppy play in the field by Oakland.

Game One stayed 2–1 Oakland until the Athletics added a final run by Bert Campaneris in the top of the eighth with the help of a Ron Cey throwing error. When I came up to bat in the bottom of the ninth with 2 outs and nobody on, and the A's leading 3–1, the great mustachioed reliever, Rollie Fingers, was astride the pitching mound rubber and looking to close the door.

I just had one last door jamb to offer.

Fingers left a breaking pitch over the plate and I caught it good. It took off for a long, high, and hard ride to my favorite landing spot in Dodger Stadium, the place in left center field that the fans earlier had renamed as Cannon Country.

It wasn't enough. And I felt little celebration in the achievement of my one and only World Series homer. The Oakland Athletics had taken Game One of the 1974 World Series by a 3–2 margin.

A similar-sized crowd of 55,989 fans showed up to watch the Dodgers square the World Series at 1–1 when we took Game Two by an identical 3–2 final score. After scratching out a 1–0 lead in the bottom of the second, Joe Ferguson gave the Dodgers a 3–0 lead with his two-run blast in the bottom of the fifth.

Don Sutton pitched beautifully for the Dodgers against Vida Blue until the top of the ninth. After giving up a couple of runs to the pesky, scrappy A's on a two-run, ninth-inning single by Joe Rudi, Mike Marshall came into the game to pitch for the Dodgers as designated pinch runner Herb Washington took the place of the slower Joe Rudi as the runner at first base. Marshall promptly picked off the surprised Washington to seal the deal on a 3–2 Dodger victory that knotted the Series at a win for each team as the games moved north to Oakland.

If we swept all three games on the road, the Dodgers could celebrate a World Series triumph on the road and also do it again when we got back to L.A. Looking at things in a more down-to-earth way, we knew we had to win at least one of the three games in Oakland to get the Series back to Los Angeles.

The dreams and the math are always the easy parts. It's winning the games on the field against the best competition in the world that's hard.

On October 15, 1974, Al Downing pitched for the Dodgers against Catfish Hunter of the Athletics before a sellout crowd of 49,375 at Oakland-Alameda Stadium in Oakland, California. The game turned out to be a real sad fizzle for the Dodgers.

The Oakland A's plated a couple of unearned runs in the bottom of the second inning. They added another single crooked number in the fourth to fill out the 3–0 lead they held over us going into the top of the eighth. Things looked bad.

Hope rises.

After Bill Buckner homered off Hunter with one out in the eighth, Rollie Fingers came in to do another door-slam job with the score now 3–1 A's. Rollie got the A's out of further trouble in the eighth, but our Willie Crawford gave Mr. Fingers and Company cause to worry when he led off the top of the ninth with a home run to narrow the margin again to that familiar 3–2 score.

Sadly, that was it. Fingers again shut us down and the final score in the World Series for the third consecutive time was 3–2, but twice in favor of the A's, and twice with Rollie Fingers on the mound, and twice with Fingers giving up a ninth-inning homer before putting out the lights.

One of the things that makes baseball players superstitious is the game's tendency to produce strange similar outcomes in a row, especially when they come about in serial packages of "three." It was too soon to tell what the three identical 3–2 final scores might mean for the future, if anything, but we Dodgers had our fingers crossed that it was a sign that our fortunes would soon change for the good.

They didn't.

With Andy Messersmith working Game Four for the Dodgers on October 16 in Oakland, A's mound opponent Ken Holtzman took Andy deep in the bottom of the third for a 1–0 Oakland lead. We answered with a two-run triple by Bill Russell in the top of the fourth to give the Dodgers a 2–1 lead that held firm through five and one-half innings of play.

One interesting comment about the Holtzman home run is in order: 1974 was also only the second year in which the American League had used the new designated hitter rule, but it still had not been approved for use in World Series play. So that means the guy who hit one here was not merely a pitcher. Ken Holtzman was a pitcher who had hardly batted at all over the entire season. I have to give him credit for coming through when his club needed him to do something he wasn't getting paid to do.

The worm turned again in the bottom of the sixth in Game Four. Led by a two-run pinch single off the bat of pinch hitter Jim Holt, the A's of manager Alvin Dark scored four times to take a 5–2 lead that would hold up as the final score.

The Oakland Athletics had taken a 3–1 lead in the Series. We had broken the 3–2 final score skein in Game Four, but we had retained the fact that the losing team in all four games always only scored two runs. As Dodger players, all we knew for sure was that we had to win Game Five or we were done.

On October 17, 1974, Don Sutton took the mound as the last Dodger hope for staying alive in the World Series. Vida Blue carried the Oakland aspirations for a post–game A's champagne championship shower.

The A's took a 2–0 lead with single tallies in the bottom of the first and second inning. We tied the game in the top of the sixth on my sacrifice fly RBI and a run-scoring single by Steve Garvey. The A's regained the lead in the bottom of the seventh when Joe Rudi smacked a leadoff home run off Mike Marshall. We had a chance to tie the game in the top of the eighth, but that chance died when Bill Buckner tried to run a single (and a missed-ball error in center field by Bill North) into a leadoff bonus trip to third base. He didn't make it. Buckner was thrown out on a perfect 9–4–5 relay throw that nailed him at third base, shutting down our last real opportunity to get back in the game and the World Series.

For the fourth time in five games, the final score was 3–2. For the fifth time in every game, the losing team scored exactly two runs. For the fourth time in five games, the Dodgers lost, yielding the 1974 World Series victory celebration to the Oakland Athletics.

For the A's, it was a third consecutive World Series victory, one that sealed their place among the elite World Series teams of all time.

For the Los Angeles Dodgers, it was a disappointment, of course, but we still had delivered on my pre–season promise to win the National League pennant.

Years after his retirement, Jimmy Wynn returned to Dodger Stadium to play in an Oldtimers' All-Star Game. Jimmy and actor Kevin Costner (left) were teammates in a contest played against actor Tom Selleck and others.

For Walt Alston, it was the last pennant year in his storied career as manager of the Dodgers. I was just proud to have been a small part of that achievement too.

For Walter and Peter O'Malley, I hoped it would be a reassurance that their confidence in Jimmy Wynn had been well placed. I know they had to be highest on the list of disappointed souls who bled Dodger Blue that we had not won it all, but we did win the pennant I promised them. I never promised either of them a World Series rose garden, but I did commit us to a mighty good whiff of our own National League pennant.

And we got it. No one could ever take that pennant year from any of us.

For me, Jimmy Wynn, it was the almost-perfect fulfillment of a lifelong baseball dream come true. Add to that satisfaction the hope that stirs the soul of every ballplayer that hangs in there for the long run.

There's always next year. Who knows what may be possible for me with just a little more time and effort?

You gotta have hope. You gotta have heart. You gotta have faith. You gotta have talent. You gotta have opportunity. And you gotta have baseball luck. I had all six of those Mojo qualities working for me going into the 1974 off-season, plus my career was now sailing full speed on a sea of Dodger Blue waves. Who could ask for more?

CHAPTER 14

The Day the Music Died

Most baseball careers die a slow death. Some players lose it overnight, suffering what amounts to the baseball version of a heart attack or stroke, but most of us lose it over a period of time, and it's pretty much up to the ballplayer to act as his personal career coroner.

Oh, if you have trouble making the final call, the clubs will help you. If your ability is dead gone, you won't be able to get a job. If you're a big enough name to help sell tickets, you may be offered a roster spot, but it will only be to do things you never would have done in your prime. In return for signing a less-than-happy deal, you may be promised something that isn't going to happen, just so you will agree to play a little longer on the club's terms.

Babe Ruth stands as the best example of a player whose name outlived his abilities to play the game of baseball. When the New York Yankees sold the Babe to the old Boston Braves prior to the 1935 season as an outfielder, Ruth was led to believe that he was in line to soon take over his new club as manager. That wasn't going to happen. The Braves got Babe Ruth for one reason only, to draw fans to the ballpark that otherwise cared nothing about going to see a bad club play baseball.

Babe figured the deal out early in the 1935 season. By then he was knee deep on his way to a .181 batting average on the season and struggling hard to simply run the bases and make the ordinary plays in right field. To those who knew and loved him, it wasn't a pretty sight at all.

Then on one very ordinary season day, May 25, 1935, in a humdrum everyday baseball game at Forbes Field, one that pitted the visiting Boston Braves against the home club and also going-nowhere Pittsburgh Pirates, Babe Ruth reached down deep inside his soul to come up with one final echo of that very natural-born talent for baseball that God had given him.

Babe Ruth hit three monster home runs that afternoon in Pittsburgh. They would be the last three home runs of his storied career and they would leave us with the number "714" as the benchmark total for a single player until the great Hank Aaron passed it by in 1974.

Some say that Ruth's 714th home run traveled about 600 feet. Others say it could not possibly have gone that far. Few argue against the probability that it was the longest home run anyone, even Josh Gibson, had ever hit at Forbes Field. Babe Ruth retired five days later, only a short blink down the line from his last unforgettable moment in baseball, but already many shadows deep past the sunlight of his last great period of everyday productivity at the highest level.

I cannot help but think back upon Ruth in 1935, and Mickey Mantle from 1965 to 1968, and Willie Mays in 1972 and 1973, when I think back upon my own last days in the major leagues. Not that I ever performed at the same level as these three baseball immortals, but because these fine superstars were heroes to so many American baseball fans and it was hard for us to read about, hear about, or watch them go out badly. Yes, baseball players can be fans too.

As a ballplayer also, I hated to see what happened to each of these men in their final days as active players, but they also awakened me to the fact that the rest of us with any long-term talent would be governed by the same rules.

Anyone can stay too long at the fair.

Chances existed for me too that my established name could outlive my actual ability to play the game of baseball at the level others expected of me on an everyday basis. Going into the 1975 season off the tremendous bump in my productivity in 1974, however, it was impossible for me to think much about endings. All I could see was the opportunity for new beginnings.

At age thirty-three in the spring of 1975, anything resembling the end of things seemed even farther from sight than it had four years ago, when I slipped into the agony of my longest and worst season of 1971. Buoyed also by the team success of our 1974 National League Dodger pennant, I also felt a sense of new belonging and identity that I may have mistaken as the healthy pulse rate of a career that was still in its prime.

Whenever you end up retiring I've since learned that you have your early moments of second-guessing yourself on those mornings you do wake up feeling physically good. "I could still be playing this game" grows easily into a round, easy thought that rolls through the mind. Over time, however, this sweet idea melts away like ice cream on a Houston summer day. It is replaced by a new thought: "I could have done myself a favor by retiring even sooner."

Then, if we're lucky, and if we're blessed, we simply come to the realization that there are no instant replay do-overs, either in baseball or in life. Things are what they are, and we either learn from our experiences or move on, or else we lock into what I see as the Devil's temptations. We fall into a life overflowing with resentment, blame, regret, and repetition of the same old mistakes.

I wasn't near to embracing all those realizations in 1975, but they were starting their awakening in me and, curiously, at about that same time I began a final, but hard-for-me-to-see slide on the playing field. Oh, I had 18 home runs in 1975, but my batting average had slipped by 23 points from our 1974 L.A. Dodger pennant season, closing the door in 1975 at .248.

My walks stayed near the same at 110 to the 108 from 1974, and I even cut my strikeouts way down from 104 to 77, but part of that was due to the fact I was now playing less. The fall that hurt the most in my productivity decline from 1974 was in runs batted in. I fell from 104 RBI in 1974 to only 77 in 1975.

That being said, I was still playing well enough in 1975 to have earned my second straight All-Star Game start in center field for the National League. The 1975 All-Star Game was played at County Stadium in Milwaukee on July 15, 1975. The honor for me marked my third and final career appearance as an All-Star.

The Dodgers, as the defending champions, were even better represented at the game in 1975 than we were in 1974. Walt Alston served as manager of the National League, while Steve Garvey started at first base; Ron Cey started at third base; and I started in center field.

Don Sutton worked a couple of scoreless frames as the second pitcher in the game for our side. Steve Garvey and I each homered to lead the National League to a 6–3 win over the American League.

By the time play resumed after the All-Star break, we had a pretty good idea about where things were going in the second half of the 1975 pennant race. As a team, the Dodgers didn't play as well together as we had in 1974. We just weren't good enough in 1975 to keep up with a now revved-up version of the Big Red Machine from Cincinnati. The Reds rolled to a 108–54 record in 1975, leaving the Dodgers twenty games back in the dust as second place finishers in the NL West with an 88–74 mark.

I don't mind telling you, the 1975 season was very disappointing. After our promising pennant year of 1974, it was hard to accept the fact that the Dodgers would not be returning to the World Series for a second straight year.

On a bittersweet note, I was proud to have played on the last Dodger club managed by Walt Alston for a complete full season. Alston would return in 1976, but he would yield the Dodger reins to Tommy Lasorda over the last four games. I'm just sad we couldn't get him one more ring in 1975, but it wasn't to be.

Walt thanked us for giving the 1975 team our best, but he didn't say much else. Walt never was much of a talker, so you pretty well knew that you were getting what he was thinking when he did speak. All he ever asked of his players was that we treat the game with the respect it deserves and that we each give the game on the field our very best at all times.

The 1975 Dodgers were kindred spirits with the 1974 club in that regard.

We respected the game. We gave it our best. With and without pennants, we were each of those two years champions of the spirit in the mirror image of the Dodger tradition, as spurred on by the special inspiration of the great Walt Alston.

I will always be grateful for my brief but very happy association with the O'Malley family, Manager Walt Alston, Coach Tommy Lasorda, all my fighting Dodger teammates, Miss Frances, and all the other wonderful fans out in Dodger Land, especially those that came in numbers and supported me so faithfully in Cannon Country during home games. As was true during my Houston years, I will never forget the L.A. people who were there for me as I gave the game my best.

If it sounds as though I am saying goodbye to Los Angeles here, I've either left you all the easy tips you need, or else you already know the basic facts of my baseball history.

Baseball is also a business. People who really care about their ball club still get traded and it was about to happen to me for the second time and, as it just so happened, at another stopping point with a second marriage that wasn't working out. Joanne and I had simply grown quietly apart over the time we lived in Los Angeles. The upcoming trade to Atlanta suddenly became an opportune time for both of us to go our separate ways by mutual agreement, and so we did.

I left my second marriage with sadness and acceptance of the fact that, no matter how lonely I may get, I needed to give myself a lot more time for thought and reflection upon what I'm expecting of marriage before I do it again. In the meanwhile, Joanne and I wished each other well and said a quiet goodbye.

My focus returned to baseball.

On November 17, 1975, the Dodgers traded me, along with outfielder Tom Paciorek and infielders Lee Lacy and Jerry Royster, to the Atlanta Braves in return for outfielder Dusty Baker and Ed Goodson, a throw-in name. The objective for the Dodgers was getting my old friend Dusty Baker for their outfield future. I was the major name player going over to the Braves in exchange, but the Braves were also getting a better group of younger players by exchange in this deal.

On April 10, 1976, another of my former Dodger teammates decided to join us on the Braves roster by way of the newly earned free agency route when Andy Messersmith signed with Atlanta. Andy was a welcome sight, believe me.

The movement of players between the Dodgers and Braves didn't stop with the deals involving Andy Messersmith and me. Once the new season had started, on June 23, 1976, Lee Lacy went back to the Dodgers from the Braves, along with pitcher Elias Sosa, in exchange for ace reliever Mike Marshall coming over from the Dodgers to the Braves. There was another welcome sight. I'm not sure how Lee Lacy felt about his merry-go-round stay in Atlanta, but I think he was glad to be going back to Los Angeles. Lee Lacy had a pretty nice career from that time forward, but more as an outfielder than an infielder.

The 1976 Atlanta Braves weren't very good, but we had a lot of fun playing for owner Ted Turner and manager Dave Bristol. Fulton County Stadium was a bandbox playing field, but it had a ballpark seating capacity with far more seats than fans during the time I was there.

Ted Turner did everything he could think of to help draw people into watching a bad ball club play. We had everything from chariot races to egg-throwing contests to cow-milking competitions and even bathtub races. Ted Turner was involved in everything that took place there too. He did it to

In 1976, Jimmy found his bicentennial home with the Braves (National Baseball Hall of Fame Library, Cooperstown, NY).

help the gate, but he also seemed to really enjoy these planned activities for the fans.

The year after my stay in Atlanta, 1977, Ted Turner finally got into trouble with the commissioner by putting himself on the bench as manager of the Braves. The commissioner stopped that move after one game and Turner was forced back upstairs to think of something else.

By stopping Ted Turner from managing as an owner, Commissioner Bowie Kuhn was taking the position that it made a farce of the game. He may as well have said out loud what everybody else knew he was thinking: It made no sense to have someone with a lot of ego and money, but no direct baseball experience, managing a big league club.

Personally, I've never seen any kind of list of qualifications for managing. Does playing a few seasons of minor league ball make you a better manager of people than a guy like Turner who has turned over millions of dollars in business?

How much does the success of a manager hinge upon his knowledge of people versus his knowledge of baseball? I doubt that's a question that anyone will ever seriously try to answer, but it's out there anyway. Anytime a club sends a guy out there to manage, he'd better have some kind of working handle on both the people and the baseball issues that are going to arise for sure.

This much I know for certain: We'll never know how good or bad a manager Ted Turner might have actually turned out to be.

As an owner, Ted Turner took care of his ballplayers as though they were his own family. He had big parties for us on weekends over at the WTBS television Superstation studios, whenever possible, and he got us whatever we needed. All we had to do was tell him and Ted would swing into his Big Daddy mode.

Sometimes a free lunch comes along. Just don't count on it ever happening.

My free lunch came in the form of finding a place to live, with help from Ted Turner. Through Ted I met a guy who happened to own an upscale complex of condos in nearby DeKalb County, Georgia. This fellow decided that having me live in one of his units would help raise the general value of the property. He offered to let me live there for free during my year in Atlanta in exchange for the right to use that fact as a selling point to potential buyers. It couldn't have been forever. After all, at some point he would have needed to sell my unit too, but with no other strings attached when I moved in, that deal became an offer I couldn't refuse.

Ted Turner's marketing wheels never stopped revolving.

At one point, Ted decided to have all of us players put our nicknames on the backs of our jerseys. Of course, mine was simple enough. It read "The Toy Cannon," with the number 24 underneath. Yep! Getting my old number back was one of the perks that came with the Atlanta trade.

Some players didn't have nicknames, however, so Turner just told them, "If you don't have a nickname, get one!" It was about here that we guessed what he probably had been angling to do all along. You see, Ted Turner knew that pitcher Andy Messersmith, who wore number 17, had no baseball nickname, so he sort of not-so-naively suggested that "Channel" would be a good choice for Andy.

Lo and behold! By Messersmith's acceptance of the boss's suggestion, Ted Turner could then place a jersey directly on the field during games that literally promoted Channel 17, the television channel number of his WTBS Superstation.

Andy Messersmith always understood who buttered his bread and he readily went along with Ted Turner's nickname suggestion. The nickname uniforms lasted about two games before Commissioner Bowie Kuhn put a stop to them too, just as he would later put the screws to Ted's managerial career.

As an entrepreneur, Ted Turner was, and still is, an American classic!

As for the serious baseball side of my Atlanta year, there wasn't much to write home about in 1976. The Braves were on their way early to a last-place finish in the National League West with a 70–92 mark. Oh, we had Messersmith and Marshall, and future Hall of Fame knuckleballer Phil Niekro, all right, but we really had no firepower or speed in our lineup at all.

My own productivity, except for my 17 season home runs, had mostly fallen to the level of my worst previous season, that awful year of 1971. In 148 games in 1976, I batted only .207 and knocked in only 66 runs. I had 127 walks, but walks were always easy for me to get when there was no one else in the lineup that opponents felt they had to pitch around. In the '76 Braves lineup, I was the guy they pitched around.

I don't know how Ted Turner missed the marketing boat on my "17" HR total. He could've had me running TV promos at season's end saying something like: "Hi, I'm Jimmy Wynn. I stopped at 17 homers in '76 because that's the channel number for WTBS-TV, America's Number One Superstation!"

That didn't happen. The season ended with my Atlanta future in a cloud.

One day, it cleared up. I got a call from Ted Turner that changed everything.

Turner was a nervous kind of talker. When I went over to WTBS to see him, he came out to receive me and we walked together back to his office. All this time he was talking ninety miles an hour about everything under the sun. It was late November and everything from holiday plans, programs, world situations, and the Braves in general were on his mind. When he arrived in his office, Ted closed the door, but he continued pacing back and forth, almost talking to me, almost talking more to himself. Meanwhile, I'm just standing there watching.

"Sit down, Jimmy!" Ted finally said with a few fluttering downward waves of his right hand. I took a chair as he sat down behind his desk and lit a cigar.

"George Steinbrenner of the Yankees just called me, Jimmy," Ted said. "He wants you to come to New York and be his right-handed designated hitter. How do you feel about that?"

I was taken a little back by the idea. I don't know if any ballplayer ever gets used to the news that his current club is thinking about moving him. Unless you have walked in our shoes, you just can't imagine all the thoughts that race like wildfire through your mind at these times.

Aside from feeling unwanted, again, there's all the stuff you have to take care of immediately just to make a move work before your name can move from one team's roster to another's.

In this case, the idea of moving from a last-place team to a World Series club overnight was appealing, but I wasn't happy about the thought of becoming a DH and just playing the offense side of the game. It sounded exactly like it was going to be a lot of time sitting on the bench, waiting for my next time at bat.

Turner saw my hesitation and, whether he meant it or not, he told me that the decision on dealing me to the Yankees was entirely up to me. I finally said, "OK, if you really want me to go, I'll go. Pull the string."

Turner said the deal had nothing to do with him wanting me to go, but that the Yankees needed a right-handed DH and they were willing to pay the Braves fair market value for my contract.

In other words, business is business.

All owners share one approach in common with each other. When an owner wants to acquire or keep you, it's personal. You're like a son or little brother to him. When he wants to trade or sell you, it's nothing personal. It's strictly business.

On November 29, 1976, and with my expressed consent, Braves owner Ted Turner sold my contract to the New York Yankees for whatever the fair market value may have been during the 1976–77 off-season. I never learned the amount. It didn't matter. What mattered most to me was the fact that I was changing clubs again. This time I was moving to the most storied franchise in baseball, but it was to the American League, and to a position that didn't even feel like real baseball to me at all, the position of designated hitter.

As spring training in Fort Lauderdale, Florida, turned out, I had one of the best, most fun camps of my career, second only to the Dodger camp of 1974. I will also never forget the first day of camp. We were all there, dressed out for practice and just milling around with Elston Howard, the bench coach, and the two base coaches, Bobby Cox and Dick Howser, when I began to wonder, almost out loud, "Where's the manager?"

All of a sudden, manager Billy Martin appeared, but he wasn't dressed out for practice. He was wearing slacks and a golf shirt, plus sunglasses and a Yankee cap. He didn't smile or say much to anybody. He just walked up and said to Elston Howard, "OK, let spring training begin." Then he turned and walked off the field with former Yankee great Mickey Mantle, who was standing nearby. Where they went, we had some idea, but that was Martin's business. Our business was to carry out the order that our manager had left with his coaching staff. As practices go, it wasn't too grueling at all. In fact, we had lot of fun for a first day, and the tempo of things stayed cool even when our manager found the time to catch up with us on Day Two.

As we got into the season, however, the trade began to feel more like the complete downfall of my career. I hadn't wanted to be a DH, but my problem with the idea worsened once I realized that the Yankees had several guys already under contract that they could insert as right handed DH's.

Lou Piniella and I were the only two extra guys on the club who could bat right and also play the outfield when the new season began, but then the Yankees went out and acquired catcher Cliff Johnson from the Astros on June 15. Once Johnson joined the club, he took over as the designated hitter. My designation from that point on was to the Yankees bench.

I wasn't surprised. After going six for twelve in my first four games, including a home run (.500 BA), and nine for twenty-six (.346 BA) in my first nine games, I fell into the biggest slump of my career. I went a not-so-mighty two for fifty-one in my last official trips to the plate for the New York Yankees. By July 3, I closed the books on my ever-so-brief Yankee baseball life with a total of eleven hits in seventy-seven times at bat (.207 BA). My Yankee hits included two doubles, one triple, and one very-special-to-me home run.

The year 1977 also marked the infamous "Son of Sam" summer in New York. As a result, my one partial season in New York unfolded at the same time that a deranged young man named David Berkowitz was out there running around with a handgun, randomly shooting people, and especially young lovers, on the streets and sidewalks of the city. The man was committing murder whenever he felt the need and saw a chance to get away with it.

No one was feeling safe on the streets of New York until Berkowitz was finally identified and caught. The random insanity by which the Son of Sam went about things and placed fear in the hearts of millions was tough for the city to bear. It proved too that, in contrast to the nicknames sports stars earn, some people acquire nicknames for the bad things they do.

At the same time the insane Son of Sam was grabbing the New York City limelight, tensions were building in the Yankee clubhouse because of all the soap opera stuff going on between owner George Steinbrenner, manager Billy Martin, and right fielder/superstar Reggie Jackson.

All this was happening too while I was slumping and riding the bench for the first time in my career. One day I finally snapped. I came out of the batting cage at Yankee Stadium prior to a game and ran into Coach Bobby Cox. Bobby simply tapped me on the shoulder in passing and said, "You're not playing today."

That's all he did. And I was ready to explode.

The first thing I did was walk over to the bat rack. Once there, I proceeded to destroy two of my bats by slamming them against the concrete wall. Then I just drifted off to the clubhouse, dressed, and started walking out of the stadium. No one stopped me, but I had an answer prepared for anyone who might try to hold me up long enough to ask, "Where are you going, Jimmy?" No one did ask or even seemed to notice that I was leaving. I gave my answer to the four winds: "I can't take it anymore!" I kept repeating the words aloud as I walked away.

I was in a strange mental place that afternoon as I left the stadium. I drove all the way to my apartment in New Jersey. Once inside my place, I began to give my actions a few second thoughts. In a very short while, I went back out to my car and drove back across the Hudson and East Rivers to the Bronx, walked back into the stadium, back into the clubhouse, dressed again for the game that was already going on, found my way to the Yankee dugout, and took my place alone at the end of the bench.

No anyone ever said anything to me.

No fine was ever levied against me. I was left to suppose that these silences were not out of indifference, but out of some commonly shared realization among most ballplayers about where I was heading with my career. It hurt bad, and I'm not talking here about missing the game scheduled for that particular day. I'm talking about the writing I saw on the wall at the sound of Bobby Cox's earlier words, "You're not playing today."

My career was done and I knew it, but I kept in shape to play by running with the pitchers. I began to use the increasing pine time to think about what I wanted to do with my life at age thirty-five. First base coach Bobby Cox and third base coach Dick Howser became my listening buddies and guideposts during this period. I shall forever be grateful to these two men for being there for me at that point in my career.

All the while this was going on with me, Reggie Jackson was establishing himself firm and tight as the new Yankee with the biggest ego. Ironically, Jackson had signed with the Yankees as a free agent on the same date the Braves sold my contract to the club, on November 29, 1976, but that's where any similarity in our two Yankee careers comes to an end.

While *The Demise of Jimmy Wynn: Cry Me a River* was figuratively playing far off Broadway, or maybe even further away and across the Hudson River in an East Orange, New Jersey, little theatre company, the Really Big Show in town, *Look at Me, Billy! No, You Listen to Me, Reggie!*, starring Reggie Jackson and Billy Martin, was playing deep-in-the-bright-lights heart of Broadway.

Reggie Jackson was his own self-appreciation club. He just loved talking about how important he was to the team's chances of winning. As you probably remember, Reggie became famous in spring training in 1977 for that line, "I am the straw that stirs the drink," when someone asked him to summarize his value to the Yankee club.

Catfish Hunter may have summed up Reggie's personality best when he made up a joke about Jackson's new Reggie candy bar.

"You know how you can tell Reggie's candy bar from all the others?" Catfish once asked. "It's the only one that comes straight out of the wrapper telling you how good it is!"

Then, of course, we had the famous incident in Boston on Saturday, June 18, 1977, that went out to the whole country over national television.

Late in the game that day, the Boston Red Sox were well on their way to an eventual 10–4 stomping of the Yankees in Fenway Park, a bad enough day in itself. It got worse fast when the slow-footed Jim Rice of Boston dropped a dying quail into right field that looked pretty catchable from the time it left the bat, but Reggie Jackson, who was playing right field, just sort of made a lazy jogging attempt to reach the ball.

Instead of being caught, the ball hit the ground in front of Reggie and bounded away far enough to help even the slow-moving Rice reach second base with what amounted to a cheap double in the eyes of many who saw it. And two of those eyes belonged to Billy Martin.

Martin was livid. He immediately sent Paul Blair out to right field as a defensive replacement for Jackson. That's when things really heated up. Now the equally angry and publicly embarrassed Reggie Jackson came roaring into our dugout on the first-base side. He went storming after manager Martin.

"What's the big idea?" Reggie screamed. "Why did you show me up in front of these people like that?"

As soon as Martin sensed the attack, he sprang into action to get at Reggie, leaving coaches Yogi Berra and Elston Howard with the rough job of keeping the two men apart while the rest of us tumbled around in the dugout as the closest front-row spectators to a scene that NBC-TV carried to all of America. At this one moment in time, Mr. Reggie Jackson's future stature as New York's "Mr. October" seemed as improbable as snowfall in Houston on the Fourth of July.

Speaking of the Fourth of July, it was near that time in 1977 that I made my last appearance in a Yankee game. It happened on July 3, 1977, when I failed to reach base while pinch hitting for Fred Stanley in the nightcap game of a 16–10 losing cause against the Tigers at Yankee Stadium. It was on the twilight side of a lazy double-header that I would have otherwise completely missed as an active player.

That pretty much covers my Yankee year. Billy Martin and his coaches must have thought so too. They called me in the next day for a little talk in Billy's office. The Yankees wanted me to drop down to AAA ball to get my batting eye back, all the while assuring me that my pay would remain the same.

I didn't have to think that over very long. It had been thirteen years since I played for my last minor league team at Oklahoma City and I sure didn't want to do it again, not for even one more day.

I guess my pride was hurt, but that wasn't the major reason I said "No" to the Yankees' offer. I knew that I had reached something larger than a slump in my physical life as a ballplayer and it wasn't something that was going to be cured by a little rehab time in the minors. I had reached the end of the road as far as my abilities to physically play the game were concerned. I'd lost bat speed, timing, and the ability to lay off unhittable pitches. All the qualities that had made me able to play the game proudly as the Toy Cannon were now gone from me.

The music of my God-given physical talent had died. And I was left dancing alone in the silence of a rainy, but strangely quiet afternoon at baseball's one and only cathedral. Who knows when it started happening for me, Jimmy Wynn? I guess it's always happening all the time to all ballplayers. We just never know it until it gets here.

Nobody wants to find the truth by falling down on a routine fly ball catch or by going nothing-for-five with four strikeouts against pitchers you used to own. In that regard, just hearing "You're not in the lineup today" was a pretty easy way to get the message, if there is such a thing. I guess it still bugged me that, like almost everyone else, I hadn't seen it coming until it slapped me in the head.

Back then, I just knew that my decline had started earlier than July 3, 1977, and that it wasn't curable by a trip to Toledo. Now I know that my dip had started in earnest in 1975, the year following my World Series year with the Dodgers.

The Yankees did what they had to do in response to my minor league assignment refusal. They gave me my unconditional release.

I thanked the Yankees for the opportunity and made a point to say good-bye to all of my teammates, extending each of them my best wishes for team success.

Dad had taught me the right way to go into the game. And now I was trying to leave it in the right way too.

I think I did OK with the surface things in that moment, but I will never find the words to describe what was going on deep inside me. I think you'd have to walk a few years in my shoes to understand how a ballplayer feels when he says goodbye to the game and, even then, you would have your own feelings about things and not mine.

This would have been the perfect moment to just go back to my home in Los Angeles, but pride derails us from many perfect opportunities for letting go. I had been making my peace for weeks that 1977 would be my last year as a player, but the Yankees had pushed up the date for me by giving me an early release.

Pride said: "This was not your decision. Find a way to finish the season somewhere else. If you don't improve there, then go ahead and retire after this full season is over."

I signed to play the rest of the 1977 season with the Milwaukee Brewers, now managed by one of my respected Cincinnati role models, former shortstop Alex Grammas. All I got from the experience was the satisfaction of finishing the whole season and total affirmation by my Milwaukee stats that yes indeed, it was time for Jimmy Wynn to hang 'em up.

In thirty-six games for the 1977 Brewers, I added twenty-three hits in one hundred and seventeen times at bat for a Milwaukee batting average of .197. Of my twenty-three hits, I had three doubles and one triple, but no more homers.

Anytime Jimmy Wynn goes to bat one hundred and seventeen official times and fails to hit a single home run, it's time to quit. And so I did.

I went back to Los Angeles to take it easy, play a little golf, and just give myself time to take stock of what I wanted to do with the rest of my non–playing life. I wasn't entertaining any thoughts of a comeback in the spring, nor was I trying to fill the void by finding another woman to marry.

I had matured. The next woman who came into my life was going to have to be very special. If she reached me at all, and if I reached her, it was going to have to be on the Lord's terms, not mine or hers. She might come tomorrow. She might come years from this moment. Or she might never come at all. It wasn't up to me to make it happen. I just had to stay open to meeting someone that filled my life on a much deeper spiritual plane.

Meanwhile, the Yankees didn't forget me. When they traveled to Los Angeles to play the Dodgers in the 1977 World Series, they made sure I had tickets for the game and even more. The Yankees wanted me to know that they had voted me a partial share of their player winnings.

I was really humbled by the Yankee team gesture, but I refused the money. "Give it to a deserving charity," I said, before adding a request of my own.

"There is something I'd like to have as a short-time member of the 1977 club," I said. "You guys are standing on the brink of something that always eluded me as a player. If you win this thing, and you're willing to include me for my small part in helping you get here, I would more than anything love to have a New York Yankees World Series Championship ring."

The Yankees were all over me with pats and hugs on that one. When they went on from there to take the 1977 World Series in six games from the Dodgers, I got my ring too. It remains on my finger today as one of my most treasured baseball possessions.

The greater treasure for me, however, is my memory of the last day the music played strongly in my baseball life. If I were writing a movie script of *The Jimmy Wynn Story*, it would have been the day I should've said goodbye to baseball forever and never again stepped forth on the field as an active player.

That last big moment happened on Thursday, April 7, 1977. The New York Yankees were celebrating a very special Opening Day in the newly remodeled Yankee Stadium against the visiting Milwaukee Brewers. After playing their 1976 games around the Mets at Shea Stadium, the Yankees were back in The House That Ruth Built in 1923, but in a more modernized, safer structure.

In the Opening Day lineup, I was scheduled to hit sixth as the DH.

I awakened that morning with all the butterflies of a school kid on the Saturday of a big sandlot game. Since I had taken an apartment in New Jersey, I wasn't sure how long the drive over to Manhattan and then on to the Bronx was going to take. I wasn't even sure of when I was supposed to be there for the start of a night game, so I left early.

As it turns out, I was the first player on hand, but that was fine with me. I dressed out quickly so I would then have some time to explore the playing field and visit the monuments of all the great players in Yankee history.

As I walked from the Yankee dugout across the infield, I gazed over at home plate, to the very spot where Ruth, Gehrig, DiMaggio, Berra, Dickey, Maris, and Mantle all had stood in their time. What a rush that was. I was awed deep inside from my head to my toes.

They don't call Yankee Stadium the "Cathedral of Baseball" for no reason. I walked across that sacred grass in measured reverence for all the great souls of baseball whose own music had played here since 1923.

When I reached the monuments, I tried to read the inscriptions and spend a little time with each, but, of course, I was drawn like a magnet to the image of the great Babe Ruth. Stillness came over me as a power I've never before felt or known at any other ballpark. A wind rushed over me as a source of some strange untapped energy. I felt at once strong, at peace, and totally focused.

All of a sudden my quiet, solitary meditation was shattered by the loud voice of an approaching teammate. It was Reggie Jackson.

"What are you doing here?" I asked.

"Hey, man," Reggie answered, "I play for the Yankees too. I just thought I'd come out and join you here at the monuments."

"I didn't need your company," I said in a flat-out unfriendly voice. "I came out here to have a quiet moment alone. Now you've spoiled it for me."

I turned and walked away, heading back to the clubhouse as Reggie stood alone and offered one parting shot from his own hurt feelings, I suppose.

"Well, excuse me!" Reggie said.

Maybe he needed to get back at me, but later, near game time, Reggie came up to me and started talking some trash.

"So, they called you the Toy Cannon over in that other league, did they?"

Reggie was a master of the one-liner putdown.

"That's right, Reggie," I answered, "and that other league you're talking about is the National League, or as it's sometimes called among those who have good sense to show it proper respect, the Senior Circuit!"

"That right?" Reggie shot back. "Well, it really don't matter what they call that other league 'cause you are misnamed, anyway! You ain't no home run cannon! You ain't big enough to hit no real home runs! Not like the ones I hit!"

"Just you watch!" I muttered as I walked away. I wanted nothing further to do with Reggie Jackson. He riled my blood in ways that didn't feel good at all.

The game got underway to a tumultuous roar, as the writers like to write. Catfish Hunter was pitching for the Yankees and we were going up against 6'6" Bill Travers of the Milwaukee Brewers. (Remember, Milwaukee was a member of the American League back in 1977.)

Going into the bottom of the second inning in a scoreless tie, I came up to bat for my first time in Yankee Stadium with none on and one out. I remember feeling calm, strong, focused, and relaxed as I stood in to face Travers. I let the first inside pitch go, but I was aware that the ball looked to be about the size of a cantaloupe as it passed me.

The second cantaloupe came in fast over the plate. It did not pass. If it had been a real cantaloupe, I would have in that moment cut it in half with my bat.

With one sweet swing of my Louisville Slugger, the ball took off on a high arching flight to deep center field. I saw the Brewers' center fielder make a couple of steps back before he froze to simply watch. The ball left the field and fell into the darkened section of deepest center. The first run of the season, and the first home run in the new Yankee Stadium, forever belonged to me, Jimmy Wynn, the Toy Cannon. It was also the 291st and last home run of my major league career.

1977: "The Day the Music Died" was also the day that Jimmy Wynn hit his 291st and last major league home run (Courtesy Brace Photo, Chicago).

I floated around the bases, soaking up the roar of a Yankee crowd that still plays on today at will in my brain's baseball memory iPod. My happiness in that moment is forever there for me upon any reminder of that happening so long ago.

As I approached home plate, all my teammates had come out to greet me because of everything that home run represented as a symbol of success in our new season and, I guess too, because of how far it traveled. Reggie Jackson was among the first to greet me, but I brushed past him, high-fiving and hugging with all the others as I made my way to the end of the dugout and sat down alone.

A few minutes later, here came Reggie at me a second time. I really give Reggie Jackson credit now for reaching out to me back then, even though I was still too hot at him at the time to accept what he would then say with any instant outpouring of graciousness.

"Look, Jimmy," Reggie said. "I take back all the mean things I said. You must have been the Toy Cannon in that other league after all, man! You can hit home runs with anybody!"

"As I said earlier, Reggie, that 'other league' is the National League, the *Senior Circuit*." I was still pretty wound up over Reggie's earlier trash words. I couldn't pass on laying out a few final digs. "Remember those names the next time you decide to take lightly what we do over there!"

I'm sorry, Reggie. None of us are perfect, are we? Thirty-three years after the fact, we are both entitled to the lessons of humility that only age can bring in full doses. I'm just grateful that I could leave the game with my own final blast of home-run joy back in April 1977. If I'd had enough humility in me that same day, I'd have hung 'em up on the spot right there.

But I didn't leave on the high note of my Opening Day homer. I stayed long enough to crash and burn in New York. Then I took the toast of what was left of me to Milwaukee and provided breakfast for a few more pitchers until I took myself off the menu at season's end.

We just don't get it when it happens to us personally, and who knows? Maybe that's especially true of home run hitters. All home run hitters want that opportunity to put their career signature on one last great game, but we don't always recognize when it just happened for the last time. Look at history for the best example I can recall. Had Babe Ruth known for sure he was done on that day in Pittsburgh back in 1935 that he hit the three home runs in one game for the Braves against the Pirates, he would have done what William Bendix did in the 1948 movie version of that moment in his life story. He would have walked off the field and never taken another time at bat. In reality, Ruth went on to Cincinnati for a little more meaningless and hitless play before he finally hung it up a few days later for all time.

I would have done well to have walked away after that last home run in 1977 too, but I had to go through a little period of extended futility in New York and Milwaukee to reach that deal with my own ego, but that's OK too. None of us are perfect.

In my mind, and in the heart of my soul of souls, that last Opening Day for me in 1977 was the day the music died. First it soared on the wings of one last big and far-traveling home run in the House of Ruth. Then it died steadily within me as a player, even as I slumped on the Yankee bench, belligerently accepting the swallowed-pride congratulations of one Reggie Jackson.

After this moment, the baseball music for me as a player stayed dead, but the joy of that one last moment as a home run hitter lives on forever. It remains solidly in my reverie as a symphony of soulful joy and triumph, an honest and repeatable spiritual trip that always takes me back to Opening Day in Yankee Stadium on April 7, 1977, anytime I choose to go there.

It was what it was, once upon a time.

By late September 1977, it was time to go home.

Going back to my house in Los Angeles, I put it all in God's hands.

CHAPTER 15

Rounding Third, Headed for Home

We make a living by what we do. We make a life by what we give.

Sir Winston Churchill

God must have invented golf and the southern California weather on the same day of Creation. Those two things come together hand and glove and they both fit me and my needs to the hilt during the winter of 1977–78.

Back in L.A., single again, and no longer prepping for another spring training jaunt in four short months, I was really just into little more than chilling out and sleeping in. Most of the time, only an early tee time got me out of bed any sooner than necessary.

I had taken a job representing an L.A.-based beverage company, but that work panned out mainly as a celebrity-show-up deal. It quickly proved to be not very demanding on my schedule of other things to do.

It felt a little strange come spring, of course. After all, I had been going to spring training somewhere for sixteen years in a row, all of my adult life, and 1978 was different.

Spring 1978 was just a stream of endless days on the golf links of L.A.

In all modesty, I got to be an excellent golfer with a powerful long game after my retirement from baseball. Driving a golf ball 300 yards down the fairway came as normally to me as hitting a baseball for distance. Although I haven't done any studies on the subject, I think that my driving strengths in the long game are a fairly typical result for baseball power hitters who seriously take up golf.

If you were a guy who was prone to hitting home runs, chances are higher that you will be able to use many of the same muscles and moves to drive a golf ball for distance. Unfortunately, these long game abilities do not help your putting skills one iota. Maybe baseball contact hitters are better putters. I don't know. I just know that golf was a great game for me, and one

Jimmy met Marie, the love of his life, after his 1977 retirement.

that was very important to me in my transition from baseball to civilian life.

Of course, hitting a baseball and hitting a golf ball are very different in a few important ways. Baseballs are larger, of course, and they come at you at various heights, paths of trajectory, and speeds. Golf balls are smaller. They are more like hitting a baseball pitch in the dirt that's already come to a dead stop and shrunk in size about four or five times.

No problem. Right?

I still hung out with some of my old Dodger buddies in 1978, and mostly on the golf course, but I was at peace with the idea that my baseball playing days were done. That is, I was OK and, I thought, settled with the idea of retirement until a group from Mexico approached me about playing again in 1979 for the Coahuila Mineros of the AAA Mexican League. This all came about during the time that Mexican League ball was recognized by Major League Baseball.

I said no to the Mexican League offer until they waved enough money at me. Then I gave in and signed up to play. Maybe I should have guessed that the good pay also came with great expectations. These people didn't just want the name of Jimmy Wynn on their roster. They wanted Jimmy Wynn at the peak of his home-run hitting power, and they wanted him to hit home runs in a ballpark in Coahuila that was about the size of the Grand Canyon. If memory serves, it was 360 feet down the foul lines and it just got far worse from there as the fences moved to the power alleys and deep center.

The playing field was hard as stone with little to no grass.

For the record, the Coahuila manager was a fellow named Victor Favela, a Mexican national whom I'd never heard of, but that was the norm down there. I didn't know any of these guys, giving me, at least, something else in common with the rest of the larger world: No one else would ever get to know these guys on a larger baseball stage either.

I finally tagged one last monster-shot home run for Coahuila, but that was it. I left on good terms with the club after that homer, explaining as best I was able that I just couldn't do this sort of thing anymore. I think they understood, but even if they didn't get it, it was of no matter to me. I was done.

Going down south to play Mexican baseball in 1979 was a mistake, but I tried to mine this experience for all the lessons it was worth. "Jimmy," I told myself, "from here on in, down the road into the deep twilight, try not to do any other kind of work that is just for the money. It's not worth it."

Thirty-two years later, I think I've kept that promise to myself.

Sometime in the early 1980s, I got a call that turned my life upside down. Mom called me from Cincinnati to let me know that Dad had died in the hospital following a short stay. I never knew the exact cause of his death. He had been suffering from a number of things, any one of which could have taken him out. All I knew for sure was that I was being forced to hear words I never wanted to hear. And I never wanted to remember the date it actually happened.

Dad was dead, gone from my life forever.

About a year later, around the time that I was just beginning to accept the fact that my dad's physical presence in my life was gone forever, I got another call. This time the call from my brother carried the news that Mom had died too. The way I figured it, Mom just didn't want to be here any longer without Dad, so she checked out to join him in Heaven. Now they were together again, both gone from us Wynn kids forever in worldly form, but together with each other as they always wanted to be.

In the end, even when we can't see it, things turn out as they need to be.

If we have loving parents, and we live long enough, we eventually have to let them go from our everyday physical lives. If we allow ourselves to accept the loss, over time, we learn that some things don't pass away from us completely with the deaths of our loving parents. We learn that we get to keep all the love and lessons they ever gave to us while they were here.

Over time, I came to understand the fact that my parents, Joe and Maude Wynn, were still with me forever in the name of God's love, even after death. From that realization, I came to embrace a three-part understanding that the matters of God, love, and forever are all tied together.

God is forever. Love is forever. God is Love.

We are free to see that formula or not. We are also free spiritually to feast or starve. How we resolve all the great questions of life for ourselves remains our individual challenge. All I'm doing here is sharing what came to me from my own personal experience on the path of spiritual search for meaning in life.

Losing Mom and Dad in the early 1980s helped me make the decision to move back to Houston from Los Angeles. If my two kids were going to receive the benefits of all the love I felt for them, I needed to make a life for myself closer to where they lived. Joe and Maude Wynn had been my everyday parents. I wasn't even living in the same town with Kimberly or Jimmy Jr.

I wasn't going back to Houston to be a copy of Joe Wynn. I was going back to Houston to be every ounce of the entire father that I knew Jimmy Wynn could be under these very different life circumstances. Life's too short to be separated from the people we claim to love and care about.

Years after the fact, I will say this much about my return to Houston: I never want to be apart from my kids and grandkids again, not for as long as I still live on this earth as part of God's plan.

Somewhere, in a time beyond the death of my parents, I started getting some strong tugs from several old friends back in Houston about coming home. They all bore the same independent and unified message, but one voice was especially strong. An old friend named Dr. Mazique put it this way: "C'mon back to Houston, Jimmy! This is where your real home is! This is where your real friends are! And this is where your family is!"

I listened. I wanted more than the sunshine, golf, and late-night poker games that had become the major track of my L.A. life. So, about 1985, I put my L.A. home on the market and moved back to Texas. I first took an apartment. Then I leased a condo, and I continued my happy single life in Houston, again living in the area of town where I had come of age as a ballplayer, socializing once more with many of the same people I had gotten to know here many years earlier.

It's funny how mindsets often cause us to disregard changes in old social conditions. When I first came to Houston in 1963, segregation still laid a heavy hand upon the public movements of black people in the city. There were still movies and restaurants where black people weren't welcome back then.

Heck! Allow me to take it where it belongs. In 1963, there were still whole neighborhoods in Houston where the simple presence of a black man was looked upon by many whites with great suspicion. That fact remains today, I'm sure, but I would hope that the good and fair-minded people of Houston now far outnumber the old racists who used to run things during the era of legal and socially formal segregation.

What I'm saying here is not meant with any disrespect for any of my many white Houston friends. I just felt more comfortable living again in the area that was once the heart of Houston's black professional community back

Jimmy Wynn's kids, Jimmy Jr. and Kimberly, have grown up happy and close to their famous ballplayer dad!

in the pre–Civil Rights era. That would be the area of Houston known for years as the Third Ward, near Texas Southern University. I felt safe, accepted, and at home there.

Hey! I was living pretty well in my new circumstances. I was now taking my Major League Baseball pension; I had money from the sale of my L.A. house; and I was now working as sort of a celebrity bartender at a high-class black social cafe called the McGregor Club. The place was owned by Tully Tuttle, a lady who ran a high-class bar there for years in that area on McGregor Drive.

I enjoyed the bartender work too because it involved listening to people and talking baseball. In the short time I did the bartender thing, I was good at listening, and I was also good at mixing drinks with advice and fast opinions on baseball. The drink-mixing itself wasn't hard. I could fix everything from gin and vermouth to Scotch on the rocks to bourbon and Coke. How hard is that?

Most importantly of all, being back in Houston gave me the opportunity to find the long road home of rebuilding my relationships with my two nearly grown kids. It didn't happen overnight. Their mother was still living back then, and Ruth remained pretty cool to the idea of letting me back into the children's lives on a regular basis. When I would call and ask about them, Ruth would usually answer my questions about the kids with a quick and cool "They're doing fine" tone of voice. She always spoke these words in a way that made me feel she was really saying, "Back up, Jimmy. Don't ask for more than that."

Moving back to Houston only removed the mileage barriers to regular contact with Kimberly and Jimmy Jr. Once back here, I had to deal with all of the unhealed psychological wounds between Ruth and me that made it difficult for us to get along and for me to see the children. Of course, the age of the kids played a big part in things too by the time I moved back to Houston. They were both into their teenage years by then and they were not too interested in spending their time with a dad who hadn't been around much while they were growing up, anyway. Ruth's coolness toward me just made it easier for me to stay away too.

There were all kinds of tolls on this road to reunion with the kids and not all of them had been placed there by Ruth. My absence on a daily basis over the time of my baseball career played a big part in the problem. Then there was the clock itself. Time may be a great healer, but the absence of a father from his children's everyday lives over time creates a need for healing from the damage of absence.

I was responsible for my part in healing a breach of trust with the kids that only God could eventually mend in peace. We had an ocean of distance to cover, but I was dedicated to the idea that love and contact would win the day.

Sadly, it would not be until Ruth died young from cancer that I would have a clear chance to rebuild my relationships with both of my then young adult kids. I never blamed Ruth for her feelings toward me, and I was saddened for the kids when their mother passed away. Our divorce had to be, but it left a trail of hurt for all of us.

As for my children, we all loved each other as family, but the emotional and physical distance that piled up over time had robbed us of a lot of early bonding opportunities. We had to find it together anew, over a new stretch of years, against the pain of the earlier lost time, but in the name of love, after I moved back home to Houston.

I feel now, and I certainly hope my two grown kids agree, that everything is much better between us today. I also know that we shall always need to keep the fires of good contact going between us for the rest of our time together here on God's good Earth. If we can each do our parts, we can have what a loving family needs to have. And that's each other's love and devotion until our deaths do us part.

We can have the part of God's love that flows most freely through the love of family members for each other. It takes two loving hearts to find that kind of love. Sad to say, neither their mom nor I were capable of owning that kind of love for each other, but the love between parents and their children is different.

My love for my kids is flesh-and-blood unconditional. No matter how well we now have learned to get along and be together, I would have always loved Kimberly and Jimmy Jr. anyway, no matter what.

One other thing is very important to me here. I was aiming for something beyond simply "getting along better" in the matter of Kimberly and Jimmy Jr. I wanted to be something of the father to my kids that I never was while they were growing up. I wanted to be there for them, even if it were only in a ghostly whisper of the way that my father was there for me the whole time I was growing up in Cincinnati.

I had to try. And I asked God to help me get there as best I could. Only Jimmy Jr. and Kimberly know for sure if I have succeeded in any way, but that's all that matters. I'm their dad, for better or worse, forever, even beyond the day Our Lord calls me home.

My whole life seemed to be unfolding in a different direction once I moved back to Houston. Sometimes, when you're yearning to find your spiritual mission in life, it reaches out to find you. I think that's what happened to me.

Somewhere near the end of the 1980s, I started getting calls from Rob Matwick and Jamie Hildreth of the Houston Astros administrative staff. They both wanted my help with some of the community outreach programs that the club was trying to produce for neighborhood groups, especially with school-age kids.

The Astros were having trouble finding players who would volunteer their time to community service. Things were changing in the big league scene and it was getting harder at that time to find active players who were willing to go out and talk to groups on top of their direct jobs of playing baseball.

The problem was fairly short term with the Astros. A young fellow on their club named Craig Biggio was about to break out as a future Hall of Famer on the humanitarian side too. Craig Biggio got on board early in support of Houston's Sunshine Kids Foundation. Biggio now serves as their national spokesperson in addition to all the other things he does to help raise money for kids with cancer.

By 2008, and largely through the tireless efforts of Ms. Marian Harper and the support of owner Drayton McLane Jr., the Houston Astros had put together the Astros in Action Foundation to help inner-city kids by bringing new first-class baseball fields and equipment to the kids of Houston who would otherwise never have a chance to play the game of baseball.

In 1988, I started working in community service for the Astros. I went to many schools in the Houston area on a regular basis, just to talk about everything from how I got started in baseball, the Astros, the importance of following their own dreams, the value of learning from their own mistakes, avoiding drugs, bad company, and crime, the value of healthy self-esteem, and the importance of having a life plan for themselves that is built around what they really care about.

You always hope that you were able to reach somebody along the way, but the payoff for me over the past twenty-two years has been the personal discovery that an old expression from my own childhood is really true: "It is better to give than to receive." I always try to sprinkle that message into my talks as though it were salt on a good home-cooked meal.

Nothing is worth it if you're just doing it for the money alone. We all need to find the gift that only comes from giving of ourselves, if we wish to own any real happiness in life. We all hunger to find something in life we feel passionately about. If our hunger is just for making money, any way we can, however, it will eventually disappoint us, even if we never publicly admit the fact to another soul.

As I see it, real peace in life is about giving, not taking. In fact, I will add to that belief even this much room: A life without giving is not worth living.

My post–retirement work with the Astros in community service has been all about *giving* for two decades and counting. I could not be happier with the path I've taken. It's a road that has produced a state of mind that has dovetailed nicely into my awakened need to be a real father to my now two adult children as well as a real grandfather to my grandkids.

I'm very proud of both my son and daughter today. Jimmy Jr. works as a valued long-term delivery person for UPS; Kimberly is employed as a health care professional at M.D. Anderson Hospital. Like Jimmy Jr., she also has built a good name for herself over years of faithful service to her career.

My post–playing career reunion with baseball has been interesting. For a while after my return to Houston, I didn't even go to games or keep up with the Astros very closely. I was still in that phase of my adjustment where I needed a break from the game, but that soon enough changed. I got involved in the Major League Baseball Players Alumni Association and fairly quickly found myself serving on the Board of Directors.

Working for the MLBPAA was a good experience for me. I started traveling around the country as a planner and participant in various teaching clinics and golf tournaments that we supported or help sponsor. I really liked the teaching part of the job and, of course, I always loved the camaraderie with others in the name of a good cause. Realize it or not at the time, I was on my way to the great bell call of my playing career retirement years. That was, and still is, service to others.

Card shows were starting to grow in popularity by the late 1980s and early 1990s, but I only did a couple of these events a year. Back then, the emphasis was on bringing Hall of Fame members to the public for autographs. As time went by, people's memories of me as a player seemed to sharpen and I became more in demand at card shows. Funny how that works, isn't it? I guess I sort of had to be away from the active game long enough to grow into the "Legend of Jimmy Wynn."

Whatever the reason, I was glad to have the attention and the opportunity for a little card show money. I didn't play baseball under the "Pennies from Heaven" skies of today's MLB salary structure. I played for far less money, with no way to set myself up for life just for getting paid to play the game I loved. If today's deals had been around when I played, I would have taken one gladly and been set for life too, but that's OK. Being lazy-rich has never been the major fire in my heart anyway.

I did the card shows for the people-contact opportunity it gave me as much as I did them for the money. I saw these shows as a chance for the fans and me to come together and share our memories of those times when I played the game. I like to think that the fans had a pretty good idea going into our contact that I was appreciative and glad to have the time with them too. Along with my autograph on items, and for no extra charge that could ever be put upon my signature, the individual fans also always received my thanks from the heart for their support. Without the fans, there never would have been a Jimmy Wynn the baseball player.

As I walked deeper into the autumn of my life, I started to notice that I was beginning to develop words and thoughts to go along with the earliest images of my childhood. These increased in my mind after the death of my parents, and the pattern continued following my return to Houston. I see these haunting images now as further lessons from Joe and Maude Wynn. They were clearly images of the mind, but they were images that gave birth to new words about the most important lessons of my childhood.

All those little moments when a look on my dad's face told me everything from "try harder" to "good job" came rushing at me. The look on Mom's face when she told us that we simply needed to adopt our brother William came back to me too. The new words that now attached to these old images were these:

> I am so grateful that I had parents who helped me find and develop my passion in life at an early age; so happy that I had parents who taught me to take responsibility for my actions; and so fortunate to have had parents who taught me love was forever when it was about giving, not taking.

I learned these things from Joe and Maude Wynn:

"We believe in you. You are here to fulfill God's purpose for you in this life. You have both a right and a personal responsibility to do what it takes to get yourself there.

"Give to others and try to do no harm along the way. If you make a mistake, admit it. If you cause damage, apologize and make up for it as best you can.

"Learn from your pain so that you don't keep repeating the same painful experiences over and over again.

"Don't look for peace and happiness anyplace outside your own heart.

"See love as giving. Once you see that much, you will be ready to receive it."

Jimmy and Marie Wynn with grandkids (l-r) Chastity, Darren, and Kennedi, the children of Jimmy's daughter, Kimberly Wynn Davis.

That being said, I rolled into the 1990s feeling pretty content with the idea of staying single and never getting married again. I enjoyed getting up each day when I pleased; fixing breakfast at home or going out to eat as the mood struck me; and dating a variety of pretty ladies, or else just playing golf with my buddies, as I preferred on a particular day.

Never say never.

Although it took the death of my parents to pull me totally into the lessons of my purpose in life, I met a very attractive lady in 1992 who turned my world upside down on my commitment to the middle-aged bachelor life. A lady named Marie turned out to be the love of my life, the beautiful soul mate I had waited forever to meet and almost missed. It was the presence of Marie in my life that helped me spiritually get through with better understanding the earlier loss of my parents. It was the presence of Marie that also helped me find and clarify my faith and relationship with God and also the lessons of love from my parents.

For the grace of God that brought me Marie, I shall be forever grateful.

Marie and I met in 1992 at the Wunder Bar, a mainly black social club that was quite popular among black professional people back in the late 1980s and early 1990s. Marie had just happened to come there one night with a niece to have a drink and just get a little air from the divorce she was going through at the time.

It was a meeting straight out of that song, "Some Enchanted Evening." As soon as I laid eyes upon this tall, slim, and attractive stranger with the long flowing straight hair, I wanted to meet her. Before I could make my first move, however, I looked up and some other guy had already asked her to dance.

I'm a competitor. I wasn't going to let something like a fast draw dance invitation stand in the way of the desire I had to meet this special lady. I walked out there about halfway through their dance and cut in. The other guy was a little shocked, but he yielded the way—which is what he needed to do. This feeling I was having for this new lady was not going to be stopped short by anything less than the hand of God, and this other guy didn't look like God's agent at all.

Dancing with Marie felt right from the very start, even in the short time we danced before I learned her name and told her mine. My name was vaguely familiar to Marie, but she was not a baseball fan. That was fine with me too. I didn't have to worry that she was going to be attracted to me because of my baseball celebrity. Marie was either going to like me for myself or not at all.

After our dance, I asked to sit and talk with Marie and she was OK with the idea. I thoroughly enjoyed it and I ended up letting her know that I would love to see her again. She was open to the idea, but she didn't seem overjoyed by the prospect of further contact on a social basis. I exchanged telephone numbers with Marie on drink napkins and we soon got together for a planned date.

We've been together ever since.

Marie later explained that she wasn't immediately attracted to me because of the height factor. "At first, I couldn't get past the fact you were so short," she later admitted. Well, I'm not that short, am I? I'm 5'9" tall, but Marie is 5'8" without her shoes. When she puts on her long high heels, like the ones she was wearing on the night we met, she towers over me.

"Over time, as I was getting to know you, Jimmy," Marie also admitted, "my attraction grew. I realized that I couldn't base my feelings for you on your stature. I had to base my feelings on your heart. I fell in love with a good-looking guy who also happened to be walking around with the biggest heart that ever ticked!"

How could I ever forget a quote like that? The strange, or not so strange, thing is that my always-growing love for Marie goes way beyond her physical beauty. She's a walking heart in her own right and the most spiritually centered person I've ever met. Just being with Marie has brought me closer to God than I ever thought I could be. She's my partner in every way.

Marie and I dated for eight years. We finally married on March 4, 2000, while we were on a business/pleasure trip to Hawaii on behalf of the Field of Dreams event, a program skillfully planned by a fellow named Bob Tur-

Jimmy Wynn (l) with daughter Kimberly (top) and son Jimmy Jr. (second from right), plus grandkids (l-r) Kennedi and Chastity Davis.

nauckas, the director of a company known as Beyond Meetings and Incentives. We were staying at the Ritz Carleton on the big island of Hawaii.

We weren't planning on getting married in Hawaii, but word had gotten around that Marie and I had been thinking about a wedding in Las Vegas. Bob Turnauckas pushed the envelope on that one. "If you guys want to get married here in Hawaii, I'll help you arrange it," he offered.

After going through some mutual reflection on our true intentions, and with some down-to-earth gut checking, Marie and I together decided to accept Bob Turnauckas's offer. We obtained the wedding license, put on Hawaiian shirts, and enlisted the support of other Field of Dreams friends as our wedding party.

Trudy Grant, the wife of Jim "Mudcat" Grant, stepped forward to serve as Marie's maid of honor. All the other former major leaguers who were on the trip with us, namely Gaylord Perry, Tommy Davis, Mudcat Grant, Ferguson Jenkins, and Steve Carlton, all stood up for me as my best men. Talk about an All-Star cast. Hey! I'd put my wedding party up against any other that ever formed to compete in a game of baseball—any year, any season, any month, any day of the week, or any time of day.

Right after the moment that Marie and I said our "I do's," a gentle wind swept through the room that no one there could ignore. It reminded me of that wind I felt in Yankee Stadium back in 1977 on the date of my visit to Monument Valley.

Jimmy Wynn with all his grandkids and some of their friends. The girl with glasses is granddaughter Tiara. Clockwise from the little girl at lower left, a friend, we have Chastity with a big smile; another friend in back ducking his head; granddaughter RhondKetia; grandson Darren (Little "D"); and granddaughter Kennedi.

Marie told me later that she felt that wind as the presence of the Holy Spirit sweeping over us. I said it was probably the soul of my late mom, showing up for the wedding, just in time to give us her blessing. Most likely, we were both right.

After we exchanged vows, we enjoyed a beautiful reception in the hotel gazebo, where we were served with the finest food and drink available, caviar and champagne, the works, and also nice music and great photography. When all this ceremony and celebrating were said and done, Bob Turnauckaus took Marie and me aside and informed us that the hotel sponsoring the event was picking up the tab on the entire wedding.

Marie and I were both blown away with gratitude. We weren't planning to be married on that Hawaiian excursion, but I know we were both ready for our trip to be more than something beyond the baseball clinic it was scheduled to be.

Time flies.

On March 4, 2010, we celebrated our tenth wedding anniversary. This year is also the eighteenth anniversary of our first meeting at the Wunder Bar.

What else can I say? True love came late for Jimmy and Marie Wynn, but it got here, nevertheless, and with the power of the Holy Spirit guiding

The Gilbos: Marie Wynn's son Bo and his wife Rhonda, with daughters (l-r) Jaz, Jade and Jordyn.

us, we didn't let it slip through our fingers. That fire of our love is still growing stronger by the moment with each passing new day. A sunrise does not go by that I don't thank God for sending Marie into my life.

I'm also very proud of Marie's development as a spiritual writer. Her new book, *Empowered by Prayer*, is now in print and she is getting out there in the community, talking with groups about the powerful messages it contains.

Marie was scheduled to make an appearance in Houston to hit some talking points about her book on the *CwJTV* (Choices with Jeanette TV) program, but that appearance had to be rescheduled due to Hurricane Ike. For those of you who may be interested, please check out what Marie G. Wynn has to say about this very special work at her own website, www.empoweredbyprayer.com.

Although nothing exceeds my gratitude to God for the love of Marie and family, I am deep in appreciation to Him also for all the many blessings that have sprouted forth in the garden of my life during this autumn of my time on Earth.

Baseball has been very good to me. (There. I've said it.) My story would not feel complete had I not expressed that classic, but genuine line. I can even flesh it out further in very honest, specific terms.

Baseball, and especially the Houston Astros organization, has been very good to me. Thanks to owner Drayton McLane Jr.; Business President Pam Gardner; Baseball President Tal Smith; former Vice-President Rob Matwick; and current Vice-President Marian Harper; and too many others to mention here, my working role with the Astros has grown in many positive ways over the decade of the 1990s and the first decade of the 21st century.

As an employee of the Astros, I still do a lot of community speaking and public greeting work for the club.

In 1997, the year that Larry Dierker took over as manager of the Astros, I got the bug to coach. Larry didn't have a spot for me on the big league club, but I took a job as the hitting coach for the club's 1997 AAA team, the New Orleans Zephyrs. I didn't really want to get into that minor league travel cycle again, but Astros General Manager Gerry Hunsicker convinced me that taking the job in New Orleans could be a pathway to moving up later to the Astros staff.

Although I enjoyed many aspects of the actual teaching assignment as a hitting coach, that one year of minor league travel was enough to settle any remaining question I may have had about donning a uniform again for whole seasons of flying or bussing around the country. After 1997, I said no thank you to the idea of continuing in New Orleans.

I'm a home guy now, and Houston is my home. Let the younger fellows bite the dust of the open road over the course of a 162-game schedule. That one year in New Orleans is now way, way up there on the "Been There/Done That" shelf of my baseball memories.

Another joy came my way in 1992. In the same year I found Marie, I also learned that I had been inducted into the Texas Baseball Hall of Fame for my years of play with the Houston Astros. This honor would prove in time to be only the beginning of my association with an organization created in 1978 by the late George Schepps of Dallas for the purpose of preserving history and honoring excellence in Texas baseball.

In 2004, I received a phone call from my friend, Dr. Bill McCurdy, the Board President of the Texas Baseball Hall of Fame. Bill explained that his organization wanted to name an annual award for exceptional community service in my honor. The TBHOF wanted to call this presentation the Jimmy Wynn Toy Cannon Award and they also wanted me, Jimmy Wynn, to serve as both the first recipient and the annual presenter to all future honorees.

Bill expressed his own vision of the award in this way: "Complete service to community isn't possible through any single program. It takes the sum of much individual and small group effort to get the job done, with all these smaller efforts firing away at human needs and issues like so many toy cannons of caring."

The Jimmy Wynn Toy Cannon Award was born in 2004. I am now pleased also to report that I also served on the Board of Directors for the Texas Baseball Hall of Fame from January 2007 through August 2009.

Marie Wynn and sisters (l-r) Pat Mahan and Angelina Mitchell.

Although he doesn't want me to make this mention, I insist: I want to thank Bill McCurdy for the role he has played in bringing honor to my name as both a player and a man of dedication to community service. I also want to thank Bill for the help he has given me in the editing of this book, and even more for his deep and abiding friendship. Loyalty and honesty are the keys to real friendship and those qualities abide as the conditions that have brought Bill and me together as friends and co-workers on this project. I didn't want my story to just be a talking box score on my baseball life. I'm hoping I've helped you get to know me better.

My cup overflows in recent years too. Maybe it's been overflowing forever and I've simply grown old enough to realize the fact, but some nice things have come sunshining their way into my life during these latter days of Jimmy Wynn. I would be hard-pressed and soul-dead not to see and recognize how grateful I am for the happiness and satisfaction these blessings have brought to me.

In the spring of 2005, Astros owner Drayton McLane, Jr., pulled me aside at a benefit luncheon at Minute Maid Park for some news that practically caused me to faint on the spot. Short of induction into the National Baseball Hall of Fame, it was the sort of news for a former ballplayer that ranks way up there beyond all others as a form of ultimate honor.

Mr. McLane wanted me to know that the Houston Astros had decided to add my old number 24 to the franchise list of retired numbers. This meant that no other Astros player could ever again wear #24. That number had been retired in honor of Jimmy Wynn.

The retirement ceremony took place on Saturday, June 25, 2005. I was

In 2005, the Houston Astros retired Jimmy Wynn's Number 24.

presented with framed copies of the Colt .45s and Astros jerseys I had worn during my career with the club; I was acknowledged and duly honored at home plate prior to the game that was played that day; and I was congratulated by Mr. McLane, the whole Astros organization, and a whole army of former teammates like Joe Morgan, Larry Dierker, Jose Cruz, Bob Aspromonte, and Carl Warwick, just to name a few.

I joined some rarified company that summer afternoon in 2005 and I shall be forever humbled to walk in spirit among the others who also have been duly honored by the Houston organization. Including a couple of guys who've now come after me, the complete list of retired Houston MLB Club numbers at this writing is as follows—and presented here in the order of their retirement:

32—Jim Umbricht
40—Don Wilson
25—Jose Cruz
33—Mike Scott
34—Nolan Ryan
42—Jackie Robinson (retired by all Major League clubs)
49—Larry Dierker
24—Jimmy Wynn
5—Jeff Bagwell
7—Craig Biggio

At his uniform #24 retirement ceremony at Minute Maid Park on June 25, 2005, club owner Drayton McLane Jr. presented Jimmy Wynn with copies of all three uniform jerseys he wore in Houston, plus a real toy cannon that actually fires.

See what I mean by "forever humbled"? I'm walking in some tall company here, but I still thank Mr. McLane and the Houston Astros for deciding I belong in the same row of numbers that now flanks the big scoreboard in right center field at Minute Maid Park. I'm especially honored to have my number standing in line with the great Jackie Robinson. Because of Jackie's courage, the door of racism, the one always described in baseball circles as "the color line," was busted down for all the Jimmy Wynns of this world who grew up just wanting to play baseball at the most competitive level.

Thank you too, Jackie Robinson! Had you not gone before me, I could have been denied this whole wonderful baseball life in the major leagues. In respect for my interest in numbers, it's also not lost on me that our two numbers, 42 and 24, are inversely made up from the same two digits, just one more reason to feel the kind of special connection with Jackie Robinson that only another baseball player would probably understand. So many other good things have happened in recent years. In 2003, we started the Jimmy Wynn annual golf tournament for the benefit of the Urban League. The tourney has been a lot of fun and a big help to the support of Urban League programs. We are hoping to keep it going, beyond my lifetime, if possible.

In 2007, and thanks to Pam Gardner, President of Business Operations for the Houston Astros, I finally resumed my long-ago-abandoned broad-

Top: In 2006, Jimmy Wynn started working as an analyst for the FOX Sports Houston telecasts of Houston Astros home games at Minute Maid Park. FOX analyst and broadcaster Greg Lucas was Jimmy's first on-the-air partner. *Bottom:* As of 2010, Jimmy is still going strong at FOX and is also working hard for the community relations program arm of the Houston Astros. Here he is enjoying a beautiful workday at the ball park with FOX co-analyst Kevin Eschenfelder.

casting career, but this time, instead of KYOK-AM, I was on a live telecast of several Houston Astros home games from Minute Maid Park. The FOX Sports Network used me as one of their alternating analysts on a number of the pre–and post–game comment shows. From my point of view, at least, I took to the TV work like the proverbial duck to water.

On the FOX Sport Net shows, I have been privileged to work the 2007 through 2010 seasons with two consummate media professionals, Greg Lucas and Kevin Eschenfelder. I have to tip my cap to both men. They have taught me much in a short time and they have made my new break-in period on TV both easy and enjoyable. I shall look forward, hopefully, to further work with both men in future seasons at the ballpark. People like Greg and Kevin are the ones who put the icing on the cake that is TV baseball.

I'm still pretty active working some out-of-town charity events and also some revenue-producing card shows, but I'm a little too old and deep into the permanent DL list for any more old-timer games.

One of the most enjoyable of times has been my work for the Negro League Baseball Museum in Kansas City. That's a slice of unique baseball history that needs to be preserved in a first-class way for all time. Those pioneer curators of black history in Kansas City do a great job with a limited budget. They could use a lot more help than they are getting from the public, but that seems to be the universal cry of all historical societies, especially those that aim to preserve the history of regional or special interest baseball groups. The Negro League Baseball Museum will continue to have my help for as long as I am up to traveling and able to provide some support by my participation in their various fundraising functions.

I'm running out of things to say here. I guess that means that my story is pretty much coming to an end, except for the business of continuing to get up with each new dawn I'm blessed to see and then make the most of what time I have left to give back of myself to this world.

Beyond family, I want to thank all my past managers for all they each taught me about baseball and/or life, and sometimes in ways I would've sooner escaped altogether. Hershell Freeman (Tampa, 1962) probably saved my career in the bud when he took on the racial bully in Palatka, Florida, in my behalf. Harry Craft (Houston, 1962–64), Luman Harris (Houston, 1964–65), and Grady Hatton (Oklahoma City, 1963; Houston, 1966–68) taught me baseball. Harry Walker (Houston, 1968–72) and Leo Durocher (Houston, 1972–73) taught me patience with arrogance. And the wonderful Walt Alston (Los Angeles, 1974–75) taught me that it really was possible for Jimmy Wynn to finally have a manager that inspired him to greatness.

I forgive Harry Walker and all others who've ever deeply offended me, and I ask for genuine forgiveness from all those that I've ever unintentionally harmed or disappointed. Life isn't easy. We all have to learn and recover from the pains we've both caused and received.

I'm hoping that my story reads clearly. I've told it as straightforwardly and as honestly as I am able, not as a perfect person, but as someone who has tried to learn from his experiences and his mistakes for the sake of becoming a better version of the person I really am.

Before I say goodbye, there is one thing left I'd like to say to young people everywhere. The same words here apply to those of you who are older and just now waking up to the fact that you may not be living as you'd like to be living. It's never too late to make things right, even if it does mean that you may have to crawl out of a deeper hole at an older age to get your life turned around. You can still do it, one day at a time, if it's really important to you.

Here's my parting message: Never give up on your dream. If it's something doable that's important to you, don't allow creature comforts, laziness, impatience, the fear of rejection or failure, bad habits, addictions, or loneliness on the long road of effort get in the way.

The answer is simple: You have to be willing right now to do what's true and right for you. That's only hard if you're unwilling to get rid of whatever now stands in your way of having the life you deserve to live.

Where do you start? Start wherever you are, but organize the effort. None of us gets anywhere without a plan—and you deserve to have one too.

If you don't know what you want to do as a career, look around for anything you feel passionately about. Unless it's something that's harmful to you or others, or something against the law, go talk to people who are working with anything that pertains to your areas of interest. Get help from a career counselor. Do whatever it takes to start narrowing down what your choices may include.

Whenever you come up with a reasonable career goal, start focusing upon what you have to do to get there. Don't procrastinate. Organize a written plan for getting there without thinking too long on the subject.

Become willing to sacrifice the presence of anything or anyone who stands in the way of the work you will need to do to get the job done.

Surround yourself as much as possible with positive, supportive people. You don't need anybody feeding you messages of fear or guilt about a passionate goal that is neither immoral or against the law.

I don't push my religious views on anybody, but this step will also help you get there, if you are a believer: Ask God to help you be clear about your passion in life. Ask Him to help you turn your abilities and your will over to the bigger goal of getting them into line with His Will for you in this life.

Then, if you allow yourself to carry out your plan this far, listen and act upon the familiar advice of Nike: "Just do it!"

If your goal is right for you, you will get there, but even it doesn't happen, you will be able to live OK with the knowledge that you gave it your very best shot.

In the end, what matters most is the knowledge that we gave ourselves the best shot at life we could take. We don't live well with the regret that comes from living with an ongoing dream that we know in our hearts we never even tried to fulfill. And that's the lesson that soaked deep into my soul long ago from Joe and Maude Wynn. I pass it on freely to all of you out there who have ears to hear:

Follow your dream. Live your dream. Be your dream. Take it down the road as far as it will take you. That's the only way to live in peace with yourself once the long shadows of life's evening begin to fall and stretch. That much I know.

The game of baseball was my teacher.

Jimmy Wynn Biographical Data

Birth Name:	James Sherman Wynn	College:	Central State University
Nickname:	Jimmy or The Toy Cannon	Bats:	Right
Born On:	03-12-1942	Throws:	Right
Born In:	Cinicinnati, Ohio	Height:	5-09
Zodiac:	Pisces	Weight:	170
		First Game:	07-10-1963 (Age 21)
		Last Game:	09-27-1977

Major League Career Hitting Statistics by Season

Year	Team	G	AB	R	H	2B	3B	HR	RBI	BB	SO	HBP	AVG	OBP	SLG	SB
1963	HOU	70	250	31	61	10	5	4	27	30	53	0	.244	.319	.372	4
1964	HOU	67	219	19	49	7	0	5	18	24	58	1	.224	.301	.324	5
1965	HOU	157	564	90	155	30	7	22	73	84	126	5	.275	.371	.470	43
1966	HOU	105	418	62	107	21	1	18	62	41	81	1	.256	.321	.440	13
1967	HOU	158	594	102	148	29	3	37	107	74	137	2	.249	.331	.495	16
1968	HOU	156	542	85	146	23	5	26	67	90	131	5	.269	.376	.474	11
1969	HOU	149	495	113	133	17	1	33	87	148	142	3	.269	.436	.507	23
1970	HOU	157	554	82	156	32	2	27	88	106	96	1	.282	.394	.493	24
1971	HOU	123	404	38	82	16	0	7	45	56	63	2	.203	.302	.295	10
1972	HOU	145	542	117	148	29	3	24	90	103	99	2	.273	.389	.470	17
1973	HOU	139	481	90	106	14	5	20	55	91	102	4	.220	.347	.395	14
1974	LAD	150	535	104	145	17	4	32	108	108	104	0	.271	.387	.497	18
1975	LAD	130	412	80	102	16	0	18	58	110	77	1	.248	.403	.417	7
1976	ATL	148	449	75	93	19	1	17	66	127	111	0	.207	.377	.367	16
1977	NYY	30	77	7	11	2	1	1	3	15	16	0	.143	.283	.234	1
1977	MIL	36	117	10	23	3	1	0	10	17	31	0	.197	.294	.239	3

Major League Career Hitting Totals

Games: 1,920; At Bats: 6,653; Runs: 1,105; Hits: 1,665; 2BH: 285; 3BH: 39; HR: 291; RBI: 964; BB: 1,224; IBB: 84; SO: 1,427; SH: 32; SF: 74; HBP: 27; GIDP: 117; AVG: .250; OBP: .366; SLG: .436; SB: 225.

Statistics compliments of www.baseball-almanac. com

The famous seat where Jimmy Wynn slammed his far and deep homer to the fourth level left field upper deck in 1970 was on display at the "Baseball as America" Exhibit at the Houston Museum of Fine Arts in 2005.

Key to Team Name Abbreviations

HOU = Houston, National League. The team was nicknamed the Houston Colt .45s from their 1962 initial year through 1964. The club was renamed the Houston Astros in 1965.

LAD = Los Angeles Dodgers, National League.

ATL = Atlanta Braves, National League.

NYY = New York Yankees, American League.

MIL = Milwaukee Brewers, American league. Milwaukee moved to the National League in 1998.

Bibliography

Articles

Doyle, Al. "Jimmy Wynn: Former Dodger has many memories of his 15 years in the majors, including his grand slam in 1974 to help L.A. win the N.L. West Division—The Game I'll Never Forget." *Baseball Digest*, March 2003.

Hulsey, Bob (uncredited). "Jimmy Wynn, 'The Toy Cannon,' # 24." *Astros Daily*, www.astrosdaily.com.

Wilson, John. "Wynn Packing Cannon on his Spindly Frame." St. Louis: *The Sporting News*, August 26, 1967.

Books

Ankenmann, Fred N. *Four Score and More: The Autobiography of Fred N. Ankenmann, Sr., 1887–1979*. Houston: Publication Supported by the Joseph Stephen Cullinan Publication Fund, 1979.

Bouton, Jim. *Ball Four*. New York: Dell Publishing, 1971.

Chapman, Burton. *Telephone Road, Texas: A History and Guide to Telephone Road and Southeast Houston*. Friendswood, TX: Baxter Press, 2007.

Dierker, Larry. *This Ain't Brain Surgery: How to Win the Pennant Without Losing Your Mind*. New York: Simon & Schuster, 2003.

Johnson, Lloyd, and Miles Wolff, eds.; Steve McDonald, assoc. ed. *The Encyclopedia of Minor League Baseball*. 2nd edition. Durham, NC: Baseball America, Inc., 1997.

Morgan, Joe, and David Falkner. *Joe Morgan: A Life in Baseball*. New York and London: W.W. Norton, 1993.

Palmer, Pete, and Gary Gillette. *The 2005 ESPN Baseball Encyclopedia*. New York: Sterling, 2005.

Reed, Robert. *Colt .45s, a Six-Gun Salute: An Illustrated History of the Houston Colt .45s*. Houston: Gulf Publishing, 1999.

Ruggles, William B. *The History of the Texas League of Professional Baseball Clubs: 1888–1951*. Dallas: The Texas Baseball League, 1951.

Testa, Judith. *Sal Maglie: Baseball's Demon Barber*. DeKalb: Northern Illinois University Press, 2007.

Varela, Christopher. *Kotton, Port, Rail Center: A History of Early Radio in Houston*. Houston: Fez Publishing, 2004.

Witte, Jerry, with Bill McCurdy. *A Kid from St. Louis: Jerry Witte's Life in Baseball.* Houston: Pecan Park Eagle Press, 2003.

Internet Narrative and Database Sites

Astros.Com. The Official Site of the Houston Astros. www.astros.com
Astros Daily. www.astrosdaily.com
Baseball Almanac. www.baseball-almanac.com
Old-Time Data, Inc. The Professional Baseball Player Databases. http://www. baseball-almanac.com/minor-league/

Interviews

McCurdy, Bill, with Jimmy Wynn: Fourteen one-hour tape sessions, June 20, 2008, through October 2, 2008.

Research Notes

McCurdy, Bill. Copious library research notes from newspaper files on the history of Houston baseball, 1861–1961, were made available as background information on the local sporting and social culture that existed when Jimmy Wynn joined the Houston professional baseball club in 1963.
McCurdy, Bill. Notes from direct and peripheral information obtained over the years from a variety of everyday Houstonians, special people mentioned by Jimmy Wynn, Texas history scholars, former Wynn teammates, local baseball community figures, former team officials, managers, other former players.

Index

Numbers in *bold italics* indicate pages with photographs.